COURT
OFFICER
EXAM

COURT
OFFICER
EXAM

2nd Edition

LEARNINGEXPRESS®

NEW YORK

Library of Congress Cataloging-in-Publication Data:
Court officer exam / by LearningExpress, LLC.—2nd ed.
   p. cm.
ISBN-13: 978-1-57685-786-1
ISBN-10: 1-57685-786-7
1. Courts—United States—Officials and employees—Examinations, questions, etc. I. LearningExpress
(Organization)
 KF8770.C599 2011
 347.73'16—dc22

                                                        20010026504

Printed in the United States of America

9 8 7 6 5 4 3 2 1

Second Edition

ISBN: 978-1-57685-786-1

For information on LearningExpress, other LearningExpress products,
or bulk sales, please write to us at:
  2 Rector Street
  26th Floor
  New York, NY 10006

Or visit us at:
  www.learnatest.com

LIST OF CONTRIBUTORS ▶

Dr. Kimberly Collica has a Ph.D. in Criminal Justice and is a Professor in the Justice Studies Department at Berkeley College. She has many years of experience working within the state prison and county jail systems. Her consulting expertise is in the area of corrections, HIV and women's health, and Criminal Justice curriculum development. Her research focuses on HIV, correctional populations, rehabilitation, and reintegration.

Gregory Saffady holds the office of Michigan District Court Officer/Bailiff. Appointed in 1984, he is a court-certified expert witness in civil process, execution against property, and writs of replevin/claim and delivery. He has also been appointed receiver in U.S. District Court—Eastern District State of Michigan and many Michigan Circuit and District Courts, resulting in the recovery of more than $1,500,000 in debtor assets. Saffady is a frequent guest speaker and lecturer on court officer practice and procedure.

CONTENTS ▶

HOW TO USE THIS BOOK ▶

Congratulations on your decision to become a court officer! You will find this career path both rewarding and financially beneficial. The work is interesting, sometimes exciting, and, as we all know, extremely important. However, there are some hurdles ahead of you. Indeed, you have to beat out the competition and succeed at each step of an arduous selection process before you can be appointed.

Court Officer Exam will guide you through each stage of the selection process and will help you strengthen your test-taking skills to improve your chances of success. The following chapters are filled with useful information, advice, and practice exercises that will help you understand both how the hiring process works and how you can best meet the requirements.

The hiring process for selecting court officers varies among districts. Getting through each phase of the hiring process will require determination and a commitment to your goal of becoming a court officer. The selection process can be challenging, especially for those who don't know what to expect. You'll probably have serious competition, but you will have an edge over your competition if you use this book and study it thoroughly. It will provide you with the practice and information you need to succeed.

While there may be some variation among court systems, most court systems require applicants to complete each of the following steps successfully (although not necessarily in this exact order):

1. Application
2. Written exam
3. Physical fitness test
4. Interview
5. Psychological evaluation
6. Medical evaluation, which includes drug testing
7. Extensive background investigation

Failure to pass any one of these stages can result in disqualification. In many jurisdictions, candidates who fail the physical agility exam are given a second opportunity to retake the exam within 90 days. However, anyone who tests positive for illegal drugs or who has a felony conviction in his or her background will be prohibited from proceeding any further in the hiring process. Please be sure that you can meet these basic qualifications before applying for the position.

Prepare yourself by taking the practice tests in this book and reading each chapter, so you can avoid the pitfalls that prevent many court officer candidates from being hired.

Diligent study and review of this book will help you to appreciate *how* the exam is structured and *what* you are being asked to do. Make sure to complete all of the practice exams and review your answers, both correct and incorrect, carefully. By doing so, you will see a noticeable increase in your test scores, thereby allowing you to score higher than candidates who did not adequately prepare for the exam. Remember, a prepared test taker is a better test taker.

Court Officer Exam will help you find out as much as you can about the hiring process and practice the skills you need to succeed at each stage. This book will give you an inside look at the entire process, so you will be less nervous when facing tests, interviews, and procedures that can sometimes be intimidating. You will know what to expect, which is likely to lead to better choices and better results than those of other candidates who are just rushing ahead blindly.

1 ▶ BECOMING A COURT OFFICER

C ourt officers assist in the effective operation of federal, state, and local courts. Their duties vary, but their principal function is the undertaking of tasks assigned by the court, either inside the courthouse or in the field.

Some of these tasks may include the following:

- maintaining the orderly conduct and security of the courtroom, hearing room, all adjacent rooms, and the court grounds
- taking appropriate action to subdue aggressive or escaping prisoners
- acting as the first responder in emergency situations
- arresting a law-violating individual when necessary
- escorting judges from their chambers to the courtroom
- maintaining security of the court detention center
- escorting prisoners to and from the courtroom
- admitting and taking control of prisoners from the county jail for court proceedings
- operating security equipment such as a magnetometer or other types of screening devices
- screening all those who enter the court's facilities

- enforcing court decisions by executing court orders and serving legal orders or documents (e.g., summonses and subpoenas)
- summoning potential jurors to court
- opening and closing court and hearing room proceedings
- calling on witnesses
- administering the oath to jurors and witnesses
- maintaining the security, control, and integrity of jury panels
- announcing the beginning and end of court sessions
- administering the jury roster
- opening hearing rooms
- posting court lists on notice boards
- allocating rooms for use by legal practitioners
- preparing audiovisual equipment for court and hearing rooms
- recording and protecting exhibits tendered in the court
- keeping records of court processes (e.g., summons, warrants, etc.) served
- maintaining and updating court records
- running the court registries and maintaining the court files
- replenishing court forms and supplies
- making sure all of the judge's rules are adhered to in the courtroom
- liaising with judiciary, police, corrections, and legal officials

The job title given to individuals who complete these tasks may vary from state to state. In this book, however, the general term **court officer** shall be used for ease of understanding.

Other titles commonly used include **court security officers**, **bailiffs**, and **field officers**. The next few paragraphs provide common job descriptions for these titles.

Court Security Officers

The first line of defense at the courthouse is maintained by court security officers. These uniformed workers are responsible for screening all visitors who come through the front doors of the courthouse. They typically operate the metal detectors, X-ray conveyors, and hand-held screening devices, searching all individuals and their packages/items for contraband. These officers are the first to have contact with the public when they enter the court building; hence, their professionalism is vital, as it is reflective of the overall image of the court.

Court security officers also patrol the grounds and building, open and close the courthouse, and provide courtroom security as needed. At times, they are required to escort court employees and judicial officers when they travel on court business and when they make daily banking runs.

Bailiffs

This is the best-known court officer position. Bailiffs are uniformed courtroom attendees charged with courtroom security, judicial security, and attending and securing juries. Bailiffs are assigned to a particular judge, rather than a specific courtroom. It is not uncommon for a bailiff to serve his or her entire career with one judge. In smaller venues, bailiffs also perform many court security officer functions.

Field Officers

Field officers, or whatever title afforded this position by the court, perform their duties away from the courthouse. They are responsible for civil and criminal court-issued processes that include serving summonses, complaints, subpoenas, wage and bank garnishments, orders of eviction, writs of execution (property seizures/levies), and bench warrants

The typical job responsibilities of a court officer can vary from court system to court system. However, the skills and ability needed for a successful court officer candidate are basically the same, regardless of legal or procedural court differences. *Court Officer Exam* can be used by potential court officers throughout the United States. Its reviews and practice questions consist of skills that will benefit all court officer candidates.

Basic Qualifications

Desired qualifications are as varied as the duties of the court officer. It's worthwhile to research the qualifications of the court system you want to serve. Some qualifications are standard:

- **A minimum age requirement:** In most states, candidates must be at least 18 years old to be appointed as a court officer. However, in some states, the minimum age could be as high as 22 years of age. If you are younger than the state's age requirement, you can still take the court officer exam. You will be placed on a waiting list until you reach the required age.
- **A high school diploma or equivalent:** A college education in criminal justice or a legal-related discipline, such as paralegal, public administration, or court administration, is a plus. Law school graduates frequently take positions as court officers. Graduation from a state-certified police academy can often be substituted for a college degree.
- **A clean criminal record:** Anyone with a felony conviction is prohibited from being a court officer. If you have a felony arrest that did not result in conviction, you are still eligible for the position. Your background investigator will ask you for an explanation of the events that led up to your arrest. It is in your best interest to obtain a disposition from the original court that presided over your case prior to meeting with your investigator. Misdemeanor convictions are examined on a case-by-case basis; they will not automatically disqualify you from employment. However, if any of the misdemeanors are for domestic violence, you will most likely be ineligible.
- **Excellent physical and mental health:** After passing the written exam, candidates undergo a medical and psychological exam, as well as a physical fitness test.

- A valid driver's license and a satisfactory driving record
- U.S. citizenship
- A clean drug screening test

Many states require previous experience as a sworn law enforcement officer. Military service with specified training is also considered in the qualification process; however, candidates with dishonorable discharges will not be considered.

In any instance, applicants should possess maturity and an ability to interact with the public. Potential court officers should feel comfortable in a legal environment and should possess an aptitude for clerical duties. In most cases, candidates should be legally eligible to carry a firearm.

Many field officers who are responsible for collecting civil money judgments must obtain a public official surety bond. Therefore, their personal credit should be acceptable to a surety company. Please be advised that a credit check will be performed on all potential candidates. If you have outstanding debts such as overdue bills, bankruptcy claims, loan defaults, or even unpaid parking tickets, it will most likely eliminate you from the applicant pool. Make sure to rectify all financial matters prior to meeting with a background investigator. Good credit is symbolic of integrity and responsibility, which are two important qualities sought during this selection process.

Hiring

Many states offer a competitive civil service examination, while others use a standard hiring process consisting of an application and interview. In some venues, court officers are appointees who are preselected by judges or courts. These appointees usually have special qualifications that the court desires or needs.

Hiring may be completed by a panel of judges and members that make up the court's management team, by an individual judge, or, in smaller venues, by a court administrator. The final hiring process will always consist of an interview or oral examination, an extensive background investigation, and a satisfactory physical examination.

The Exam or Position Announcement

Beginning with the exam or position announcement, you will immediately notice that applying to be a court officer differs from applying to any other type of position. You rarely see court officer openings advertised in the help wanted ads. Instead, court systems usually start looking for potential court officers by means of a special announcement. In most instances, this announcement will outline the basic qualifications for the position, as well as the steps you will have to go through in the selection process. It often tells you some of the duties you will be expected to perform. It may give the date and location of the exam, which is usually the first step in the selection process. Some jurisdictions will post exam announcements on their state's civil service home page. It is important to check the state's website frequently for such exam announcements. If you miss the exam, it may be years before another exam is offered.

Make sure you obtain a copy of the exam or position announcement. Study it closely in order to be fully prepared for the selection process.

Training

Many states offer a formal training academy, on-the-job training, or a combination of both. Areas of study include:

- **Understanding state and federal statutes**
  Purpose: Court officers should have a basic knowledge of the law, including how to read and interpret case law. Knowing how laws are made and which laws are applicable to a court officer's daily work is important and will enhance job performance. Knowing how to find state and federal statutes and court decisions, either in the law library or on the Internet, will answer many questions that arise in work-related situations.

- **Civil practice and procedure**
  Purpose: The core of field officers' work consists of process service, property seizures, and evictions. Mastering these assignments *outside* the courthouse results in steady case flow *inside.* The court should not be burdened with meritless complaints that clog dockets because of procedural errors in the field. Experience gained in training and in the field assures excellent docket control.

- **Criminal law** (including execution of arrest/bench warrants)
  Purpose: Officer safety ranks first in completing criminal assignments successfully. Making correct arrests within the law eliminates liability nightmares. Field officers must be properly trained in arresting suspects on criminal process.

- **Principles of judicial security**
  Purpose: Court security officers and bailiffs are guardians of the judiciary, not only when court is in session, but also when judges and staff travel on court business. They must know how to safeguard persons and property in and out of the courthouse.

- **Firearms and self-defense tactics**
  Purpose: Court officers are more often than not required to carry firearms while they perform their job duties. Proficiency with a firearm is not a luxury. Less lethal tactics and use of nonlethal force reduces liability and enhances officer safety.

- **First aid and CPR**
  Purpose: Inside the courthouse, court officers are first responders. When seconds count, the ability to tend to the sick and injured competently and correctly may result in lives saved. Basic and advanced emergency medical procedures are emphasized.

- **Ethics and professional conduct**
  Purpose: The image of the judiciary is tantamount to integrity of the justice system as a whole. Court officers are representatives of the judicial system. Stellar and exemplary conduct is expected and stressed not only daily, but throughout a career.

- **Report writing**
  Purpose: Words said are forgotten as quickly as they are said. Words written last a lifetime, and how they are written exceeds importance. Being able to accurately and clearly document events is a skill that must be sharpened because as reports form the basis for legal actions. Clear and competent reporting shines.

Many departments require that you serve as a court officer trainee for your first two years on the job. Once you successfully complete the probationary period, you will typically be rewarded with permanent status and an increase in salary. Be advised that as a trainee, you will be under the direct supervision of a court officer sergeant and the general supervision of the court clerk; both will probably be required to make recommendations on whether you have successfully completed the probationary period.

Even after attending a formal state-certified academy, court officers receive extensive work experience from qualified training officers. Many courts also require their court officers to attend continuing education seminars and training classes annually.

Your Application

Often, one of the first steps in the process of becoming a court officer is filling out an application. Applications vary among court systems, but usually, they request basic information about you that will show whether you may proceed to the next step in the selection process. Questions about your previous education, employment, and military experience are common. In addition, you may find questions that ask about factors that could prove disqualifying, such as felony convictions or noncitizen status.

Here are some tips for completing your application:

- Neatness counts! Typing your application is a good idea.
- Double-check your application for accuracy before you submit it.
- Do not send your resume in lieu of an application; this not only shows a disregard for instructions, but also ensures that it probably won't even be read.
- If you are sending your application in the mail, make sure you mail it (and any supporting documentation) to the proper address. Follow all instructions in the exam announcement *exactly*.
- If you download an application from the Internet, make sure your printer produces a high-quality copy. If possible, fill out the downloaded application in a word-processing program, and run the spell-check feature before printing it out. (To be safe, you should also have someone else review your application to catch any errors that the computer missed.)

Salary and Benefits

As with nearly every job, court officers earn different salaries depending on where they work and for whom they work. In most cases, entry-level court security officers and bailiffs can expect to earn $30,000 to $35,000 annually, depending on where they are hired and whether the position is civil service rated. Veteran court officers with more than five years' experience earn more than $45,000. Supervisors and command officers can earn up to $75,000, including benefits and government retirement programs.

Many states offer entrepreneurial ventures to court officers who are willing to accept fee-based compensation. In lieu of a salary and benefits, these officers earn their compensation from fees generated from attorneys and judgment creditors for recovery of civil money judgments, executing evictions, and service of civil process. In many of these self-employment ventures, court officers have the opportunity for unlimited income. It is possible to earn more than $100,000 per year, depending upon location and volume of assignments. There are both tax advantages and disadvantages associated with self-employment. Nonetheless, obtaining private health insurance can be quite costly. Working evenings, weekends, and long hours is to be expected, which poses the question of sacrifice, as well as stability. Those considering fee-based compensation should weigh all factors before undertaking this position.

Employee benefit packages also vary for court officers from district to district. Common benefits include a comprehensive healthcare package with medical, dental, prescription drug, and vision plans; a generous state retirement plan and deferred compensation program; sick leave; vacation and holiday pay; and educational incentives.

Helpful Resources

Here is one of the major professional organizations in the court officer field. You may want to take advantage of the information and assistance that organizations like CODA have to offer regarding court officer opportunities, training and education, and other career-related matters.

**Court Officers' and Deputies'
Association (CODA)**

1450 Duke Street
Alexandria, VA 22314
1-800-424-7827
www.sheriffs.org/coda

2 ▶ ABOUT THE COURT OFFICER WRITTEN EXAM

Just as the appointment and hiring process varies from state to state, so does the written examination. Although there is no standard, national court officer exam, most written exams share many similarities. They test fundamental skills and aptitudes, such as your reading comprehension, memory skills, ability to follow directions, and judgment and reasoning skills. Court officers have to be able to read and understand complex materials. They have to write reports and materials in clear and correct language. The written exam measures basic skills that court officers use every day. The exam or position announcement should tell you what subjects are on your exam. The most commonly tested subjects are covered in detail in later chapters.

In any event, the purpose of the examination is universal: to determine the skill sets of potential candidates. The higher the test score, the more likely the candidate will succeed in the position. There are exceptions, as many court officers who excel in the job once hired fared average on the initial written examination. Many excellent employees are not naturally good test takers. However, the court officer exam is one of the most competitive civil service exams. If you want to have an interview, you need to score within the top 5% to 10%. Don't worry—*Court Officer Exam* will guide you every step of the way.

The examination process is governed by either a civil service system (federal, state, or local) or an at-will employment process. Many examinations are scheduled according to position availability; others are scheduled on a designated timetable to create an eligibility hiring list. The lists become valuable when multiple openings are expected due to attrition or an increase in staffing. Eligibility lists are usually active for a two- to five-year period. If no openings occur in that time, the list expires and the examination process recommences. If the number of job openings exceeds the list of eligible candidates, an expedited hiring process can be expected with the examination given on an as-needed basis to generate a pool of eligible candidates.

For the courts, selecting a testing process is like buying a suit: off the rack or custom. Many states select a generic examination process that measures candidates' verbal, written, and reasoning skills. This process satisfies either legislative or individual committee requirements. Others prefer a job-specific examination for two purposes:

1. to assess the candidates' ability to comprehend the job *prior* to hiring
2. to use the test as a minicourse prior to any formal training. A candidate with some knowledge of the work to be performed will likely take to the formal training with greater interest.

What the Written Exam Is Like

Unless there is a central education/testing center, the tests are usually given at multiple locations in an auditorium or classroom setting, depending upon the number of candidates. In the era of modern technology, it is very likely that the written examination will be computerized and given in a computer laboratory. Although the method may change, the purpose of administering the examination will remain unchanged. Regardless of your feelings about computers, there is an advantage to taking a computerized examination—scores are typically generated directly after you answer the last question, thereby allowing you to know your score before you leave the testing center. The traditional pencil and paper test may feel more comfortable, but it can take anywhere from four to six months to receive your test scores.

With few exceptions, the test totals 100 points. Some jurisdictions may grant additional points for state or county residency or for military experience. The scoring formula for the exam typically depends upon the type of test administered. Most exams are multiple choice; you have probably encountered such exams when you were in school.

Some court systems are supplementing multiple-choice tests with other test formats. Because writing is an important part of a court officer's job, some tests require candidates to write a response to five essay questions totaling 50 points, in addition to answering 50 multiple-choice questions worth one point each.

The time limit for the court officer exam varies. Some jurisdictions will allot three to four hours, with a 15-minute break after 90 minutes. Other jurisdictions allot six hours, with no break. If you need to use the bathroom, raise your hand and you will be escorted by a test proctor. These jurisdictions also recommend that you bring a bag lunch. Eating breakfast before the test and having snacks (if allowed) during the test will help you to obtain a better score. If you are hungry, you will not be able to concentrate. Make sure you eat a balanced meal, but don't overeat before the exam—it could leave you feeling lethargic.

How to Prepare for the Written Exam

In the time before you take the exam, gather as much information about it as you can. Ask if the court system to which you are applying has a study guide. If it does, be sure to allow yourself time to read it and complete any practice questions. If the court has a website, you may find sample test questions online.

Practice, practice, practice! Review the material in the instructional chapters of this book, which offer tips on how to improve in each skill area on your exam. Take all the practice exams in this book. Candidates preparing for the examination should spend time with a legal dictionary to familiarize themselves with legal terminology and common legal phrases. Brushing up on basic spelling, reading, and verbal skills is also recommended. If possible, you may want to find people who have taken the exam recently and ask them for any insight. Their hindsight—"I wish I had . . ."—can be your foresight.

On the day of the written exam, listen carefully to all directions given by the person who administers the test. Budget your time during the exam. Don't spend too much time on any one question. Read the entire question before answering it, and make sure you check out each answer before choosing one. Do not leave any blank answers. If you leave an answer blank, you will get a zero for that question. If you take a guess, you have a 25% chance of getting the answer right. Stop and check every now and then to make sure you are filling in the correct bubble or spot for each answer. You don't want to fail the test because of misplaced marks! If there is time left after you finish, double-check your answers.

3 ▶ THE LEARNINGEXPRESS TEST PREPARATION SYSTEM

CHAPTER SUMMARY

Taking the court officer exam can be tough, and your career in law enforcement depends on passing it. The LearningExpress Test Preparation System, developed exclusively for LearningExpress by leading test experts, gives you the discipline and attitude you need to succeed.

First, the bad news: Taking the court officer exam is no picnic, and neither is getting ready for it. Your future career in law enforcement depends on your passing the test, but there are all sorts of pitfalls that can keep you from doing your best on this all-important exam. Here are some of the obstacles that can stand in the way of your success:

- being unfamiliar with the format of the exam
- being paralyzed by test anxiety
- leaving your preparation to the last minute
- not preparing at all!
- not knowing vital test-taking skills: how to pace yourself through the exam, how to use the process of elimination, and when to guess
- not being in tip-top mental and physical shape
- arriving late at the test site, having to work on an empty stomach, or shivering through the exam because the room is cold

What's the common denominator in all these test-taking pitfalls? One word: control. Who's in control, you or the exam?

Now the good news: The LearningExpress Test Preparation System puts you in control. In just nine easy-to-follow steps, you will learn everything you need to be in charge of your preparation and your performance on the exam. Other test takers may let the test get the better of them; other test takers may be unprepared or out of shape—but not you. You will have taken all the steps to get a high score on the court officer exam.

Here's how the LearningExpress Test Preparation System works: Nine easy steps lead you through everything you need to know and do to get ready to master your exam. Each of the steps listed below includes both reading about the step and one or more activities. It is important that you do the activities along with the reading, or you won't be getting the full benefit of the system.

Step 1. Get Information
Step 2. Conquer Test Anxiety
Step 3. Make a Plan
Step 4. Learn to Manage Your Time
Step 5. Learn to Use the Process of Elimination
Step 6. Know When to Guess
Step 7. Reach Your Peak Performance Zone
Step 8. Get Your Act Together
Step 9. Do It!

If you have several hours, you can work through the whole LearningExpress Test Preparation System in one sitting. Otherwise, you can break it up and do just one or two steps a day for the next several days. It is up to you—remember, you are in control.

Step 1: Get Information

Activities: Read Chapters 1 and 2. Knowledge is power. Therefore, first, you have to find out everything you can about the court officer exam. Once you have your information, the next steps will show you what to do about it.

Part A: Straight Talk about the Court Officer Exam

It is important for you to remember that your score on the exam does not determine how smart you are or even whether you will make a good court officer. There are all kinds of things a written exam like this can't test: whether you are likely to show up late or call in sick a lot, whether you can be patient with the public, or whether you can be trusted with confidential information. Those kinds of things are hard to evaluate on a written exam. Meanwhile, it is easy to evaluate whether you can correctly answer questions about your job duties.

This is not to say that correctly answering the questions on the written exam is not important! The knowledge tested on the exam is knowledge you will need to do your job, and your ability to enter the profession you have trained for depends on your passing this exam. And that's why you are here—to achieve control over the exam.

Part B: What's on the Test

If you haven't already done so, stop here and read Chapter 2 of this book, which gives you an overview of the exam. Later, you will have the opportunity to take the sample practice exams in Chapters 4, 10, 11, and 12.

Step 2: Conquer Test Anxiety

Activity: Take the Test Anxiety Quiz on page 14.
Having complete information about the exam is the first step in getting control of the exam. Next, you have to overcome one of the biggest obstacles to test success: test anxiety. Test anxiety cannot only impair your performance on the exam itself, but it can even keep you from preparing! In this step, you will learn

stress management techniques that will help you succeed on your exam. Learn these strategies now, and practice them as you complete the exams in this book so that they will be second nature to you by exam day.

Combating Test Anxiety

The first thing you need to know is that a little test anxiety is a good thing. Everyone gets nervous before a big exam—and if that nervousness motivates you to prepare thoroughly, so much the better. Many well-known people throughout history have experienced anxiety or nervousness—from performers such as actor Sir Laurence Olivier and singer Aretha Franklin to writers such as Charlotte Brontë and Alfred, Lord Tennyson. In fact, anxiety probably gave them a little extra edge—just the kind of edge you need to do well, whether on a stage or in an examination room.

Stop here and complete the Test Anxiety Quiz on page 14 to find out whether your level of test anxiety is something you should worry about.

Stress Management before the Test

If you feel your level of anxiety getting the best of you in the weeks before the test, here is what you need to do to bring the level down again:

- **Get prepared**. There's nothing like knowing what to expect and being prepared for it to put you in control of test anxiety. That's why you are reading this book. Use it faithfully, and remind yourself that you are better prepared than most of the people taking the test.
- **Practice self-confidence**. A positive attitude is a great way to combat test anxiety. This is no time to be humble or shy. Stand in front of the mirror and say to your reflection, "I'm prepared. I'm full of self-confidence. I'm going to ace this test. I know I can do it." If you hear it often enough, you will come to believe it.

- **Fight negative messages**. Every time someone starts telling you how hard the exam is or how it is almost impossible to get a high score, start telling them your self-confidence messages. If the someone with the negative messages is you, telling yourself you don't do well on exams or you just can't do this, don't listen.
- **Visualize**. Imagine yourself reporting for duty on your first day as a court officer. Imagine coming home with your first paycheck. Visualizing success can help make it happen—and it reminds you of why you are working so hard to pass the exam.
- **Exercise**. Physical activity helps calm down your body and focus your mind. Besides, being in good physical shape can actually help you do well on the exam. Go for a run, lift weights, go swimming—and do it regularly.

Stress Management on Test Day

There are several ways you can bring down your level of test anxiety on test day. They will work best if you practice them in the weeks before the test, so you know which ones work best for you.

- **Deep breathing**. Take a deep breath while you count to five. Hold it for a count of one, then let it out for a count of five. Repeat several times.
- **Move your body**. Try rolling your head in a circle. Rotate your shoulders. Shake your hands from the wrist. Many people find these movements very relaxing.
- **Visualize again**. Think of the place where you are most relaxed: lying on the beach in the sun, walking through the park, or whatever makes you feel good. Now close your eyes and imagine you are actually there. If you practice in advance, you will find that you need only a few seconds of this exercise to experience a significant increase in your sense of well-being.

Test Anxiety Quiz

You need to worry about test anxiety only if it is extreme enough to impair your performance. The following questionnaire will provide a diagnosis of your level of test anxiety. In the blank before each statement, write the number that most accurately describes your experience.

0 = Never   1 = Once or twice   2 = Sometimes   3 = Often

_____ I have gotten so nervous before an exam that I simply put down the books and didn't study for it.

_____ I have experienced disabling physical symptoms such as vomiting and severe headaches because I was nervous about an exam.

_____ I have simply not shown up for an exam because I was scared to take it.

_____ I have experienced dizziness and disorientation while taking an exam.

_____ I have had trouble filling in the little circles because my hands were shaking too hard.

_____ I have failed an exam because I was too nervous to complete it.

_____ **Total:** Add up the numbers in the blanks above.

Your Test Stress Anxiety Score

Here are the steps you should take, depending on your score. If you scored:

- **Below 3**, your level of test anxiety is nothing to worry about; it's probably just enough to give you that little extra edge.
- **Between 3 and 6**, your test anxiety may be enough to impair your performance, and you should practice the stress management techn ques listed in this chapter to try to bring your test anxiety down to manageable levels.
- **Above 6**, your level of test anxiety is a serious concern. In addition to practicing the stress management techniques listed in this chapter, you may want to seek additional, personal help. Call your local high school or community college and ask for the academic counselor. Tell the counselor that you have a level of test anxiety that sometimes keeps you from being able to take the exam. The counselor may be willing to help you or may suggest someone else you should talk to.

When anxiety threatens to overwhelm you right there during the exam, there are still things you can do to manage your stress level.

- **Repeat your self-confidence messages.** You should have them memorized by now. Say them quietly to yourself, and believe them!
- **Visualize one more time.** This time, visualize yourself moving smoothly and quickly through the test, answering every question correctly and finishing just before time is up. Like most visualization techniques, this one works best if you have practiced it ahead of time.
- **Find an easy question.** Skim over the test until you find an easy question, and answer it. Getting even one circle filled in gets you into the test-taking groove.
- **Take a mental break.** Everyone loses concentration once in a while during a long test. It is normal, so you shouldn't worry about it. Instead, accept what has happened. Say to yourself, "Hey, I lost it there for a minute. My brain is taking a break." Put down your pencil, close your eyes, and do some deep breathing for a few seconds. Then you will be ready to go back to work.

Try these techniques ahead of time, and see if they work for you!

Step 3: Make a Plan

Activity: Construct a study plan.
One of the most important things you can do to get control of yourself and your exam is to make a study plan. Too many people fail to prepare simply because they fail to plan. Spending hours poring over sample test questions the day before the exam not only raises your level of test anxiety, but it also will not replace careful preparation and practice over time.

Don't fall into the cram trap. Take control of your preparation time by mapping out a study schedule. On the following pages are sample schedules, based on the amount of time you have before you take the written exam. If you are the kind of person who needs deadlines and assignments to motivate you for a project, here they are. If you are the kind of person who doesn't like to follow other people's plans, you can use the suggested schedules here to construct your own.

Even more important than making a plan is making a commitment. You can't review everything you learned in your law enforcement courses in one night. You need to set aside some time every day for study and practice. Try for at least 20 minutes a day. Twenty minutes daily will do you much more good than two hours on Saturday—divide your test preparation into smaller pieces of the larger work. In addition, making study notes, creating visual aids, and memorizing can be quite useful as you prepare. Each time you begin to study, quickly review your last lesson. This act will help you retain all you have learned and help you assess if you are studying effectively. You may realize you are not remembering some of the material you studied earlier. Approximately one week before your exam, try to determine the areas that are still most difficult for you.

Don't put off your study until the day before the exam. Start now. A few minutes a day, with half an hour or more on weekends, can make a big difference in your score.

Schedule A: The Long-Term Plan

You have taken the first practice test in Chapter 4 and know that you have at least six months in which to build on your strengths and improve in areas where you are weak. Do not put off your preparation. In six months, five hours a week can make a significant difference in your score.

TIME	PREPARATION
Exam minus 6 months	Pick the one section in which your percentage score on the practice exam was lowest to concentrate on this month. Read the relevant chapters from among Chapters 5–9 and work through the exercises. When you get to that chapter in this plan, review it.
Exam minus 5 months	Read Chapter 5, "Memory and Observation," and work through the exercises. Practice studying pictures or newspaper articles and quiz yourself to see how much you remember. Find other people who are preparing for the exam and form a study group.
Exam minus 4 months	Read Chapter 6, "Reading Texts, Tables, Charts, and Graphs," and work through the sample questions. All this reading is a good time to practice your reading comprehension skills, too.
Exam minus 3 months	Read Chapter 7, "Legal Definitions," and work through the exercises. Use the resources on page 92, or your old textbooks, to review topics you are shaky on.
Exam minus 2 months	Read Chapter 8, "Applying Court Officer Procedures," and work through the exercises. Give yourself additional practice by making up your own test questions in the areas that give you the most trouble.
Exam minus 4 weeks	Read Chapter 9, "Clerical Ability," and work through the exercises. Read Chapter 14 so you are prepapred for the physical, medical, and psychological exams.
Exam minus 2 weeks	Take the practice exams in Chapters 10 and 11. Use your scores to help you decide your focus for this week. Go back to the relevant chapters, and get the help of a teacher or your study group.
Exam minus 1 week	Review the sample tests you've taken, especially the answer explanations. Then, take the practice exam in Chapter 12 for extra practice. As you study this week, concentrate on the areas you're strongest in and decide not to let any areas where you still feel uncertain bother you. Go to bed early every night this week so you can be at your best by test time.
Exam minus 1 day	Relax. Do something unrelated to your court officer exam. Eat a good meal and go to bed at your new early bedtime.

Schedule B: The Short-Term Plan

If you have just two to four weeks until the exam, you have your work cut out for you. Carve two hours out of your day, every day, for study. This schedule shows you how to make the most of your time if you have just two weeks.

TIME	PREPARATION
Exam minus 14 days	Read Chapter 6, "Reading Text, Tables, Charts, and Graphs," and work through the exercises.
Exam minus 12 days	Read Chapters 7 and 8, "Legal Definitions" and "Applying Court Officer Procedures," and work through the exercises. Use the resources on page 92, or your old textbooks, to review topics you're shaky on.
Exam minus 10 days	Read Chapter 5, "Memory and Observation," and work through the exercises.
Exam minus 8 days	Read Chapter 9, "Clerical Ability," and work through the exercises. Go to bed early every night this week so you can be at your peak by test time.
Exam minus 6 days	Take the practice tests in Chapter 10 and 11. Choose one or two areas to review until the day before the exam, based on your scores. Go back to the relevant instructional chapters, and get the help of a teacher or friend.
Exam minus 4 days	Take the practice exam in Chapter 12 for extra practice.
Exam minus 1 day	Relax. Do something unrelated to your court officer exam. Eat a good meal and go to bed at your new early bedtime.

Learning Styles

Each of us absorbs information differently. The way that works best for you is called your dominant learning method. If someone asks you to help them construct a bookcase he or she just bought, which may be in many pieces, how do you begin? Do you need to read the directions and see the diagram? Would you rather hear someone read the directions to you—telling you which part connects to another? Or do you draw your own diagram?

The three main learning methods are visual, auditory, and kinesthetic. Determining which type of learner you are will help you create tools for studying.

1. **Visual learners** need to see the information in the form of maps, pictures, text, words, or math examples. Outlining notes and important points in colorful highlighters and taking note of diagrams and pictures may be key in helping you study.
2. **Auditory learners** retain information when they can hear directions, the spelling of a word, a math theorem, or poem. Repeating information aloud or listening to your notes on a tape recorder may help. Many auditory learners also find working in study groups or having someone quiz them is beneficial.
3. **Kinesthetic learners** must *do*. They need to draw diagrams, write directions, or copy important information. Rewriting notes on index cards or making margin notes in your textbooks also helps kinesthetic learners retain information.

Mnemonics

Mnemonics are memory tricks that help you remember what you need to know. Acronyms (words created from the first letters in a series of words) are common mnemonics. One acronym you may already know is **HOMES**, for the names of the Great Lakes (Huron, Ontario, Michigan, Erie, and Superior). **ROY G. BIV** reminds people of the colors in the spectrum (Red, Orange, Yellow, Green, Blue, Indigo, and Violet). Depending on the type of learner you are, mnemonics can also be colorful or vivid images, stories, word associations, or catchy rhymes such as "Thirty days hath September . . ." created in your mind. Any type of learner, whether visual, auditory, or kinesthetic, can use mnemonics to help the brain store and interpret information.

Step 4: Learn to Manage Your Time

Activities: Practice these strategies as you take the sample tests in this book.

Steps 4, 5, and 6 of the LearningExpress Test Preparation System put you in charge of your exam by showing you test-taking strategies that work. Practice these strategies as you take the sample tests in this book, and then you will be ready to use them on test day.

First, you will take control of your time on the exam. Most court officer exams have a time limit, which may give you more than enough time to complete all the questions—or may not. It is a terrible feeling to hear the examiner say, "Five minutes left," when you are only three-quarters of the way through the test. Here are some tips to keep that from happening to you.

- **Follow directions.** If the directions are given orally, listen to them carefully. If they are written on the exam booklet or the computer screen, read them thoroughly. Ask questions before the exam begins if there's anything you don't understand. If

you are allowed to write in your exam booklet or a piece of scratch paper, write down the beginning time and the ending time of the exam.

- **Pace yourself.** Glance at your watch every few minutes, and compare the time to how far you have gotten in the test. When one-quarter of the time has elapsed, you should be a quarter of the way through the test, and so on. If you are falling behind, pick up the pace a bit.
- **Keep moving.** Don't spend too much time on one question. If you don't know the answer, skip the question and move on. Circle the number of the question in your test booklet in case you have time to come back to it later. (Note that you may not have the option to return to a skipped question on a computer-based test. Pay special attention to the directions provided at the testing location.)
- **On a paper test, keep track of your place on the answer sheet**. If you skip a question, make sure that you also skip the question on the answer sheet. Check yourself every five to ten questions to make sure that the number of the question still corresponds with the number on the answer sheet.
- **Don't rush.** Though you should keep moving, rushing won't help. Try to keep calm and work methodically and quickly.

Step 5: Learn to Use the Process of Elimination

Activity: Complete Process of Elimination Quiz (see pages 21–22).

After time management, your next most important tool for taking control of your exam is using the process of elimination wisely. It is standard test-taking wisdom that you should always read all the answer choices before choosing your answer. This helps you find the right answer by eliminating wrong answer choices. And, sure enough, that standard wisdom applies to your court officer exam, too.

Let's say you are facing a question that goes like this:

Which of the following lists of signs and symptoms indicates a possible heart attack?
a. headache, dizziness, nausea, confusion
b. dull chest pain, sudden sweating, difficulty breathing
c. wheezing, labored breathing, chest pain
d. difficulty breathing, high fever, rapid pulse

You should always use the process of elimination on a question like this, even if the right answer jumps out at you. Sometimes, the answer that jumps out isn't right after all. Let's assume, for the purpose of this exercise, that you are a little rusty on your signs and symptoms of a heart attack, so you need to use a little intuition to make up for what you don't remember. Proceed through the answer choices in order.

- **Start with choice a.** This one is pretty easy to eliminate; none of these signs and symptoms is likely to indicate a heart attack. Mark an **X** next to choice **a** so you never have to look at it again.
- **On to choice b.** "Dull chest pain" looks good, although if you are not up on your cardiac signs and symptoms, you might wonder if it should be "acute chest pain" instead. "Sudden sweating" and "difficulty breathing"? Check. And that's what you write next to choice **b**—a check mark, meaning "good answer, I might use this one."
- **Choice c is a possibility.** Maybe you don't really expect wheezing in a heart attack victim, but you know "chest pain" is right, and let's say you are not sure whether "labored breathing" is a sign of cardiac difficulty. Put a question mark next to **c**, meaning "well, maybe."
- **Choice d is also a possibility.** "Difficulty breathing" is a good sign of a heart attack. But wait a minute. "High fever?" Not really. "Rapid pulse?" Well, maybe. This doesn't really sound like a

heart attack, and you already have a better answer picked out in choice **b**. If you are feeling sure of yourself, put an **X** next to this one. If you want to be careful, put a question mark. Now your question looks like this:

Which of the following lists of signs and symptoms indicates a possible heart attack?
X a. headache, dizziness, nausea, confusion
✓ b. dull chest pain, sudden sweating, difficulty breathing
? c. wheezing, labored breathing, chest pain
? d. difficulty breathing, high fever, rapid pulse

You have just one check mark, for a good answer. If you are pressed for time, you should simply mark choice **b** on your answer sheet. If you have the time to be extra careful, you could compare your check mark answer to your question-mark answers to make sure that it is better.

It is good to have a system for marking good, bad, and maybe answers. We recommend this one:

X = bad
✓ = good
? = maybe

If you don't like these marks, devise your own system. Just make sure you do it long before test day—while you are working through the practice exams in this book—so you won't have to worry about it during the test.

Key Words

Often, identifying key words in a question will help you in the process of elimination. Words such as *always, never, all, only, must,* and *will* often make statements incorrect.

Words like *usually, may, sometimes,* and *most* may make a statement correct.

Even when you think you are absolutely clueless about a question, you can often use the process of elimination to get rid of at least one answer choice. If so, you are better prepared to make an educated guess, as you will see in Step 6. More often, you can eliminate answers until you have only two possible answers. Then you are in a strong position to guess.

Try using your powers of elimination on the questions in the following worksheet, Using the Process of Elimination. The questions are not about law enforcement work; they are just designed to show you how the process of elimination works. The answer explanations for this worksheet show one possible way you might use the process to arrive at the right answer.

Using the Process of Elimination

Use the process of elimination to answer the following questions.

1. Ilsa is as old as Meghan will be in five years. The difference between Ed's age and Meghan's age is twice the difference between Ilsa's age and Meghan's age. Ed is 29. How old is Ilsa?
  a. 4
  b. 10
  c. 19
  d. 24

2. "All drivers of commercial vehicles must carry a valid commercial driver's license whenever operating a commercial vehicle."
   According to this sentence, which of the following people need NOT carry a commercial driver's license?
  a. a truck driver idling his engine while waiting to be directed to a loading dock
  b. a bus operator backing her bus out of the way of another bus in the bus lot
  c. a taxi driver driving his personal car to the grocery store
  d. a limousine driver taking the limousine to her home after dropping off her last passenger of the evening

3. Smoking tobacco has been linked to
  a. increased risk of stroke and heart attack.
  b. all forms of respiratory disease.
  c. increasing mortality rates over the past ten years.
  d. juvenile delinquency.

4. Which of the following words is spelled correctly?
  a. incorrigible
  b. outragous
  c. domestickated
  d. understandible

Answers

Here are the answers, as well as some suggestions as to how you might have used the process of elimination to find them.

1. d. You should have eliminated choice **a** off the bat. Ilsa can't be four years old if Meghan is going to be Ilsa's age in five years. The best way to eliminate other answer choices is to try plugging them in to the information given in the problem. For instance, for choice **b**, if Ilsa is 10, then Meghan must be 5. The difference in their ages is 5. The difference between Ed's age, 29, and Meghan's age, 5, is 24. Is 24 two times 5? No. Then choice **b** is wrong. You could eliminate choice **c** in the same way and be left with choice **d**.

2. c. Note the word *not* in the question, and go through the answers one by one. Is the truck driver in choice **a** "operating a commercial vehicle"? Yes, idling counts as "operating," so he needs to have a commercial driver's license. Likewise, the bus operator in choice **b** is operating a commercial vehicle; the question doesn't say the operator has to be on the street. The limo driver in choice **d** is operating a commercial vehicle, even if it doesn't have a passenger in it. However, the cabbie in choice **c** is not operating a commercial vehicle, but his own private car.

3. a. You could eliminate choice **b** simply because of the presence of the word *all*. Such absolutes hardly ever appear in correct answer choices. Choice **c** looks attractive until you think a little about what you know—aren't fewer people smoking these days, rather than more? So how could smoking be responsible for a higher mortality rate? (If you didn't know that mortality rate means the rate at which people die, you might keep this choice as a possibility, but you would still be able to eliminate two answers and have only two to choose from.) And choice **d** doesn't make much sense, so you could eliminate that one, too. You are left with the correct choice, **a**.

4. a. How you used the process of elimination here depends on which words you recognized as being spelled incorrectly. If you knew that the correct spellings were *outrageous*, *domesticated*, and *understandable*, then you were home free.

Step 6: Know When to Guess

Activity: Complete worksheet on Your Guessing Ability (see pages 23–24).

Armed with the process of elimination, you are ready to take control of one of the big questions in test taking: Should I guess? Some exams have what's called a "guessing penalty," in which a fraction of your wrong answers is subtracted from your right answers. Other exams don't tend to work like that. Before test day, research whether or not your court officer exam has a penalty for guessing.

The more complicated answer to the question "Should I guess?" depends on you—your personality and your guessing intuition. There are two things you need to know about yourself before you go into the exam:

1. Are you a risk-taker?
2. Are you a good guesser?

You will have to decide about your risk-taking quotient on your own. To find out if you are a good guesser, complete the Your Guessing Ability worksheet on pages 23–24.

Step 7: Reach Your Peak Performance Zone

Activity: Complete the Physical Preparation Checklist.
To get ready for a challenge like a big exam, you have to take control of your physical, as well as your mental, state. Exercise, proper diet, and rest in the weeks prior to the test will ensure that your body works with, rather than against, your mind on test day, as well as during your preparation.

Exercise

If you don't already have a regular exercise program going, the time during which you are preparing for an exam is actually an excellent time to start one. And if you are already keeping fit—or trying to get that way—don't let the pressure of preparing for an exam fool you into quitting now. Exercise helps reduce stress by pumping feel-good hormones called endorphins into your system. It also increases the oxygen supply throughout your body, including your brain, so you will be at peak performance on test day.

A half hour of vigorous activity—enough to raise a sweat—every day should be your aim. If you are really pressed for time, every other day is OK. Choose an activity you like and get out there and do it. Jogging with a friend always makes the time go faster, or take a portable radio or MP3 player.

But don't overdo it. You don't want to exhaust yourself. Moderation is the key.

Diet

First of all, cut out the junk. Go easy on caffeine and nicotine, and eliminate alcohol from your system at least two weeks before the exam. What your body needs for peak performance is simply a balanced diet. Eat plenty of fruits and vegetables, along with lean protein and complex carbohydrates. Foods high in lecithin (an amino acid), such as fish and beans, are especially good "brain foods."

The night before the exam, you might "carbo-load" the way athletes do before a contest. Eat a big plate of spaghetti, rice and beans, or whatever your favorite carbohydrate is.

Rest

You probably know how much sleep you need every night to be at your best, even if you don't always get it. Make sure you do get that much sleep, though, for at least a week before the exam. Moderation is important here, too. Extra sleep will just make you groggy.

If you are not a morning person and your exam will be given in the morning, you should reset your internal clock so that your body doesn't think you are taking an exam at 3 a.m. You have to start this process

Your Guessing Ability

The following are ten really hard questions. You are not supposed to know the answers. Rather, this is an assessment of your ability to guess when you don't have a clue. Read each question carefully, just as if you did expect to answer it. If you have any knowledge of the subject, use that knowledge to help you eliminate wrong answer choices.

1. September 7 is Independence Day in
   a. India.
   b. Costa Rica.
   c. Brazil.
   d. Australia.

2. Which of the following is the formula for determining the momentum of an object?
   a. $p = MV$
   b. $F = ma$
   c. $P = IV$
   d. $E = mc^2$

3. Because of the expansion of the universe, the stars and other celestial bodies are all moving away from each other. This phenomenon is known as
   a. Newton's first law.
   b. the big bang.
   c. gravitational collapse.
   d. Hubble flow.

4. American author Gertrude Stein was born in
   a. 1713.
   b. 1830.
   c. 1874.
   d. 1901.

5. Which of the following is NOT one of the Five Classics attributed to Confucius?
   a. *I Ching*
   b. *Book of Holiness*
   c. *Spring and Autumn Annals*
   d. *Book of History*

6. The religious and philosophical doctrine that holds that the universe is constantly in a struggle between good and evil is known as
   a. Pelagianism.
   b. Manichaeanism.
   c. neo-Hegelianism.
   d. Epicureanism.

7. The third chief justice of the U.S. Supreme Court was
   a. John Blair.
   b. William Cushing.
   c. James Wilson.
   d. John Jay.

8. Which of the following is the poisonous portion of a daffodil?
   a. the bulb
   b. the leaves
   c. the stem
   d. the flowers

9. The winner of the Masters golf tournament in 1953 was
   a. Sam Snead.
   b. Cary Middlecoff.
   c. Arnold Palmer.
   d. Ben Hogan.

10. The state with the highest per capita personal income in 1980 was
    a. Alaska.
    b. Connecticut.
    c. New York.
    d. Texas.

Answers

Check your answers against the correct answers below.

1. c.
2. a.
3. d.
4. c.
5. b.
6. b.
7. b.
8. a.
9. d.
10. a.

How Did You Do?

You may have simply gotten lucky and actually known the answers to one or two questions. In addition, your guessing was probably more successful if you were able to use the process of elimination on any of the questions. Maybe you didn't know who the third chief justice was (question 7), but you knew that John Jay was the first. In that case, you would have eliminated choice **d** and therefore improved your odds of guessing right from one in four to one in three.

According to probability, you should get two and a half answers correct, so getting either two or three right would be average. If you got four or more right, you may be a really terrific guesser. If you got one or none right, you may be a really bad guesser.

Keep in mind, though, that this is only a small sample. You should continue to keep track of your guessing ability as you work through the sample questions in this book. Circle the numbers of questions you guess on as you make your guess; or, if you don't have time while you take the practice tests, go back afterward and try to remember which questions you guessed at. Remember, on a test with four answer choices, your chance of guessing correctly is one in four. So keep a separate "guessing" score for each exam. How many questions did you guess on? How many did you get right? If the number you got right is at least one-fourth of the number of questions you guessed on, you are at least an average guesser—maybe better—and you should always go ahead and guess on the real exam. If the number you got right is significantly lower than one-fourth of the number you guessed on, you might feel more comfortable if you guessed only selectively, when you can eliminate a wrong answer or at least have a good feeling about one of the answer choices.

Physical Preparation Checklist

For the week before the test, write down what physical exercise you engaged in and for how long and what you ate for each meal. Remember, you're trying for at least half an hour of exercise every other day (preferably every day) and a balanced diet that's light on junk food.

Exam minus 7 days

Exercise: _____ for _____ minutes
Breakfast: _____
Lunch: _____
Dinner: _____
Snacks: _____

Exam minus 6 days

Exercise: _____ for _____ minutes
Breakfast: _____
Lunch: _____
Dinner: _____
Snacks: _____

Exam minus 5 days

Exercise: _____ for _____ minutes
Breakfast: _____
Lunch: _____
Dinner: _____
Snacks: _____

Exam minus 4 days

Exercise: _____ for _____ minutes
Breakfast: _____
Lunch: _____
Dinner: _____
Snacks: _____

Exam minus 3 days

Exercise: _____ for _____ minutes
Breakfast: _____
Lunch: _____
Dinner: _____
Snacks: _____

Exam minus 2 days

Exercise: _____ for _____ minutes
Breakfast: _____
Lunch: _____
Dinner: _____
Snacks: _____

Exam minus 1 day

Exercise: _____ for _____ minutes
Breakfast: _____
Lunch: _____
Dinner: _____
Snacks: _____

well before the exam. The way it works is to get up half an hour earlier each morning, and then go to bed half an hour earlier that night. Don't try it the other way around; you will just toss and turn if you go to bed early without having gotten up early. The next morning, get up another half an hour earlier, and so on. How long you will have to do this depends on how late you are used to getting up.

Step 8: Get Your Act Together

Activity: Complete Final Preparations worksheet.
You are in control of your mind and body; you are in charge of test anxiety, your preparation, and your test-taking strategies. Now it is time to take charge of external factors, like the testing site and the materials you need to take the exam.

Find out Where the Test Is and Make a Trial Run

The testing agency will notify you when and where your exam is being held. Do you know how to get to the testing site? Do you know how long it will take to get there? If not, make a trial run, preferably on the same day of the week at the same time of day. Make note, on the Final Preparations worksheet on page xx, of the amount of time it will take you to get to the exam site. Plan on arriving at least 10–15 minutes early so you can get the lay of the land, use the bathroom, and calm down. Then figure out how early you will have to get up that morning, and make sure you get up that early every day for a week before the exam.

Gather Your Materials

The night before the exam, lay out the clothes you will wear and the materials you have to bring with you to the exam. Plan on dressing in layers; you won't have any control over the temperature of the examination room. Have a sweater or jacket you can take off if it is warm. Use the checklist on the Final Preparations worksheet on the following page to help you pull together what you will need.

Don't Skip Breakfast

Even if you don't usually eat breakfast, do so on exam morning. A cup of coffee doesn't count. Don't eat doughnuts or other sweet foods, either. A sugar high will leave you with a sugar low in the middle of the exam. A mix of protein and carbohydrates is best: Cereal with milk or eggs with toast will do your body a world of good.

Step 9: Do It!

Activity: Ace the court officer exam!
Fast forward to exam day. You are ready. You made a study plan and followed through. You practiced your test-taking strategies while working through this book. You are in control of your physical, mental, and emotional states. You know when and where to show up and what to bring with you. In other words, you are better prepared than most of the other people taking the court officer exam with you. You are psyched.

Just one more thing . . . When you are done with the exam, you deserve a reward. Plan a celebration. Call up your friends and plan a party, or have a nice dinner for two—whatever your heart desires. Give yourself something to look forward to.

And then do it. Go into the exam, full of confidence, armed with test-taking strategies you have practiced until they are second nature. You are in control of yourself, your environment, and your performance on the exam. You are ready to succeed. So do it. Go in there and ace the exam. And look forward to your future career as a court officer!

Final Preparations

Getting to the Exam Site

Location of exam site: _____

Date: _____

Departure time: _____

Do I know how to get to the exam site?   Yes ____   No ____   (If no, make a trial run.)

Time it will take to get to exam site: _____

Things to Lay out the Night before

Clothes I will wear   ____

Sweater/jacket   ____

Watch   ____

Photo ID   ____

Four #2 pencils (for paper-based exam)   ____

Other Things to Bring/Remember

_____   _____

_____   _____

_____   _____

C H A P T E R

4 ▶ PRACTICE TEST 1

CHAPTER SUMMARY
This is the first practice test in the book based on the most commonly tested areas on the court officer exam. By taking Practice Test 1 before you begin studying for the court officer exam, you will get an idea of how much you already know and how much you need to learn.

The skills tested on this practice test are the ones that have been previously tested on court officer exams that focus on job-related skills. The exam you take may look somewhat different from this one, but you'll find that this practice test provides vital practice in the skills you need to pass a court officer exam.

The practice test consists of 100 multiple-choice questions in the following areas: memory; reading text, tables, charts, and graphs; legal definitions; court officer procedures; and clerical ability. You should give yourself three hours to take this practice test. The number of questions and the time limit of the actual court officer exam can vary from region to region.

1.	(a)	(b)	(c)	(d)
2.	(a)	(b)	(c)	(d)
3.	(a)	(b)	(c)	(d)
4.	(a)	(b)	(c)	(d)
5.	(a)	(b)	(c)	(d)
6.	(a)	(b)	(c)	(d)
7.	(a)	(b)	(c)	(d)
8.	(a)	(b)	(c)	(d)
9.	(a)	(b)	(c)	(d)
10.	(a)	(b)	(c)	(d)
11.	(a)	(b)	(c)	(d)
12.	(a)	(b)	(c)	(d)
13.	(a)	(b)	(c)	(d)
14.	(a)	(b)	(c)	(d)
15.	(a)	(b)	(c)	(d)
16.	(a)	(b)	(c)	(d)
17.	(a)	(b)		
18.	(a)	(b)	(c)	(d)
19.	(a)	(b)	(c)	(d)
20.	(a)	(b)	(c)	(d)
21.	(a)	(b)		
22.	(a)	(b)	(c)	(d)
23.	(a)	(b)	(c)	(d)
24.	(a)	(b)	(c)	(d)
25.	(a)	(b)	(c)	(d)
26.	(a)	(b)	(c)	(d)
27.	(a)	(b)	(c)	(d)
28.	(a)	(b)	(c)	(d)
29.	(a)	(b)	(c)	(d)
30.	(a)	(b)	(c)	(d)
31.	(a)	(b)	(c)	(d)
32.	(a)	(b)	(c)	(d)
33.	(a)	(b)	(c)	(d)
34.	(a)	(b)	(c)	(d)
35.	(a)	(b)	(c)	(d)

36.	(a)	(b)	(c)	(d)
37.	(a)	(b)	(c)	(d)
38.	(a)	(b)	(c)	(d)
39.	(a)	(b)	(c)	(d)
40.	(a)	(b)	(c)	(d)
41.	(a)	(b)	(c)	(d)
42.	(a)	(b)	(c)	(d)
43.	(a)	(b)	(c)	(d)
44.	(a)	(b)	(c)	(d)
45.	(a)	(b)	(c)	(d)
46.	(a)	(b)	(c)	(d)
47.	(a)	(b)	(c)	(d)
48.	(a)	(b)	(c)	(d)
49.	(a)	(b)	(c)	(d)
50.	(a)	(b)	(c)	(d)
51.	(a)	(b)	(c)	(d)
52.	(a)	(b)	(c)	(d)
53.	(a)	(b)	(c)	(d)
54.	(a)	(b)	(c)	(d)
55.	(a)	(b)	(c)	(d)
56.	(a)	(b)	(c)	(d)
57.	(a)	(b)	(c)	(d)
58.	(a)	(b)	(c)	(d)
59.	(a)	(b)	(c)	(d)
60.	(a)	(b)	(c)	(d)
61.	(a)	(b)	(c)	(d)
62.	(a)	(b)	(c)	(d)
63.	(a)	(b)	(c)	(d)
64.	(a)	(b)	(c)	(d)
65.	(a)	(b)	(c)	(d)
66.	(a)	(b)	(c)	(d)
67.	(a)	(b)	(c)	(d)
68.	(a)	(b)	(c)	(d)
69.	(a)	(b)	(c)	(d)
70.	(a)	(b)	(c)	(d)

71.	(a)	(b)	(c)	(d)
72.	(a)	(b)	(c)	(d)
73.	(a)	(b)	(c)	(d)
74.	(a)	(b)	(c)	(d)
75.	(a)	(b)	(c)	(d)
76.	(a)	(b)	(c)	(d)
77.	(a)	(b)	(c)	(d)
78.	(a)	(b)	(c)	(d)
79.	(a)	(b)	(c)	(d)
80.	(a)	(b)	(c)	(d)
81.	(a)	(b)	(c)	(d)
82.	(a)	(b)	(c)	(d)
83.	(a)	(b)	(c)	(d)
84.	(a)	(b)	(c)	(d)
85.	(a)	(b)	(c)	(d)
86.	(a)	(b)	(c)	(d)
87.	(a)	(b)	(c)	(d)
88.	(a)	(b)	(c)	(d)
89.	(a)	(b)	(c)	(d)
90.	(a)	(b)	(c)	(d)
91.	(a)	(b)	(c)	(d)
92.	(a)	(b)	(c)	(d)
93.	(a)	(b)	(c)	(d)
94.	(a)	(b)	(c)	(d)
95.	(a)	(b)	(c)	(d)
96.	(a)	(b)	(c)	(d)
97.	(a)	(b)	(c)	(d)
98.	(a)	(b)	(c)	(d)
99.	(a)	(b)	(c)	(d)
100.	(a)	(b)	(c)	(d)

Memory and Observation

Carefully examine the following court officer duty roster for ten minutes. After this time, answer questions 1 through 10 based on what you've read without referring back to the document.

Court Officer Duty Roster

DATE: June 4
LOCATION: 86TH DISTRICT COURT
CHIEF COURT OFFICER: Captain Burton Montgomery
EXECUTIVE OFFICER: Lieutenant William Hooper
CSO SUPERVISOR: Sergeant Janet Keyes
BAILIFF SUPERVISOR: Sergeant Joel Howard

JUDGE	BAILIFF	COURTROOM #
Buchanan	Kliman	210
Burke	Waldowski	212
Clinton	Gore	214
Lincoln	Sherman	216
Otis	Banks	310
Peterson	Jones	312
Pierce	Miller	314
Saunders	Bridges	316

FIELD OFFICERS

TEAM	ASSIGNMENT	RADIO CODE
Turner/Clemens	Civil Process	86-6
Morris/Shannon	Evictions	86-E
Braden/Dunlap	Seizures	86-7

MOBILE SUPPORT
VACATION: Adams, Pryzinski, Zurn
DISPATCHER: Briggs, Meckler
SICK CALL: Ripperton, Thomas
CADETS: Young, North

1. The CSO supervisor is
   a. Lieutenant Hooper.
   b. Sergeant Howard.
   c. Sergeant Keyes.
   d. Sergeant Preston.

2. The cadets are
   a. Ellison and Summers.
   b. Young and North.
   c. North and Meadows.
   d. Nicholson and Young.

3. What is the date on the roster?
   a. July 4
   b. June 24
   c. January 4
   d. June 4

4. What is the radio code for Braden and Dunlap?
   a. 86-6
   b. 86-7
   c. 86-E
   d. 86-X

5. The bailiff assigned to Judge Otis is
   a. Banks.
   b. Bridges.
   c. Miller.
   d. Thomas.

6. What is the courtroom for Judge Burke?
   a. 210
   b. 212
   c. 310
   d. 316

7. The 86th District Court has
   a. nine judges.
   b. eight judges.
   c. seven judges and one magistrate.
   d. eight judges and one magistrate.

8. According to the roster, how many court officers are on vacation?
   a. one
   b. two
   c. three
   d. four

9. To which judge is Court Officer Gore assigned?
   a. Clinton
   b. Buchanan
   c. Burke
   d. Pierce

10. Field Officers Turner and Clemens are assigned to
   a. evictions.
   b. civil process.
   c. seizures.
   d. transportation.

Carefully examine the following photograph for five minutes. After this time, answer questions 11 through 15 based on what you've observed without referring back to the photograph.

11. Based on the photo, how many people are crossing the street in front of the train?

a. one

b. two

c. three

d. undeterminable from the photo

12. Based on the photo, how many people who are crossing the street are wearing a personal music device?

a. one

b. two

c. three

d. undeterminable from the photo

13. Other than those seen crossing the street in front of the train, how many other people and non-transit vehicles can be observed in the photo?

a. one person and no vehicles

b. one person and one vehicle

c. two people and no vehicle

d. two people and one vehicle

14. What is the total number of people who are seen in the photo?

a. three

b. four

c. five

d. six

15. The two people coming toward the photographer appear to be

a. women dressed casually.

b. men dressed in jeans.

c. in conversation with each other.

d. women in business attire.

Reading Comprehension

Read the following passage, then answer questions 16 through 21 based solely on information from the passage.

A Female Serial Killer

Most of the research on serial killers has focused on men who kill multiple victims (three or more) over a period of time, on separate occasions. The paucity of research has left us with minimal information about the female serial killer. The limited research conducted on women shows that female serial killing statistically parallels rates of gender differences in the overall crime rate—women still account for a small percentage of criminal activity and a very small percentage of serial killers. Nonetheless, we should not underestimate their dangerousness or the great harm they pose to society.

Dorothea Puente is serving a life sentence in a California prison without the possibility of parole for three counts of murder but, she is believed to have killed as many as 25 victims. Puente was not a typical looking serial killer; she resembled a grandmother. At the time of her trial, she looked like an older woman in her seventies even though she was only 59 years old. She had pale skin, white hair, blue eyes, and false teeth. Puente ran a boardinghouse for society's undesirables (e.g., alcoholics/drug users, the mentally ill, the elderly). She kept an extremely beautiful boardinghouse and was known in the community for her generosity. She portrayed herself as a Hispanic woman who generously donated her time and money to Hispanic organizations. She told some people that she was a retired doctor, and some knew her as a retired nurse. Most people loved her, but others felt she was very strange, and some were the victims of her rage driven temper. Everything about her life was a complete lie. Puente was a chameleon: She could change her age, appearance, or personality at any time, and she had the ability to fool everyone and anyone around her. Puente had an extensive criminal history. She worked in various nursing homes and was accused of administering black market medication to her clients in order to steal their money. She served various prison terms for forgery and for residing in a house of ill fame. In 1978, she was convicted of illegally cashing 34 government checks. In the 1980s, Puente would also serve time in prison on charges of forgery, grand theft, and property crimes.

After her last prison term, she opened a successful boardinghouse in Sacramento. Puente was brought under suspicion for murder when one of her tenants suddenly disappeared. During their investigation, the police discovered that at least 25 of her tenants had either died of "natural causes" or had mysteriously vanished. Although these tenants were dead, she was still collecting and cashing their social security checks. Police found nine bodies buried deep in her backyard; some were under her garden, while others were found under her cement patio. Only one body was severely mutilated. All of the bodies were mummified. They were wrapped in several layers of material and plastic. They were meticulously duct-taped, sprinkled with lime, and placed in the fetal position. Police believed that she poisoned all of her victims, but the coroner was unable to determine the exact cause of death.

16. Social scientists should study female serial killers because
    a. female serial killers are a new phenomenon.
    b. the rate of female serial killing is on the rise.
    c. we have limited information about them.
    d. female serial killers are an American phenomenon.

17. Most of the bodies found in Puente's backyard were severely mutilated.
    a. true
    b. false

18. According to the passage, one of Puente's original prison sentences was for
    a. mismanaging a boardinghouse.
    b. grand larceny theft.
    c. property crimes.
    d. illegally cashing government checks.

19. Puente had a long criminal history. Which of the following crimes did she not commit?
    a. larceny
    b. robbery
    c. forgery
    d. murder

20. Puente was finally suspected of wrongdoing when
    a. money was missing from the boardinghouse.
    b. police noticed that her behavior appeared suspicious.
    c. one of her tenants was missing.
    d. one of her tenants filed a complaint against her.

21. When the police searched Puente's backyard, they found 25 bodies in her garden and/or in the cement.
    a. true
    b. false

Read the following passage, then answer question 22 based solely on information from the passage.

Court officers assigned as field officers are independent public officers of the court and are not paid a salary and benefits, but generate revenues from the private sector and public agencies that require their services in the execution of court orders. While they are not classified as employees, they are under the supervision of the court, including all judges and court management. They must also work assigned hours and shifts as established by their jurisdictional courts. They remain accountable to all superior courts and regulatory agencies set forth by statute.

22. Field officers
   a. are not employees of the court and work at their own pace.
   b. generate their own revenues the same as self-employed persons.
   c. are public officers for tax purposes.
   d. have the same access to the court as court employees.

Read the following passage, then answer questions 23 through 26 based solely on information from the passage.

Article 27-F outlines the HIV confidentiality procedures that must be followed in New York State (NYS) for medical providers and HIV social service providers. Historically, people with HIV or AIDS were severely stigmatized because of their illness. Because of ignorance and prejudice, individuals with HIV were disowned by their families ostracized by their communities, evicted from their apartments, or terminated from their employment. As a result, the NYS Department of Health wanted to make sure that all HIV-related information was held to the highest level of confidentiality. The passage of Article 27-F achieves that goal. With few exceptions, any time HIV-related information will be released to a third party, a consent form must be signed by the client. If a consent form is not signed, the release of information is unauthorized. The agency, as well as the service provider, could be fined up to $5,000 and one year in jail for each violation (i.e., each disclosure) that occurs.

23. Article 27-F was enacted by
   a. HIV social service agencies.
   b. medical providers.
   c. the NYS Department of Health.
   d. HIV-positive clients.

24. With certain exceptions, HIV-related information can be released only via
   a. a signed consent form from the client.
   b. a verbal consent from the client.
   c. a signed or verbal consent from the client.
   d. a signed consent from the medical provider.

25. Case worker Ryan inadvertently discloses his client's HIV status without a signed consent form. The person who receives this information intentionally discloses it to the client's landlord because he no longer wants the client living in the building. According to the sanctions imposed by the NYS Department of Health, Ryan's maximum punishment could be
   a. $1,000 fine.
   b. five years incarceration.
   c. $5,000 fine or one year incarceration.
   d. $10,000 fine and two years incarceration.

26. According to the passage, due to the stigma associated with HIV, many HIV-positive individuals have faced all of the following except
  a. disownment from their families.
  b. excommunication from their churches.
  c. eviction from their residences.
  d. termination from their jobs.

Read the following passage, then answer questions 27 through 31 based solely on information from the passage.

The president of the United States recommends candidates for federal judgeships at all levels of the federal judiciary. Like those suggested to become cabinet members, candidates are then given a hearing before the U.S. Senate. For judges, the Senate Judiciary Committee conducts hearings to verify their qualifications to serve on the federal bench. At the conclusion of the hearings, a recommendation is made by the committee. The nomination is then put to a vote before the full Senate to confirm or deny the judicial appointment. The nominee must receive a majority of 51% of the votes cast for confirmation. Once confirmed and sworn into office, the appointment is lifetime and subject to revocation only for violation of certain judicial canons. A vacancy occurs when a sitting federal jurist accepts "senior judge status," takes retirement, or dies while in office. Governors make judicial appointments in their respective states based upon their state constitutions, which govern the appointment process when a vacancy occurs.

27. The main theme in the reading passage is that
  a. federal judgeships are hard to obtain.
  b. state judgeships are not as prestigious as federal judgeships.
  c. the president and a governor are empowered to appoint judges.
  d. federal and state judgeships are bound by the Constitution.

28. If the full U.S. Senate votes and 51 is a majority vote, what is the total number of votes cast?
  a. 100
  b. 120
  c. 150
  d. 200

29. The term of a federal judge is
  a. ten years.
  b. 15 years.
  c. lifetime.
  d. until the next president is elected.

30. Besides federal judges, the Senate must hold hearings to appoint
  a. governors.
  b. members of the president's cabinet.
  c. anyone who applies for federal employment.
  d. anyone the president wishes to hire.

31. The reason the Senate Judiciary Committee holds hearings on judicial nominees is
  a. by order of the president of the United States.
  b. to show impartiality to the nominee.
  c. the Constitution requires a hearing to confirm the nominee.
  d. to determine if the nominee is qualified to hold judicial office.

Read the following passage, then answer questions 32 through 36 based solely on information from the passage.

Corpus delicti means the body of the crime. In a homicide case, the *corpus delicti* consists of the fact that a human being is dead and that the death was caused by the criminal act or agency of another person, and was not suicide, natural, or accidental. In an arson case, the *corpus delicti* consists of the fact that a building was burned and that the fire was caused by the criminal act or agency of another person, and was not accidental.

32. In a possible homicide case, which of the following types of evidence would most likely serve the purpose of establishing *corpus delicti*?
  a. a suicide note by the deceased person
  b. fingerprints of a stranger at the crime scene
  c. evidence of sudden heart failure
  d. evidence of a caustic foreign substance in the decedent's mouth and throat

33. In a possible homicide case in which a dead body was found with a bullet wound to the head, which of the following types of evidence would most likely serve the purpose of establishing *corpus delicti*?
  a. The gun from which the bullet was fired was found in the victim's hand.
  b. The gun from which the bullet was fired was found within ten feet of where the body fell.
  c. The victim has other gunshot wounds to the forearms and palms of the hands.
  d. The victim has another graze gunshot wound to the head.

34. In a possible arson case, which of the following types of evidence would most likely serve the purpose of establishing *corpus delicti* of arson?
  a. The building was insured.
  b. The fire started in one spot while the building was in use.
  c. The fire started in more than one spot while the building was closed.
  d. The sprinkler system did not work.

35. In a possible arson case, which of the following types of evidence would most likely serve the purpose of establishing *corpus delicti* of arson?
  a. A body was found at the scene of the fire, and the victim was the owner of the building.
  b. A body was found at the scene of the fire, and the victim died from the fire.
  c. A body was found at the scene of the fire, and the victim died of natural causes shortly before the fire.
  d. A body was found at the scene of the fire, and the victim was murdered shortly before the fire.

36. In a possible murder case in which a body was found in the remains of a building destroyed by fire, which of the following facts in evidence would most likely serve the purpose of establishing *corpus delicti* for the murder?
  a. The victim had bruises and had no carbon dioxide in the lungs.
  b. The victim had bruises and had substantial carbon dioxide in the lungs.
  c. The victim had no bruises and had substantial carbon dioxide in the lungs.
  d. The fire was intentionally set and the victim had substantial carbon dioxide in the lungs.

Read the following passage, then answer questions 37 through 43 based solely on information from the passage.

The cultural defense assumes that a defendant's criminal conduct is culturally motivated. Individuals are so strongly influenced by their cultures that they may be obliged to act in a particular way or they may not know or understand that such behavior has violated criminal law. Although this is not a formalized defense, it has become a legal strategy in which a defendant's cultural background is used to negate mens rea or to mitigate criminal culpability. Many examples of camouflaged cultural defenses exist in which evidence of a defendant's background was used to justify behavior, negate mens rea, reduce sentencing, or minimize punishment.

In *People v. Moua* (1985), a Laotion man forced a Laotion woman from a Fresno City college to have sexual intercourse with him. Moua claimed that he was engaging in a Laotion ritual known as *zij poj niam*, or marriage-by-capture. In order to be wed, the woman must resist the man's sexual advances to prove that she is virtuous and to prove that he is strong. Moua believed that the victim's protest was part of the Laotion ritual. He was originally charged with kidnapping and rape but his charge was later mitigated by cultural evidence. Moua was convicted on a misdemeanor charge of false imprisonment.

In the same year (*People v. Kimura*), a Japanese woman killed her two children by engaging in the Japanese custom of *oyako-shinju*, parent-child suicide. After learning of her husband's infidelity, Kimura tried to drown herself and her two children. Her children died as a result of her actions, but she did not. Parent-child suicide is not encouraged in Japanese tradition, but it is understood. Instead of living with shame and humiliation, suicide is considered an honorable way of dying. Those who kill themselves and leave their children behind to face a life of shame are seen as terrible human beings. In view of these facts, cultural evidence was used to establish a temporary insanity defense and Kimura was convicted of voluntary manslaughter instead of murder.

Cultural evidence should be used only to establish mens rea or to mitigate punishment. It should not excuse the defendant's actions. We can be sensitive to cultural factors, but we cannot ignore grave injustices.

37. Based on the author's tone, what is an appropriate title for this passage?
   a. Cultural Defense—A Missing Element of America's Legal System
   b. Cultural Defense—Another Excuse, Another Unacceptable Explanation
   c. Cultural Defense—A Reason for Female Victimization
   d. Cultural Defense—The Criminal Justice System's Need for Cultural Sensitivity

38. The key argument in this passage is that we should
   a. not excuse a defendant's actions based on cultural background.
   b. be more sensitive to cultural factors.
   c. allow culture to negate or mitigate *mens rea*.
   d. allow defendants from other countries to be tried in their native countries to avoid cultural misunderstandings.

39. The term *mens rea* means
   a. criminal act.
   b. jury verdict.
   c. affirmative defense.
   d. guilty mind.

40. In *People v. Moua* (1985), a Laotion man said he forced a Laotion woman to have sexual intercourse with him because
  a. she was very pretty.
  b. he was following a Laotion ritual.
  c. he was trying to kidnap her.
  d. he thought she wanted to marry him.

41. In *People v. Moua* (1985), Moua was convicted of
  a. rape.
  b. kidnapping.
  c. false imprisonment.
  d. none of the above.

42. In *People v. Kimura*, a Japanese woman killed her two children and attempted suicide because
  a. she did not like being a mother.
  b. she blamed her children for her marital problems.
  c. her husband was cheating on her.
  d. she lost her job.

43. Because a cultural defense was used, Kimura's charges were mitigated from
  a. manslaughter to murder.
  b. murder to manslaughter.
  c. murder to child endangerment.
  d. manslaughter to child endangerment.

Read the following passage, then answer questions 44 through 50 based solely on information from the passage.

The "Plain English Doctrine" has existed since 1933, when the Securities and Exchange Commission required a prospectus to be written in a style readable and understandable by laypersons interested in making investments. The short title was the '33 Act, but the act instantly took on the common name of the Truth in Securities Bill. The Plain English Doctrine gained attention in 1977 when President Jimmy Carter required that all government regulations be written in plain English. In recent years, mainly as a mandate from several state supreme courts to attorneys and legal professionals to extract "legalese" from filed pleadings in favor of plain language, the doctrine has experienced a rebirth. Its roots in the American legal community trace back to Thomas Jefferson, who, as a lawyer, wrote a criminal bill "in language for the persons for whom it was intended." For decades, laypersons who became exposed to the American system of jurisprudence were hampered by verbose sentence structure and words foreign to them. Even if these laypersons spent time with a legal dictionary, they never did get the full grasp of what was put before them. No one was expecting laypersons to take formal law classes, and lawyers were not being asked to "dumb down" their communication skills, but only to level the playing field with clear, concise phrases. Verbiage should be eliminated in an effort to make the legal system more accessible and dismiss the shallow, negative stereotypes associated with lawyers and their writings.

44. The implication of this reading passage is that
  a. lawyers have made the courts unfriendly to the general public.
  b. lawyers should not show they are smarter than laypersons.
  c. plain English will bridge the communications gap between the public and the legal profession.
  d. plain English will decrease a lawyer's intelligence.

45. "Comes Now the Plaintiff, by and through his attorney, and makes this Complaint before the Court as follows" in plain English would read
   a. "The Plaintiff says for this Complaint."
   b. "The Plaintiff, through counsel, says for his Complaint."
   c. "Plaintiff, by and through his attorney, says."
   d. "For this Complaint, the Plaintiff says."

46. The Plain English Doctrine was first formally implemented by the
   a. Securities and Exchange Commission.
   b. U.S. Supreme Court.
   c. American Bar Association.
   d. Federalist Society.

47. Who in the American legal community is said to be an innovator of plain English?
   a. John Adams
   b. Thomas Jefferson
   c. F. Lee Bailey
   d. John Jay

48. As used in the reading passage, the word *mandate* means
   a. authorization.
   b. suggestion.
   c. order.
   d. instruction.

49. The first American president to require government regulations to be written in plain English was
   a. Gerald Ford.
   b. Jimmy Carter.
   c. Ronald Regan.
   d. Richard Nixon.

50. In the passage, the word *verbiage* means
   a. excess words with little or no meaning.
   b. few words with little or no meaning.
   c. words that have multiple meanings.
   d. words that have been declared obsolete.

Legal Definitions

The following are legal terms court officers regularly use in the performance of their official duties. Answer questions 51 through 65 based on the definitions.

Summons and complaint: An official court pleading that serves two purposes: (1) The summons informs the defendant that he or she is being sued in a civil court action. The summons also identifies the parties, their attorneys, the court, and the case number, and provides other information as commencement date of the action, when the action must be served (expiration date), and a history of related prior actions. (2) The complaint is the factual account of the action in which a party is seeking money damages or other type of relief (e.g., divorce, possession of property).

Plaintiff: A party commencing a lawsuit. Also known as a *judgment creditor* if he or she is the prevailing party and money damages is awarded.

Defendant: The party being sued. Also known as a *judgment debtor* if he or she loses the lawsuit and a money damages judgment is entered against him or her.

Service of Process: The delivery of legal documents to a person who either is named as a litigant in a civil action, or is a witness in a court action. Service of process can be effectuated personally by a court officer or a private process server. Some states allow process to be served by certified/registered mail with a return receipt signed by the party to whom process is directed.

Subpoena: An order of the court that either compels a party to appear as a witness, or requires the delivery of documents or other tangible items.

Judgment: In a civil action, the decision of the court, granting relief to the prevailing party in the form of money damages, awarding title to real property, or dissolving of marriage.

Writ of execution: An order of the court commanding the seizure and sale of judgment debtors' personal and/or real property to satisfy a civil judgment. Also referred to as a *levy* or *seizure order.*

Writ of replevin: Also known as *claim and delivery* or *writ of attachment.* An order of the court that commands the return of specific property to a secured creditor.

Writ of restitution: Also known as *order of possession* or *order of eviction.* An order of the court in a real estate action that terminates the tenancy of a party and restores possession of land or premises to the owner/landlord.

Writ of garnishment: An order of the court that attaches wages or a bank account of a judgment debtor, that is in turn paid to a judgment creditor.

Satisfaction: When a judgment is paid in full or in part.

Return of service: A legal document that provides proof of the delivery of civil process to an intended party and the manner in which the process was served. The document includes the name of the party served; the location, date, and time; the fee charged for service; and the name and official title of the person who made the service. The return of service also details if service of process was not completed due to an incorrect address, inability to locate the party to whom process was directed, or other factors. The document is then filed with the court. Also known as *proof of service.*

Self-incrimination: The act of accusing oneself of a crime for which a person can then be prosecuted. Self-incrimination can occur either directly or indirectly: directly, by means of interrogation in which information of a self-incriminatory nature is disclosed, or indirectly, when information of a self-incriminatory nature is disclosed voluntarily without pressure from another person. The Fifth Amendment protects witnesses from being forced to incriminate themselves, and applies wherever and whenever an individual is compelled to testify. *Miranda v. Arizona* (1966) was a landmark case involving confessions.

Discovery: The pretrial phase in which each party can request documents and other evidence from other parties or can compel the production of evidence by using a subpoena or through other discovery devices, such as requests for production and depositions.

Remittitur: A ruling by a judge, usually upon motion to reduce or throw out a jury verdict, lowering the amount of damages granted by a jury in a civil case.

Court officer sale: A public sale, usually an auction, conducted by court officers to liquidate property seized pursuant to a writ of execution. The net proceeds of the sale, usually sale price less expenses and taxable fees, are applied to the judgment balance to satisfy the judgment in full or in part.

Amicus curiae: A Latin phrase, literally translated as "friend of the court," that refers to someone, not a party to a case, who volunteers to offer information on a point of law or some other aspect of the case to assist the court in deciding a matter before it.

Order to show cause: A legal proceeding in which a party must appear before the court and explain its conduct or reasons for its actions in a certain incident. The most common type of show cause proceeding is where a party must convince the court that its actions do not rise to the level of contempt of court, which could result in fines or jail. A show cause may be brought by a litigant or the court itself.

51. Mrs. Cox, a Bronx resident, was walking home from the grocery store on a cold January evening at approximately 6:00 PM. It had snowed the night before and three inches had fallen before 5:00 that morning. In New York City, a

homeowner is responsible for shoveling the sidewalk in front of his or her home within a reasonable period of time after the snow has ceased. As Mrs. Cox approached Mr. Conklin's home, she noticed that he had not shoveled his sidewalk. She tried to maintain her balance but slipped, fell, and broke her leg. She sued Mr. Conklin civilly for negligence. In this case, Mrs. Cox is the
a. defendant.
b. plaintiff.
c. satisfaction.
d. judgment winner.

52. Mrs. Cox sues Mr. Conklin for $15,000 in damages for his negligence. After deliberations, the jury finds in favor of Mrs. Cox. The decision of the court to grant her damages is called
a. writ of execution.
b. writ of restitution.
c. subpoena.
d. judgment.

53. A party served with a writ of garnishment is known as the *garnishee.* The most likely garnishee of the following is the judgment debtor's
a. parents.
b. ex-wife.
c. employer.
d. landlord.

54. Attorney Thomas Allen is lead counsel in the matter of *Investors Bank and Trust v. Woodsley.* Allen wants to examine federal tax returns Woodsley filed in 2001, 2002, and 2003, but Woodsley refuses to produce the documents voluntarily. To obtain the documents, Allen will issue a
a. summons.
b. subpoena.
c. writ of attachment.
d. seizure order.

55. Court Officer Frank Simmons is assigned service of a summons and complaint in the matter of *Hunnicut Medical Group, PC, v. Bruce Clark.* On June 2, Simmons is informed by Bernice Clark that Bruce died on March 17. The document Simmons would complete to report this fact to the court is the
a. death certificate.
b. *Daily News* obituary.
c. return of service.
d. affidavit of Bernice Clark.

56. Daniel Fisher is a judgment debtor in the matter of *Security Bank v. Fisher.* Fisher fails to provide documents for examination by the attorney for the judgment creditor. To get Fisher to comply, the attorney will seek a(n)
a. subpoena.
b. order to show cause.
c. bench warrant.
d. writ of execution.

57. A creditor specifically demands the return of a specific item. No other damages are sought prior to entry of judgment. The creditor is requesting from the court a
a. writ of replevin.
b. writ of execution.
c. writ of garnishment.
d. writ of mandamus.

58. Ms. Padilla is suing her boss for sexual harassment. She retains a very prominent civil rights attorney. Her attorney files papers with the court that provide the facts of the case, in addition to the money damages being sought. In a civil case, this would be known as a(n)
a. service of process.
b. complaint.
c. subpoena.
d. order to show cause.

59. The proceeding known as *summary judgment* or *summary disposition* is used to end a lawsuit when there is no dispute as to the facts of the case, or when there clearly is no evidence in support of a case and proceeding would not change the outcome, or when the law does not support a claim. A case factor that best warrants summary judgment is
   a. testimony of a witness whose credibility is questioned.
   b. scientific evidence that cannot be rebutted.
   c. nonqualified immunity.
   d. admissions of a litigant made under oath.

60. An *unlawful detainer* is a term exclusive to real estate proceedings in which a party does not have the right to occupy a dwelling and is subject to eviction proceedings. Based on this definition, an unlawful detainer is NOT a
   a. tenant whose lease has expired.
   b. family who breaks into an abandoned home.
   c. man who parks a travel trailer in the parking lot of an apartment building.
   d. party whose mortgage is in default.

61. Circumstantial evidence is evidence that proves a fact by means of inference. Based on this definition, which of the following is an example of circumstantial evidence?
   a. A manager of a company purchases a new automobile on the day $10,000 is discovered missing from the company bank accounts.
   b. A woman overdoses on prescription medication and an empty prescription bottle with her name on the label is found in her hand.
   c. A car windshield is broken and a brick is lying on the front seat.
   d. A man accused of murder has his fingerprints on the murder weapon.

62. Persons have the right against self-incrimination guaranteed under the Fifth Amendment of the Constitution. The landmark case that affirmed this right is
   a. *Terry v. Ohio.*
   b. *Miranda v. Arizona.*
   c. *Gilmore v. Utah.*
   d. *California v. Mitchell.*

63. A Latin term is used to describe the situation in which a nonparty to an action receives permission from the court to provide information that may prove helpful in the issue at bar. The legal term is
   a. *res judicata.*
   b. *actus reus.*
   c. *amicus curiae.*
   d. *ab initio.*

64. At the conclusion of a civil trial, a judge rules that the money damages awarded the prevailing party are excessive. The judge decreases the award concurrent with the evidence admitted at trial. The procedure is called
   a. *additur.*
   b. *remittitur.*
   c. judgment not withstanding the verdict.
   d. reversible error.

65. The pretrial process that requires litigants to provide documents, obtain deposition testimony, and submit interrogatories is known as
   a. discovery.
   b. case evaluation.
   c. alternative dispute resolution.
   d. case facilitation.

Court Officer Procedures

Use the following court officer procedures to answer questions 66 through 79.

Writs of Execution

Field officers serving writs of execution will be governed by administrative order #6:

- Writs will be executed between 8 a.m. and 9 p.m. all days except Sunday. Unless ordered by the court on a motion showing good cause by a judgment creditor, no writs of execution will be served on Sunday.
- Upon receipt of the writ of execution, the assigned court officers will sign the endorsement section and time stamp the writ. This will determine priority on multiple writs issued against the judgment debtor in this venue.

Prior to the actual seizure of any property in possession of the judgment debtor, the field officers will serve to the judgment debtor:

- the writ of execution
- the mini Miranda warning and list of exemptions
- the worksheet

The judgment debtor will be allowed to pay the amount due to the judgment creditor together with all taxable fees prior to the seizure of any property. Payment must be in cash, certified funds, or money order only. No personal checks will be accepted. The judgment debtor will be provided with a receipt for payment signed by the field officers.

Upon seizure of property, the field officers will use service vendors who have been approved and certified by the court. No others will be used unless circumstances exist that prohibit an approved vendor from being called by field officers.

Seized property will be noticed for court officer sale within three days of seizure. If the property is not redeemed by full payment of the amount required to satisfy writ of execution, the property will be sold no later than 15 days from the date of seizure. The sale will occur Monday through Friday between 10 a.m. and 4 p.m. at the impound facility. Field officers will disburse funds concurrent with the filing of sale report of seized property no later than three days from the date of sale.

Writs of Restitution

Field officers serving writs of restitution will be governed by administrative order #7:

- Writs will be executed between 8 a.m. and 6 p.m. all days except Sunday. There will be no service of writs of restitution on Sunday without exception.
- Prior to the removal of occupants at the property, field officers will provide the named defendants and all occupants an opportunity to vacate within 48 hours of the date of service. The field officers will serve the defendants and all occupants a copy of the writ and move out instructions sheet. If the defendants are not present at the time of service, the writ and attachment will be posted on the front door.
- The field officers will not remove any property from the eviction site. The property is to be removed by the property owner or landlord, or their agents. The field officers will remove the defendants and all occupants who have failed to vacate the property. Any person or persons who fail to vacate the property upon the lawful demand of the court officer acting pursuant to the writ of restitution shall be arrested and brought before the court forthwith on the charge of contempt of court and trespass.
- The field officers will restore peaceful possession to the plaintiff. Peaceful possession is achieved when the occupants are removed from the property, the locks are changed, and the property is secured. If the property is vacant, peaceful possession is achieved when the locks are changed and the property secure. Upon completion of the restitution process, the return of service and report of activities will be filed within three days of the date of execution.

Fee Schedule #1
Fees and costs are taxable to the judgment debtor.

Service of writ of execution or writ of replevin: $40
Mileage fee within 20 miles round-trip from court: $12
Mileage fee 21 to 50 miles round-trip from court: $25
5% execution fee of receipts to $10,000: actual
3% execution fee of receipts more than $10,000: actual
Hourly rate @ $40 for standby/impound/sale: actual
Posting of sales notices at three locations: $75
Towing and storage expenses to be added to the amount required to satisfy writ.

Fee Schedule #2
Writs of restitution expenses to be paid by plaintiff prior to service

Service of writ of restitution: $40
Mileage fee within 20 miles round-trip from court: $12
Mileage fee 21 to 50 miles round-trip from court: $25
Peaceful possession restoration fee: $35
If arrest of defendant and/or occupant is required, the arrested party—as a condition of bond—will be taxed with an arrest fee of $175 in addition to any court costs and fines.

Use the following situation to answer questions 66 through 69.

Court Officer Robert Mitchell and Sergeant Jorge Romero are assigned a writ of execution in the matter of *Hanson Finance Company v. Lawrence Luther.* The outstanding judgment balance is $8,278. On April 10, the field officers seize Luther's 2000 Chevrolet Camaro, which was located 16 miles from the courthouse. Luther fails to redeem the vehicle. The vehicle is sold at public sale for $4,300. The sale and impound process took three hours. The towing and storage charges are $300.

66. Based on Fee Schedule #1, what are the taxable court officer fees?
   a. $459
   b. $475
   c. $759
   d. $775

67. What are the net proceeds payable to Hanson Finance Company?
   a. $3,541
   b. $3,525
   c. $3,825
   d. $3,841

68. What is the latest date all proceeds would be required to be disbursed to Hanson Finance Company?
   a. April 25
   b. April 26
   c. April 27
   d. April 28

69. What is the remaining judgment balance?
   a. $4,753
   b. $4,737
   c. $4,453
   d. $4,437

70. Court Officers Thomas Yan and Marge Clinton are assigned a writ of execution in the matter of *Vazquez v. Holt.* The outstanding judgment balance is $3,129. The officers travel ten miles to spend one hour with Holt and discover that he has no attachable assets. Based on Fee Schedule #1, what is the court officer fee?
   a. $0
   b. $40
   c. $52
   d. $92

71. FYC Co-op Apartments obtains a writ of restitution against Jill Travis. Court Officers Mike Harrison and Lee Blakely travel 18 miles from the court to the location. Upon arrival, they are informed by the apartment manager that Travis vacated the apartment in the middle of the night and left the unit open and unlocked. Based on Fee Schedule #2, what is the fee to which the court officers are entitled?
   a. $52
   b. $65
   c. $100
   d. $125

72. Supreme Real Estate Management obtains a writ of restitution against All Hits Music Company, located in the Bayonne Building six miles from the court. On Friday, November 4, Court Officers Barry Nichols and Erin Roberts serve the writ of restitution and give the occupants 48 hours to vacate. Based on the administrative order of the court, the occupants will be evicted on
   a. Saturday, November 5.
   b. Sunday, November 6.
   c. Monday, November 7.
   d. Tuesday, November 8.

73. During the eviction of All Hits Music Company, a group of protestors surrounds the building and attempts to prevent the officers and the landlord from entering the building to execute the writ of restitution. The court officers arrest ten protestors and the owner of the defendant company. Based on Fee Schedule #2, what is the total fees taxed for bond purposes for each arrested party?
   a. $262
   b. $275
   c. $2,620
   d. $2,882

74. Court Officers Nichols and Roberts hold a writ of restitution in the matter of *Camptown Apartments v. Tammy Thomas.* On March 28, Nichols receives a telephone call from Detective Adam Flynn of the local police department. Flynn tells Nichols he has an arrest warrant for Thomas. Flynn says Thomas knows him and will likely run if she sees him, and he has not been able to locate her. Flynn asks if he can ride with Nichols and Roberts and make his arrest. The court officers must deviate from established procedure to accommodate Flynn. The court officers should
   a. let Flynn act as the court officer because this provides good cover and accomplishes their assignment as well.
   b. advise Flynn that he can accompany them, but can make his arrest only after they have posted the 48-hour notice and writ of restitution pursuant to rules.
   c. ask the chief judge for further instructions.
   d. deny the request and tell Flynn to find Thomas on his own time.

75. Court Officer Charles Buckley holds a writ of replevin in the matter of matter of *Major Motors Financial Corp. v. William Jason.* Buckley is searching for Jason's 2003 Nissan Altima. On September 17, Buckley locates the vehicle in a shopping center parking lot. Buckley radios the court, who informs the local police department that the vehicle is being seized pursuant to the writ. The police advise that they have a unit in the immediate area and will assist Buckley. The vehicle is seized by Buckley and is placed on a flatbed trailer to be conveyed to the impound yard. The police officer asks Buckley if he can search the vehicle. Buckley should
   a. let the officer search the vehicle while it is on the flatbed trailer.
   b. let the officer search the vehicle at the impound yard after the vehicle is impounded and the officer obtains a search warrant.
   c. let the officer search the vehicle after he summons the K-9 unit to the scene and the police dog is alerted to possible contraband.
   d. refuse the request altogether.

76. Sergeant Romero receives a writ of execution in the matter of *Griffin v. Famous Sliders Hamburgers.* The writ is on a small claims judgment for $219. Romero decides to affect a "till tap" and take the money in the cash register to satisfy the judgment and all taxable fees. Romero serves the writ to the manager and takes $96 from the register. Romero tells the manager and the four employees working in the restaurant that he will remain at the register and take the money as the 13 remaining sitting customers and all new customers pay their bills. The manager tells the customers that their meals are free. Romero should

   a. arrest the manager for obstruction and padlock the location.

   b. arrest the manager and all customers for obstructing an officer.

   c. arrest the manager, have him removed, and remain at the restaurant to collect the judgment in total.

   d. collect the balance of the judgment from the four employees.

77. The administrative rules of the court prohibit service of writs on Sunday unless "good cause is shown." An example of good cause to allow Sunday service is a

   a. defendant who works during the week and is verified home on Sunday.

   b. judgment against a church that holds Sunday services and collects cash.

   c. judgment against a tavern that does landmark business on Sunday during football season.

   d. used car dealership that is closed on Sunday, so that the management cannot interfere with the service of the writ involving seizure of property.

78. Field Officers Noel Braden and Roger Dunlap are assigned a writ of execution in the matter of *Foreman v. Top Gun Armory, Inc.,* a licensed retail dealer of firearms and ammunition. On arrival at the retail store, Braden and Dunlap find agents of the Bureau of Alcohol, Tobacco, Firearms, and Explosives (ATF) locking the location and arresting the owner for violations of the RICO Statute and various federal firearms laws. The inventory of the store has been seized and impounded by ATF. Braden asks if they can execute against the cash register and the store fixtures, and the agents refuse. The field officers should

   a. enter the store and seize the property after ATF agents leave.

   b. radio the court for a supervisor and ask for instructions.

   c. serve ATF agents with the writ of execution and take the cash and fixtures from them, because the cash and the fixtures are now in the custody and control of ATF.

   d. serve ATF agents with the writ of execution, post a copy at the store, and leave.

79. Court Officers Braden and Dunlap receive a writ of execution. While reviewing the writ, they notice that the statutory language (seize and sell according to law any of the defendant(s) nonexempt personal property that will be sufficient to satisfy the plaintiff's demand, costs, and all taxable statutory court officer fees and expenses) has been changed by the plaintiff attorney to read, "do not seize any property of the plaintiff unless instructed by this office." The court clerk has signed the writ. Braden and Dunlap should

   a. proceed because the court clerk has validated the writ.

   b. contact the chief judge and advise of the concern.

   c. contact the plaintiff attorney and determine why the statutory language has been changed.

   d. return the writ as unsatisfied because no property can be seized due to the changes.

Use the following information to answer questions 80 through 83.

Court Rule: The purpose of process is notice. Process rules are intended to satisfy statutory due process requirements to provide notice of a pending action to the defendant(s) and allow the defendant(s) an opportunity to be heard. Service must be accomplished in a manner that is reasonably calculated to furnish notice by best means available.

Policy: Service of process shall be attempted at the provided service address or at an address where the intended party is located no more than three times, encompassing an A.M., P.M., and Saturday attempt. Contact cards will be posted at the service location or left with a person of reasonable age and discretion. Upon verification of a valid address, the court on the motion of the plaintiff will issue an order for alternate service allowing service by first-class mail, posting at the last known or best address for service, delivery to a person of reasonable age and discretion, and posting at the courthouse.

80. Court Officer Henry Madison is assigned a summons and complaint for service in the matter of *Roundtree Services Corp. v. Charlene Williams*, with a provided address of 7652 Forrest Lake Drive. On December 3, at 8:10 a.m., Madison makes his first attempt at service and finds no one available at the address. A contact card is posted. Williams does not call, and on December 6, Madison makes a second attempt at 6:30 p.m. There is no activity at the address. On Saturday, December 8, Madison attempts service at 10:15 a.m. and is told by a 12-year-old girl that Williams is out for the morning and will return at 2 P.M. Madison makes another attempt at 2:05 P.M. and no one is present. On January 13, Madison is issued an order for alternate service. Madison returns to the address and discovers that it has been destroyed by fire, and the posting at the address and delivery requirements cannot be completed. Madison should

   a. return the process and write a report detailing the circumstances he discovered.

   b. complete the posting and mailing requirements of the order.

   c. execute the order as required by posting on the burned dwelling, and deliver a copy to the nearest neighbor who knows the defendant.

   d. post a copy at the post office for the address in the event Williams is picking up her mail.

81. Court Officer Madison is assigned an order for alternate service. Pursuant to the order, Madison is required to post a copy at the last known address of the defendant and serve a copy to a person at the address of reasonable age and discretion with instructions to deliver it promptly to the defendant. Of the following, who is a person of reasonable age and discretion?
- **a.** a 14-year-old boy who identifies the defendant as his parent
- **b.** a 60-year-old man who does not speak English
- **c.** a 21-year-old man who appears intoxicated
- **d.** a 30-year-old woman who refuses the papers, stating that she "doesn't understand legal mumbo jumbo"

82. Court Officer Madison attempts to serve a summons and complaint to George Fox in the matter of *Great Water Ways, Inc. v. Fox.* Fox refuses to open the door, screaming at Madison, "The service is junk if you don't touch me with it!" Madison should
- **a.** return to the court and obtain an order for alternate service.
- **b.** break down the door and arrest Fox for obstruction.
- **c.** post the summons and complaint and note Fox's conduct on the return.
- **d.** mail the summons and complaint to Fox and obtain a certificate of mailing from the U.S. Post Office.

83. Sergeant David Morris serves a writ of garnishment to the garnishee, The Aces Bar & Grill. The bar owner informs Morris that the defendant was fired two weeks earlier and that he does not want the garnishment or the $6 disclosure fee. Morris should
- **a.** assist the owner in filling out the disclosure form and take the form with him to the court.
- **b.** return the writ of garnishment to the court with the information provided by the garnishee.
- **c.** ask to see the payroll records to verify that the defendant has been fired.
- **d.** serve the writ of garnishment.

Use the following information to answer questions 84 through 87.

Fee Schedule #3
Service of process
Service of summons and complaint, subpoena, garnishment, judicial notice: $20 per named defendant, witness, garnishee, or respondent
Mileage fee within 20 miles round-trip from courthouse: $12
Mileage fee 21 miles to 50 miles round-trip from courthouse: $25
Mileage is taxed once regardless of service attempts.
Incorrect address fee: $12.50 per incorrect address plus mileage
Bench warrant: service of warrant and arrest of party, mileage and processing fee for warrant arrest team: $175 per arrested party

Court Officer Buckley is assigned five witness subpoenas in the matter of *People v. White*.

FROM WITNESS	MILES COURTHOUSE	STATUS
Carla Shane	9	Served
Sara Cass	8	Served
Victor Phillips	5	Incorrect address
Thomas Christopher	19	Cannot locate for service
Joseph Samuels	12	Served

84. Court Officer Madison receives a summons and complaint in the matter of *Fabulous Fashions v. Cheryl DeFranco*. The summons lists a service address of 656 South Pioneer Trail, eight miles from the courthouse. Madison travels to the service address and is informed that the defendant moved to 9250 Victoria Lane, ten miles from the service address. Madison completes the service at the new address. Based on Fee Schedule #3, what is the total service fee?
a. $44.50
b. $50.00
c. $57.50
d. $69.50

85. Sergeant Morris serves three bank garnishments in the matter of *Southhampton Supply Company v. Mujibar Brothers Pool Company*. Bank #1 is two miles from the courthouse, Bank #2 is one mile from Bank #1, and Bank #3 is one mile from Bank #1. What is the total service fee?
a. $72
b. $85
c. $96
d. $125

86. Court Officers Nichols and Roberts are assigned a bench warrant and ordered to arrest Nathan Baxter. Baxter's last known address is 58 Damasks Lane, which is 14 miles from the courthouse. They find Baxter at the address and take him into custody. While placing him in the transport van, Baxter's girlfriend confronts Nichols and spits on him before trying to kick him in the groin. She is pepper-sprayed and arrested. What is the total fee taxable in this case?
   a. $125
   b. $175
   c. $350
   d. $500

87. Based on Fee Schedule #3, what is the taxable fee for Thomas Christopher's subpoena?
   a. $25.00
   b. $37.50
   c. $45.00
   d. $12.50

88. Sergeant Keyes receives a request for reassignment from Bailiff Kliman. Kliman is assigned to Judge Buchanan, who is hearing a criminal case, *People v. Zeke Jones,* in which Jones is charged with manufacturing and distribution of obscene materials involving a minor. There is graphic photo evidence featuring nudity and sex acts that will be shown to the jury by the prosecution and explicit testimony from the victims. Kliman states, "I am a Christian and my eyes and ears are not garbage cans." Kliman has been assigned to Judge Buchanan 12 years and has seen hundreds of criminal trials in which profanity and graphic images have been displayed. Kliman has never complained before. The trial is expected to last eight days. Under the circumstances, Sergeant Keyes should
   a. order Kliman to complete his assignment.
   b. grant the request only if another bailiff is willing to take the assignment.
   c. ask Judge Buchanan if she wants to replace Kliman for this trial.
   d. suspend Kliman if he refuses the assignment or calls in sick.

Use the following information to answer questions 89 and 90.

> **Policy:** Cadets and non-sworn court employees may accompany field officers on their off-duty time with permission of the chief court officer or the executive officer. Under no circumstances are ride-along employees to engage in any duty-related activities. Violations of this policy will result in immediate suspension pending review.

89. Cadet Rhonda North obtains permission for a ride along with field officers Braden and Dunlap. Braden and Dunlap execute a writ of replevin in the matter of *Advance Finance v. Bouche.* Bouche is a French national with limited command of English. North speaks French. Through North, Bouche states that he does not understand why his property is being seized. The field officers should
   a. continue to allow North to act as the translator and distinguish this information on all forms provided to Bouche and in their report.
   b. radio for a court officer who speaks French, so policy is not violated.
   c. complete the writ and not mention North's involvement in the process.
   d. bring Bouche to the courthouse where he can be informed of the proceedings by a French speaker.

90. Local Auxiliary Police Officer Mark Haines obtains permission to ride along with Field Officers Turner and Clemons. When he arrives at the courthouse, Haines tells Turner and Clemons that he is armed and produces a copy of his concealed weapons license that allows him to carry a firearm legally, both in his capacity as an auxiliary police officer and as a private citizen. Turner and Clemons should
   a. allow Haines his ride along. He is licensed to carry a firearm.
   b. deny Haines his ride along unless he relinquishes the firearm.
   c. report this development to the chief court officer and the local police.
   d. ignore the firearm and tell Haines not to brandish it during the ride along.

Clerical Ability

Study the following form and answer questions 91 through 100 based on the form's content and use.

Court Officer Daily Activity Log
DAY: Tuesday
DATE: July 20, 2010
TOUR: 8 A.M. TO 5 P.M.
OFFICER: BRADEN   ID#: 35980
OFFICER: DUNLAP   ID#: 39109
RADIO CODE: 87-6
UNIT: 82
MILEAGE OUT: 32,510
MILEAGE IN: 32,634

TIME	ACTIVITY
0800	BEGIN TOUR
0818	759 WESTMORELAND, S&C, SERVED: DEFENDANT
0829	2390 CENTURY ST., EXEC, NO RECOVERY
0905	4007 PETROSIAN DR., S&C, SERVED: DEFENDANT
0924	100 BAYONNE BLDG., S&C, SERVED: DEFENDANT/AGENT
0952	1320 JADE RD., S&C, CONTACT CARD
1000	1103 PEARL ST., S&C, NON SERVE/DEF. MOVED
1025	6423 TENNESSEE, S&C, CONTACT CARD
1031	TX (TELEPHONE CALL) DEF.
1320	JADE RD., RETURN TO SERVICE ADDRESS
1050	1320 JADE RD., S&C, SERVED: DEFENDANT
1103	RADIO RUN-ASSIST, UNIT 87-2: GRAND EVICT
1145	CLEAR R/R (RADIO RUN), IN SERVICE
1210	997 BOOKER BLVD., S&C, SERVED: DEFENDANT
1217	LUNCH @ 3000 CENTRAL AVE.
1300	CLEAR LUNCH, IN SERVICE
1322	4000 AIRPORT RD., EXEC, RECOVERY: $1,300/#60902
1430	CLEAR EXEC, IN SERVICE
1500	6423 TENNESSEE, S&C, UNCHANGED
1515	PERSONAL @ 6675 BAKER ST.
1530	CLEAR PERSONAL, IN SERVICE, RETURN TO COURTHOUSE
1600	COURTHOUSE, MONEY DROP #60902
1610	CLEAR COURTHOUSE, IN SERVICE
1640	2045 SAUNDERS CT., SUBP, SERVED: WITNESS
1700	END TOUR

LOG PRINT: 1702
RECORDER: DUNLAP

91. What was the number of evictions performed by Braden and Dunlap?
a. 0
b. 1
c. 2
d. 3

92. What is the total mileage for the tour of duty?
a. 75
b. 90
c. 124
d. 135

93. What is the total number of services completed?
a. 5
b. 6
c. 7
d. 8

94. What is the writ of execution receipt number?
a. 69202
b. 60902
c. 60920
d. 60209

95. According to the log, when did Unit 87-6 go to 1320 Jade Road?
a. 0950 and 1051
b. 0952 and 1055
c. 0952 and 1050
d. 0950 and 1050

96. In the log, what does the code *R/R* refer to?
a. Railroad
b. Rest and Recreation
c. Rapid Response
d. Radio Run

97. In the log, what is the time between Unit 87-6 beginning their tour of duty and their third completed service?
a. 65 minutes
b. 89 minutes
c. 92 minutes
d. 120 minutes

98. In the log, what does the code *TX* refer to?
a. Time Expired
b. Telephone Call
c. Two Times
d. The Execution

99. According to the log, what is the number of addresses to which Unit 87-6 made repeat runs?
a. 0
b. 1
c. 2
d. 3

100. What is Court Officer Dunlap's ID number?
a. 39108
b. 39109
c. 38190
d. 39809

Answers

1. c. Sergeant Janet Keyes is listed on the roster as the CSO supervisor. Choice **b**, Sergeant Joel Howard, is the bailiff supervisor. Choice **a**, Lieutenant William Hooper, is the executive officer. Choice **d**, Sergeant Preston, is not listed on the roster.

2. b. This answer can be found on the last line. Try using a trick to remember these names, like *cadets* are *young* and from the *north*.

3. d. June 4 is the date at the top of the court officer duty roster. Choice **a** can be eliminated based on the logic that most courts would not be open on a national holiday (the Fourth of July).

4. b. Field Officers Braden and Dunlap are 86-7. Choice **a**, 86-6, is Turner and Clemens. Choice **c**, 86-E, is Morris and Shannon. Choice **d**, 86-X, is not assigned.

5. a. Banks is assigned to Judge Otis. Choice **b**, Bridges, is Judge Saunders's bailiff. Choice **c**, Miller, is assigned to Judge Pierce. Choice **d**, Thomas, is on sick call.

6. b. Judge Burke is in courtroom 212.

7. d. There is one magistrate, Freed, listed on the roster in addition to the eight judges.

8. c. Court Officers Adams, Pryzinski, and Zurn are on vacation, according to the roster.

9. a. According to the roster, Gore is paired up with Judge Clinton. You might have used the analogy of Al Gore and Bill Clinton to remember this pairing.

10. b. Turner and Clemens are assigned to civil process. Choice **d** is not part of the roster.

11. c. Three people are seen crossing the street in the photo.

12. a. The woman in the center of the photo closest to the viewer is wearing earphones that appear to be connected to a personal music device.

13. d. On the left-hand side of the photo, two people are in the corner, one partially hidden by a wall and the other crouched in front of the wall. One vehicle can be seen in the background facing the direction opposite the train.

14. c. Three people are seen crossing the tracks and two people are visible in the left-hand portion of the photo.

15. a. The two people coming toward the photographer both appear to be women who are dressed casually.

16. c. The passage states that we have limited information on female serial killers, which would be a good reason for social scientists to study them. Choice **a** is incorrect because the passage never states that female serial killers are a new phenomenon. Choice **b** is incorrect because there is no reason to infer that the rate of female serial killings has increased. Choice **d** is incorrect because the passage never states that female serial killers are unique to American culture.

17. b. This answer is false. According to the end of the passage, only one of the bodies was mutilated. All of the other bodies were mummified.

18. d. The passage states that Puente served time in prison for illegally cashing government checks in 1978. Choice **a** is incorrect because mismanaging a boardinghouse was done toward the end of her crime spree. She worked in a boardinghouse in her early years but was not responsible for its management. Choices **b** and **c** are incorrect because she served time for both of these crimes in 1980.

19. b. Robbery is taking something by force. Although she stole (larceny), there is nothing to suggest that her behavior met the requirements for a robbery charge. This is an "except" question—choices **a**, **c**, and **d** are incorrect because Puente served time for all of these charges. The question wanted you to pick the charge for which she *did not* serve time.

20. c. The passage states that she was brought up on suspicion of murder when one of her tenants suddenly disappeared. Choice **a** is incorrect because money was mishandled, not missing. Choice **b** is incorrect; the police did not suspect her of any wrongdoing until one of her tenants disappeared. Choice **d** is incorrect because the passage never states that one of her tenants filed a complaint against her.

21. b. This answer is false because although the police suspected that she killed 25 people, they found only nine bodies in her backyard.

22. b. Field officers are not paid a salary and benefits, but generate revenues from the private sector and public agencies, which is the same manner in which the self-employed earn their money. Choice **a** is incorrect because sentence 3 states that field officers must work assigned hours and shifts as established by their jurisdictional courts. Choices **c** and **d** are both incorrect, as they contain information not listed in the reading passage.

23. c. Although the passage does not explicitly state that Article 27-F was enacted by the NYS Department of Health, it can be inferred from the information provided. Choices **a**, **b**, and **d** are incorrect because medical providers, social service providers and clients were all affected by the confidentiality statute, but they were not responsible for its creation or its enactment.

24. a. The passage explicitly states that a signed consent form must be received from the client. Choices **b** and **c** are incorrect because the passage does not say that a verbal consent is sufficient to meet the requirements of Article 27-F. Choice **d** is incorrect because the passage states that medical providers must obtain consent from the client; they are not authorized to give consent on behalf of the client.

25. d. Sanctions imposed by the Department of Health include a $5,000 fine and one year incarceration for each disclosure violation. There were two violations in this case: Ryan disclosed information to someone who disclosed it to another person. Hence, the maximum penalty for two disclosure violations is $10,000 and/or two years incarceration. Choices **a**, **b**, and **c** provide viable punishments but do not include the maximum allowable punishment.

26. b. This is an except question and asks you to find the choice that is not true. Choices **a**, **c**, and **d** were all mentioned in the passage. Choice **b** may be true, but it was not mentioned by the author.

27. d. The passage describes the constitutional process for appointment to the federal judiciary. The final sentence references state constitutions, which mirror the U.S. Constitution. There is no mention of appointment difficulties or prestige in the passage, so choices **a** and **b** are incorrect. Choice **c** is incorrect because the president can only recommend a candidate for a judgeship, whereas a governor is empowered to appoint a judge to a term of office.

28. a. The full Senate consists of 100 members and 51% constitutes a majority.

29. c. A federal judge has a lifetime term. The times listed in choices **a**, **b**, and **d** do not appear in the passage.

30. b. The reading passage likens cabinet members to nominated federal judges. Nothing is mentioned about federal employment or presidential hires, so choices **c** and **d** are incorrect. Choice **a**, governors, are elected state officials.

31. d. The Senate Judiciary Committee acts as the screening panel to determine a nominee's fitness for office. Choices **a** and **c** are incorrect, as the full Senate votes to confirm or deny a judicial nomination as mandated by the Constitution, not presidential order.

32. d. It most likely could be evidence of poisoning. Choice **a** is incorrect; a suicide note would lead away from an inference of homicide. Choice **b** is incorrect; without more information, a person's presence established by fingerprints does not establish he or she committed a crime. Choice **c** is incorrect; it is more likely evidence of death by natural causes.

33. c. Such defensive wounds indicate the victim was trying to defend himself or herself from an assault. Choice **a** is incorrect; it would lead to an inference of suicide. Choice **b** is incorrect; although the gun found ten feet away could lead to an inference of homicide, it is not conclusive because the person could have staggered away from the spot of the shooting or as a reaction to the shot, or the gun could have been thrown. Choice **d** is incorrect because the person could have been attempting suicide and missed with the first shot.

34. c. A fire started in more than one spot is not likely to have been accidental, especially when it occurred while the building was closed. Choice **a** is incorrect because most buildings are insured. Choice **b** is incorrect because it is less likely to have been arson than choice **c**. Choice **d** is incorrect in that it is a lesser factor for suspicion than choice **c**.

35. d. The murder of the victim could have been the motive to set the fire in order to cover up the murder. Choices **a**, **b**, and **c** are incorrect because they offer no evidence to infer that arson occurred.

36. a. It is most likely to serve establishing *corpus delicti*; because the victim had no carbon dioxide in the lungs, he or she must have died before the fire, and the bruises indicate physical force. Choices **b** and **c** are less likely because the victim had carbon dioxide and could have died accidentally from the fire.

Choice **d** is incorrect; although the fire was intentionally set, no evidence is given of who set the fire (it may have been the victim) or whether it was set with the intention of killing the victim.

37. b. The author provides information on the use of the cultural defense as an excuse or justification defense; however, she does not find it to be an acceptable reason for criminal activity. Choices **a**, **c**, and **d** are all in favor of the defense. The author is clearly against its use in the American court system.

38. a. The author clearly maintains that cultural background should not excuse a defendant's criminal actions. Choice **b** is incorrect; even though the author suggests that we should be more sensitive to cultural issues, it is not the dominant theme of the passage. The author argues against choice **c**, and choice **d** is never mentioned as an alternative.

39. d. Choice **d** is correct. The meaning of *mens rea* is the guilty mind, one's intent, or one's criminal culpability. Choices **a**, **b**, and **c** are not the correct definitions of the term *mens rea*.

40. b. In this case, **b** is the correct answer because his defense was that he was following the Laotion ritual of marriage-by-capture. Choice **a** is incorrect; the victim's appearance was not cited by the defendant as his reason for raping her. Choice **c** is incorrect; he was actually charged with kidnapping. Choice **d** is incorrect; the victim never said she wanted to marry the defendant.

41. c. Based on a cultural defense, which mitigated the charges, Moua was convicted of false imprisonment. He was charged with rape (choice **a**) and kidnapping (choice **b**) but was not convicted of those charges. Choice **d** is obviously incorrect since one of the given answers (choice **c**) is correct.

42. c. The passage clearly states that Kimura engaged in this Japanese ritual, *oyako-shinju*, because of her husband's infidelity. She needed to escape the shame and humiliation he caused her, and if she left her children behind, she would be characterized as a horrible person. Choices **a** and **b** are incorrect; the passage never states that she did not like being a mother, nor does it state that she blamed her children for her marital problems. Choice **d** is incorrect; the reader does not know whether the defendant was employed or unemployed.

43. b. To "mitigate" charges means to lessen them. She was originally charged with murder but based on cultural factors, she was convicted of the lesser charge of manslaughter. Choice **a** is incorrect; murder to manslaughter increases or aggravates the charges, not lessens them. Choices **c** and **d** are incorrect; child endangerment was never mentioned as an option for the jury to consider.

44. c. The use of plain English will make reading and interpreting legal documents easier for those seldom involved in the legal system. Choice **a** is incorrect and assumes facts not stated. Choice **b** is also incorrect because this type of conduct is not mentioned in the reading passage. Choice **d** is incorrect because nothing in the passage suggests plain English will decrease a lawyer's intelligence.

45. b. This is the preferred style because it incorporates all key components of the opening line of the pleading: the moving party (plaintiff), the fact that the party is represented (through counsel), and what pleading is before the court (complaint). Choices **a** and **d** fail to state that the party is represented, and choice **c** does not identify what is before the court.

46. a. The Securities and Exchange Commission's 1933 Truth in Securities Act is credited with the first formal implementation of the doctrine. Choices **b**, **c**, and **d** are not mentioned in the passage.

47. b. Thomas Jefferson is identified in the reading passage as one of the first American lawyers to use plain English in recorded legal pleadings.

48. c. Used as a noun, a *mandate* is an order from a superior court to a lower court or subordinate body governed by the court. Choice **a** is also a noun, but the meaning is incorrect for this passage. Choices **b** and **d** are verbs.

49. b. In 1977, President Jimmy Carter required government regulations to be written in plain English. The remaining presidents are not mentioned in the passage.

50. a. The word *verbiage* means "excess words with little or no meaning."

51. b. In this case, Mrs. Cox is the plaintiff, which is the person who brings the lawsuit to court. Mr. Conklin is the defendant (choice **a**). Choices **c** and **d** are incorrect because the reader does not know if Mrs. Cox wins the case.

52. d. The decision of the court to grant her damages is known as the court's judgment. Choice **a** is incorrect because a writ of execution is a court order seizing a debtor's property. Choice **b** is incorrect because a writ of restitution returns property to the owner or landlord. Choice **c** is incorrect because a subpoena is a court order compelling one's presence.

53. c. A writ of garnishment attaches to a judgment debtor's wages or other tangible property. Unless the judgment debtor is owed money by an individual, or an individual is holding property of the judgment debtor, choices **a** and **b** are unlikely garnishees. The judgment debtor is indebted to his or her landlord, so choice **d** is incorrect.

54. b. The specific term in this instance would be *subpoena duces tecum* (latin for "bring with you"), which calls for the production of documents or other tangible property. Choice **d** is a post-judgment remedy, and choice **c** applies to specific property of a secured creditor. Choice **a** is issued and served at the beginning of the case.

55. c. The return of service is required when service of process cannot be completed. If the court officer could obtain choices **a** and **b**, they could be attached as exhibits in support of the return of service. This would also show diligence on the part of the court officer.

56. b. The attorney for the judgment creditor will petition the court for an order to show cause, making Fisher appear before the court and explain his conduct. Choice **c**, a bench warrant, is an order of the court, issued by a judge commanding that a party be arrested and brought before the court. Choice **a** was served to Fisher when the demand for the documents was made. Choice **d** is a post-judgment collection procedure.

57. a. This is also known as writ of attachment. Choices **b** and **c** are post-judgment collection remedies. Choice **d** is an order from a superior court to a subordinate court.

58. b. A complaint is a factual account of the occurrence; it includes the relief being sought by the plaintiff. Choice **a** is incorrect because a service of process is the delivery of legal documents to the person being sued. Choice **c** is incorrect because a subpoena orders someone to appear in court. Choice **d** is incorrect because an order to show cause forces one of the parties to appear in court and explain the reasons for his or her behavior.

59. d. The best example would involve a defendant debtor who is sued on a credit car debt for $3,000. Under oath, the debtor admits to owing the money, but offers as a defense an inability to pay. The plaintiff creditor would be entitled to summary judgment as a matter of law because no facts are in dispute as to the money owed. Choices **a** and **b** are incorrect because these are factors that could be weighed by a judge or jury along with evidence

presented. Choice **c** is incorrect because non-qualified immunity is generally insufficient to warrant summary disposition of an action.

60. d. A mortgagor may continue to occupy the property until the default results in loan foreclosure proceedings and all statutory redemption rights due the mortgagee have been extinguished. Choices **b** and **c** are also known as *squatters,* and choice **a** is the most common unlawful detainer.

61. a. This is an assumption of a crime having been committed, although there is no *direct* evidence implicating the manager who purchased the automobile. Choices **b**, **c**, and **d** are examples of competent evidence.

62. b. Aptly named "The Miranda Warning," according to *Miranda v. Arizona* 386 US 436 (1966), persons being questioned by police in connection to a criminal offense must be advised of their right to remain silent, or any statements made without Miranda cannot be used against them. Choice **a** is incorrect because this case deals with "stop and frisk" actions; choice **c** is incorrect because it deals with Gary Gilmore and his 1977 execution. Choice **d** is a First Amendment case.

63. c. This is commonly referred to as an *amicus brief.*

64. b. The opposite is choice **a**, which increases an award. Choice **c** is a procedure in a jury trial. Choice **d** is incorrect because this is a remedy provided by an appellate court.

65. a. Discovery is permitted for a period of days prior to trial. Choice **b** is a process incorporated into the litigation process at the conclusion of discovery that places a value on the case for settlement purposes. Choices **c** and **d** are the same and are an alternative to a court trial in which disputes are settled in a private forum.

66. b. The fee schedule provides for the following taxable court officer fees: $215 based on 5% of

$4,300 collected, service fee: $40, mileage fee: $25 based on 32 miles round-trip (16 miles × 2), postings of sale notices: $75, and three hours of sale and impound fees at $40 per hour: $120. The towing and storage fees are separate from the taxable court officer fees.

67. b. The taxable court officer fee of $475 is combined with the towing and storage fee of $300. So, $4,300 minus $775 equals net proceeds of $3,525.

68. d. If the sale was held 15 days after the property was seized, April 28 is the third day.

69. a. The beginning judgment balance was $8,278. Net proceeds of $3,525 is subtracted, leaving a remaining balance of $4,753.

70. c. The service fees total $52 based on $40 to serve the writ and $12 mileage fee calculated on 20-mile round-trip. Choice **b** is incorrect because no mileage fee is added to the amount due. Choice **d** is incorrect because no property was seized, and the hourly rate of $40 per hour does not apply. Choice **a** is incorrect because, at the minimum, the officers are entitled to a service and mileage fee.

71. b. The officers are entitled to $40 service fee and $25 mileage fee for the 36-mile round trip. The $35 peaceful possession restoration fee does not apply because the tenant vacated prior to service of the writ; therefore, choice **c** is incorrect. Choice **a** is incorrect because the round-trip mileage exceeds 20 miles. Choice **d** is incorrect because that amount cannot be reached based on the fee schedule.

72. c. The 48-hour period will conclude on Sunday, November 6. No evictions will occur on Sunday without an order of the court allowing Sunday evictions, so choice **b** is incorrect. Choice **a** is one day early and choice **d** is 96 hours after service of the writ.

73. b. The bond amount is based on service fee: $40, mileage fee: $25 on a total of 24 miles (12 miles round-trip × 2), $35 peaceful

possession restoration fee, and $175 arrest fee. Choice **a** is incorrect because it fails to include mileage fee for the second round-trip from the court on Monday. Choice **c** is the total for ten arrests based on the incorrect amount of $262, as is choice **d**, which is for ten arrested protestors and the arrested owner.

74. b. If the defendant is not home, the notice and order will be posted per administrative order. If the defendant is present, Flynn can make his arrest. Choice **d** is incorrect because Flynn holds a valid arrest warrant and can go to the defendant's address on his own. Choice **c** is unnecessary, and choice **a** is not good or acceptable practice and procedure and would void the writ.

75. b. The officer does not have the right to search the vehicle and must obtain a search warrant in the ordinary course (*Terry v. Ohio*). Because the officer does not have immediate probable cause, summoning the police K-9 is not an appropriate remedy, so choice **c** is incorrect. The vehicle being on the flatbed under the control of the court officer does not allow a warrantless search by the police; therefore, choice **a** is incorrect. The vehicle may be searched with a valid warrant, making choice **d** incorrect.

76. a. This is textbook obstruction. The manager should be arrested and the location secured and shuttered. The customers are not obstructing the execution process by having their meals deemed gratis by the manager, making choice **b** incorrect. Choice **c** is not practical because the employees can decide not to work, defeating Romero's purpose, and the employees are not liable for the judgment unless they are owners of the restaurant.

77. b. The church is open one day and it is very likely that there will be cash available to satisfy the judgment. Choice **a** is incorrect because there is no guarantee that the defendant will be available or have any assets. Choice **c** is not valid because the tavern is open other days and assets are available at those times. Choice **d** is incorrect because parties who interfere with a court order are subject to arrest, and the arrest should be made while court is in session.

78. d. This is a federal criminal action and ATF has jurisdiction over the firearms inventory at the store. The cash and the fixtures are subject to a RICO forfeiture claims process, and the officers should file a claim for the fixtures and the cash. The service of the writ to ATF also places the agency on notice in the event that the defendant is acquitted on the charges and is entitled to the return of the cash and fixtures, which would then be subject to the writ of execution. Choices **a** and **c** are unlawful actions and subject the offenders to federal criminal prosecution. Choice **b** does not accomplish the intended purpose of the writ of execution or resolve the immediate problem.

79. b. The chief judge, or the judge to whom the case is assigned, must be made aware of this situation. Very likely, the plaintiff attorney is subject to an order to show cause for changing a statutory form or language without an order of the court. Choice **a** is incorrect because the court clerk likely entered the writ routinely. Choice **c** is incorrect because the court will contact the plaintiff attorney. Choice **d** is improper practice and procedure.

80. b. The law does not require an act that is unreasonable or cannot be accomplished because of extraordinary circumstances (e.g., death, location no longer exists). The posting and mailing requirements of the order can be fulfilled and the court can amend the order to fit the current situation by allowing posting at

an alternate location or publication in a local newspaper. Choice **a** is incorrect because part of the order can be fulfilled. Choice **c** is incorrect because this is improper practice and procedure. Choice **d** is incorrect because the order for posting does not include the post office.

81. a. Of the parties and circumstances described, the 14-year-old is the most coherent and is a direct relative of the defendant. Most states consider 14 an age of reasonable discretion for purposes of accepting process. Choice **b** is an incorrect choice because the party does not understand English. Choice **c** is incorrect because the party is intoxicated and might not remember the instructions. Choice **d** is not an acceptable choice because the party is disinterested and might not forward the process.

82. c. It is a legal myth that the intended party must be touched with the process to validate the service. There is much case law, state and federal, that states if the parties are within speaking distance of each other and the intent of the process server's presence is clear, the intended party cannot defeat the service by refusing in hand service. The process should be left within the physical control of the intended party in a secure manner. Choice **a** is unnecessary and the court can order this method later if the service is challenged and ruled improper. Choice **b** is extreme, and this conduct does not rise to the level of obstruction. Choice **d** is incorrect because this does not accomplish personal service.

83. d. It is the responsibility of the garnishee to make a full and proper disclosure to the plaintiff and the court. Choice **b** is incorrect as the garnishee is available for process and process can be completed. Choice **a** is improper practice and procedure because the court officer should not provide legal advice or any assistance in filling out legal forms unless directed by the court. Choice **c** is incorrect because there is no obligation for the court officer to verify the statement.

84. c. The fee is computed as follows: service of summons and complaint: $20, mileage fee: $25 (16 miles round-trip on incorrect address and 20 miles round-trip from the completed service address totals 36 miles), and $12.50 is charged for the incorrect address.

85. a. The three garnishments total $60 ($20 × 3) and the mileage fee is $12 based on eight round-trip miles for the three locations.

86. b. The bench warrant was for Baxter. Baxter's girlfriend was arrested for assaulting Nichols and is not subject to a taxable fee at the time of arrest.

87. a. The mileage fee is taxable. There is no indication that the address is not valid, so choice **b** is incorrect. The process was not served, making choice **c** incorrect. In choice **d**, the incorrect address fee does not apply.

88. c. If Kliman is insistent on not working this assignment, his attitude could become obvious to the jury and possibly taint the trial. Judge Buchanan works with Kliman daily and knows him and his personality, and her input will prove invaluable. Choice **d** is extreme and choice **a** may create further problems. Assigning a different bailiff, choice **b**, is a supervision tactic that should be avoided.

89. a. North is not engaging in official duties by translating for Braden and Dunlap, who are executing the writ. If the action is noted on the forms and in their reports, North can verify the circumstances requiring her assistance if the matter is challenged in court by Bouche. Choices **b** and **d** are unnecessary if

North is at the scene. Choice **c** is improper practice and procedure.

90. b. This is sound judgment. Although Haines is licensed to carry a firearm and serves with the police auxiliary, Haines is not a court officer, and this is not an assignment from the local police. Choice **a** is incorrect because the court can dictate its own firearms policy. With choice **c**, the chief court officer and the local police will come to the same conclusion as choice **b**, and the field officers are likely to be reprimanded for even considering such a request from Haines. Choice **d** is improper practice and procedure, not to mention that it exposes the court to numerous liabilities.

91. a. The court officers assisted Unit 87-2 on an eviction, but they were not the assigned team. The call is logged as an assist.

92. c. The end mileage subtracted from the beginning mileage is 124.

93. d. There were five summons and complaints, one subpoena, and two executions served.

94. b. The receipt number is 60902.

95. c. Review the form carefully to retrieve the correct times.

96. d. The 1103 entry immediately preceding code R/R indicates a Radio Run, and Dunlap, as log recorder, uses this code to record the unit cleared from the call.

97. a. The third completed service occurred at 0905.

98. b. The 0952 entry shows a telephone call from the defendant at 1320 Jade Road.

99. c. The unit made two runs to 1320 Jade Road and 6423 Tennessee.

100. b. Dunlap's ID number is listed on the second line of the log.

5 ▶ MEMORY AND OBSERVATION

Depending upon your assignment, knowing the rules and implemented policies of the court will often be the primary responsibility of the court officer. Officers who effectuate criminal process will have the use of arrest bulletins and mug shots, but they will be required to memorize key information regarding wanted suspects, such as known associates, hangouts, distinguishing marks or scars, and types of weapons carried and used.

Exam questions use a variety of methods to test your observation and memory skills. You may be shown drawings or photographs of street scenes and then asked questions about what you observed. Often, exams will provide wanted posters of suspects with their pedigree information. You will be asked to recall the suspect's description and the pedigree information.

Some questions test your memory skills by having you read a lengthy, detailed passage within a set amount of time (five to ten minutes is common). The passage is then removed and you are asked to answer multiple-choice questions on the material.

What is Memory?

Memory is the brain's ability to obtain, store, and later retrieve information. Memory is a very complicated process. In fact, it is so complicated that researchers cannot agree on the processes involved with retaining such data, such as how memory works or where memory is actually stored. We tend to have two types of memory: short term and long term. You will be honing your skills to increase your short term memory for the exam. Try to remember as much as you can about the picture or reading you are asked to study, but do not overwhelm yourself. Humans can hold only a certain number of items in their short term memories. If you try to retain too much information, the initial information you obtained will be replaced by the newer information. You can increase your memory storage capacity by practicing your observation skills daily. Try being more observant on your daily walks, train commutes, or drives. Later, see how many items you can recall. You can practice these skills at home as well. Take a deck of playing cards and practice your short term memory with a game of concentration (trying to find matched pairs). Skills practice, coupled with confidence, can go a long way in improving your test score on this part of the exam.

Memorization Tips

Memorization is much easier if you approach the task with the expectation that you *will* remember what you see or read. When you run through practice questions in this book, prepare your mind before you start. Tell yourself over and over that you will remember what you see or read. Your performance level will rise to meet your expectations.

Yes, it's easy for your brain to seize up in a stressful testing situation. But if you've programmed yourself to stay calm, stay alert, and execute your plan, you'll remember the details when you need them.

Your goal is to retain the information long enough to get through this test.

Although memory skills are developed at an early age, they can be enhanced throughout a lifetime. How memory skills are enhanced is as individualized as memory itself. Some are blessed with photographic memory: They look at a passage or picture once and the brain records it like a snapshot. It can be recalled on demand and the information retrieved in detail.

For the majority of the population, other methods are required. The most common time-proven, effective, and inexpensive learning tools are flash cards. They are easily developed with a set of 3" × 5" index cards and can be drafted on any subject matter to be used by the court officer (e.g., general orders, security policies, or legal definitions).

Observation Tips

Some people are naturally observant. However, it's never too late to sharpen, or acquire, strong observation skills.

Newspaper photos make great observation tools. News photos are action oriented and usually have more than one person in the scenes. Sit down in a quiet place, clear your mind, remind yourself for several minutes that you will retain all the details you need when you study the picture, and then turn to the picture and study it for about five minutes. At the end of the time, turn the picture over and write down all the details you can think of in the picture. Make yourself do this as much as possible before test day.

You can practice your observation skills on the way to work or school, too. Instead of sitting in your car waiting for a light to change, look around and say what you see aloud. If you're on a bus or train, you can observe these things silently. You are not only practicing a basic skill you will need to become an excellent court officer, but also training your mind to succeed at whatever memory question the test throws your way.

Practice Questions

Study the following passage for ten minutes. Then, answer questions 1 through 15 based upon what you have just read. Do not refer back to the passage when answering these questions.

On October 9, Court Officer Edmund Bursa of the 16th Municipal Court was assigned an order of eviction for a residential property at 96 Bloomfield Lane, in the matter of *Exclusive Property Management v. Cage and all occupants of 96 Bloomfield Lane.*

Bursa traveled to the property and met with the plaintiff's agent, Mark Lewandowski. Lewandowski informed Bursa that the address was vacant and the defendants had moved. What was left at the address was furniture and miscellaneous personal effects. Bursa advised that he must examine the address before returning possession to the plaintiff. Lewandowski advised that his company would remove the contents from the property.

96 Bloomfield Lane is a six-room colonial-styled two-story home. There are three bedrooms located on the second floor. There is no basement and no garage. In the utility room on the first floor, Bursa located three plastic storage containers. Bursa opened the first container and discovered stacks of money encased in clear plastic storage bags. Bursa then opened the other two containers and found more money in plastic bags.

Bursa immediately called the city police department. The police responded to the location. Upon examining the money, the officers called for a K-9 unit to determine if any drugs were present. The K-9 arrived and detected the scent of narcotics in the container and on the currency. The police impounded the currency, which totaled $1,489,236. Laboratory tests confirmed the presence of cocaine residue on the packaged currency.

On December 22, the police commenced a narcotics forfeiture proceeding in first Superior Court. On December 23, Bursa retained Melissa Hodges of the Mandrich Law Firm and filed a claim for the cash in his individual capacity. The 16th Municipal Court did not file a claim for the money. The city filed an answer to Bursa's claim and moved for summary disposition because the money was generated from narcotics activities and subject to criminal forfeiture. Bursa was acting as the court officer in an official capacity and was not entitled to claim found money as a private citizen.

On March 13, the first Superior Court found for the city and dismissed Bursa's action. The court agreed with the city that the money was a result of a criminal enterprise and was forfeited to the city. The court held that Bursa was acting in his capacity as a court officer and discovered the currency in that capacity. Accordingly, Bursa was not to be rewarded for performing his office. Bursa appealed to the 1st District Court of Appeals.

The Court of Appeals unanimously affirmed the trial court decision 18 months later. The lead opinion was written by Judge Davis Bryant II. The State Supreme Court denied leave to appeal.

1. The jurisdictional court is
   a. 1st Superior Court.
   b. 7th Superior Court.
   c. 6th Municipal Court.
   d. 16th Municipal Court.

2. What is the case title of the eviction action?
   a. *Executive Management Services v. Cagle*
   b. *Exclusive Property Management v. Cage*
   c. *Exclusive Management Company v. Cage*
   d. *Excellent Property Management v. Cartman*

3. What was the address where the order of eviction was served?
   a. 96 Bloomfield Lane
   b. 96 Bloomfield Court
   c. 906 Birmingham
   d. 900 Buckingham Court

4. The plaintiff's agent is
   a. Michael Lewis.
   b. Morris Lewandowski.
   c. Mark Lewandowski.
   d. Bernard Marks.

5. Bursa discovered the containers in the
   a. garage.
   b. basement.
   c. master bedroom.
   d. utility room.

6. The money inside the containers was stored in
   a. plastic storage bags.
   b. plastic wrap.
   c. shoe boxes.
   d. aluminum foil.

7. After arriving at the address and examining the money, the city police
   a. inventoried the currency and removed it to the station.
   b. called for a K-9 unit to detect the presence of narcotics on the money.
   c. called for surveillance units to stake out the house and arrest the tenants.
   d. called for crime scene investigation team to mark the evidence.

8. The laboratory confirmed the presence of
   a. heroin.
   b. marijuana.
   c. cocaine.
   d. methamphetamine.

9. The city commenced the forfeiture action for the money on
   a. November 12.
   b. December 22.
   c. December 23.
   d. January 1.

10. The forfeiture action was commenced in
    a. First Municipal Court.
    b. 16th Municipal Court.
    c. First Superior Court.
    d. Sixth Superior Court.

11. The attorney retained by Bursa is
   a. Melissa Hodge.
   b. Melissa Hodges.
   c. Melinda Hodges.
   d. Melissa Howe.

12. What is the amount of money sought by Bursa?
   a. $1,489,236
   b. $1,498,263
   c. $1,499,623
   d. $1,499,826

13. The city received summary judgment on
   a. January 10.
   b. January 23.
   c. March 11.
   d. March 13.

14. The Court of Appeals affirmed the trial court decision in
   a. 12 months.
   b. 16 months.
   c. 18 months.
   d. 19 months.

15. The lead opinion in the Court of Appeals was written by
   a. Brian David Jr.
   b. Davis Bryant II.
   c. Bryant Daniels II.
   d. David Bryant III.

On pages 73 and 74 is a street scene like those found on some Court Officer exams. Following are several questions about details of the scene. Use this scene to practice your memory skills. Take exactly five minutes to study the picture, and then answer the questions that follow without looking back at the picture.

Check your answers by looking back at the scene. If you get all the questions right, you know you're well prepared for memory questions. If you miss a few, you know you need to spend more time practicing, using the tips previously outlined. Remember, you *can* improve your memory with practice.

16. What type of sale is advertised at Howard Jeweler?
   a. 50% off
   b. 2 for 1
   c. going out of business
   d. 20% to 60% off

17. Which of the following is true about the man wearing the Artie's Deli shirt?
   a. His sunglasses are black.
   b. He has a shaved head.
   c. He has a tattoo on his right arm.
   d. He wears an earring in his right ear.

18. What is the complete name of the store located directly to the left of Howard Jeweler?
   a. Photo by Joe
   b. Photo Discount
   c. Joe's Photo
   d. Joe's Discount Photo

19. What is Howard Jeweler's address?
   a. 2 Cortlandt
   b. 2A Cortlandt
   c. 3 Cortlandt
   d. 3A Cortlandt

20. What is Salon & Spa's phone number?
   a. 212–555–1605
   b. 212–555–1606
   c. 212–555–1506
   d. 212–555–1505

21. How many bicycles are there in the photograph?
   a. 0
   b. 1
   c. 2
   d. 3

22. There are two young women talking to each other in the photo. Where are they standing?
   a. at a pay phone kiosk
   b. next to a rack of sunglasses
   c. near a bicycle rack
   d. outside the Salon & Spa entrance

23. What phrase is written on Sushi-Time's awning?
   a. Sushi & Noodle Restaurant
   b. Sushi & Noodle
   c. Sushi
   d. Sushi Restaurant

24. What is the man wearing the backpack doing in the photograph?
   a. talking on a cell phone
   b. looking at the Howard Jeweler window display
   c. crossing the street
   d. exiting from Salon & Spa

25. What is the phone number of Artie's Deli?
   a. 212–555–0856
   b. 212–555–5086
   c. 212–555–8605
   d. 212–555–6805

Answers

1. **d.** Court Officer Edmund Bursa was from the 16th Municipal Court.
2. **b.** Although these answer choices contain similar names, choice **b** is the correct case title.
3. **a.** The order of eviction was served to 96 Bloomfield Lane.
4. **c.** Mark Lewandowski is the plaintiff's agent.
5. **d.** The containers were in the utility room.
6. **a.** Plastic storage bags held the money.
7. **b.** They called for a K-9 unit to detect the presence of narcotics on the money.
8. **c.** Cocaine was detected.
9. **b.** This is the date mentioned in the passage.
10. **c.** The first Superior Court commenced the forfeiture action.
11. **b.** Although these answer choices contain similar names, Melissa Hodges is the correct choice.
12. **a.** Bursa sought $1,489,236.
13. **d.** This is the correct date mentioned in the passage.
14. **c.** The Court of Appeals affirmed the trial court decision in 18 months.

15. **b.** Davis Bryant II wrote the lead opinion in the Court of Appeals.
16. **d.** A "20% to 60% off" sale is advertised at Howard Jeweler.
17. **b.** The man wearing the Artie's Deli shirt has a shaved head.
18. **d.** The complete name of the store located directly to the left of Howard Jeweler is "Joe's Discount Photo."
19. **b.** The address of Howard Jeweler is 2A Cortlandt.
20. **a.** Salon & Spa's phone number is 212–555–1605.
21. **b.** There is only one bicycle visible in the photograph.
22. **a.** The two young women talking to each other are standing at a pay phone kiosk.
23. **b.** "Sushi & Noodle" is written on Sushi-Time's awning.
24. **b.** The man wearing the backpack is looking at the Howard Jeweler window display.
25. **d.** The phone number of Artie's Deli is 212–555–6805.

CHAPTER

6 ▶ READING TEXT, TABLES, CHARTS, AND GRAPHS

CHAPTER SUMMARY

Court officers need to have the ability to read—pure and simple. They also need to be able to understand what they are reading. Reports, procedures, forms, petitions, and many other documents are regularly referred to in the court officer profession. This chapter provides tips and exercises that will help you improve your reading comprehension and improve your test score in this area.

The reading comprehension portion of the written test is designed to measure how well applicants understand what they read. The tests are usually multiple choice and will likely have questions based on brief passages, much like the standardized tests offered in schools. This chapter focuses on the specifics you will need to know to ace the reading comprehension questions on your exam. Once you are armed with the strategies that are explained in this chapter, you will be better able to understand what you read. Be sure to spend plenty of time with this chapter so that you can accurately assess your reading comprehension ability and increase your level of skill in this area.

Types of Reading Text, Tables, Charts, and Graphs Questions

You have probably encountered reading comprehension questions before, where you are given a passage to read and then have to answer multiple-choice questions about it. This kind of question has two advantages for you as a test taker:

1. Any information you need to know is right in front of you.
2. You're being tested only on the information provided in the passage.

The disadvantage, however, is that you have to know where and how to find that information quickly in an unfamiliar text. This makes it easy to fall for one of the incorrect answer choices, especially since they're designed to mislead you.

The best way to excel on this passage/question format is to be very familiar with the kinds of questions that are typically asked on the test. Questions most frequently fall into one of the following four categories:

1. fact or detail
2. main idea or title
3. inference or interpretation
4. vocabulary definition

In order to succeed on a reading comprehension test, you need to understand each of these four types of questions thoroughly.

Fact or Detail

Facts and details are the specific pieces of information that support the passage's main idea. Generally speaking, facts and details are indisputable—things that don't need to be proven, like statistics (18 million people) or descriptions (a green overcoat). While you may need to decipher paraphrases of facts or details, you should be able to find the answer to a fact or detail question directly in the passage. This is usually the simplest kind of question; however, you must be able to separate important information from less important information. The main challenge in answering this type of question is that the answer choices can be confusing because they are often very similar to each other. You should read each answer choice carefully before selecting one.

Main Idea or Title

The main idea of a passage is the thought, opinion, or attitude that governs the whole passage. It may be clearly stated, or only implied. Think of the main idea

as an umbrella that is general enough to cover all of the specific ideas and details in the passage. Sometimes, the questions found after a passage will ask you about the main idea, while others use the term *title*. Don't be misled; main idea and title questions are the same. They both require you to know what the passage is mostly about. Often, the incorrect answers to a main idea or title question are too detailed to be correct. Remember that the main idea of a passage or the best title for a passage is general, not specific.

If you are lucky, the main idea will be clearly stated in the first or last sentence of the passage. At other times, the main idea is not stated in a topic sentence but is implied in the overall passage, and you will need to determine the main idea by inference. Because there may be a lot of information in the passage, the trick is to understand what all that information adds up to—what it is that the author wants you to know. Often, some of the wrong answers to main idea questions are specific facts or details from the passage. A good way to test yourself is to ask, "Can this answer serve as a net to hold the whole passage together?" If not, chances are you have chosen a fact or detail, not a main idea.

Inference or Interpretation

Inference or interpretation questions ask you what the passage means, implies, or suggests, not just what it says. They are often the most difficult type of reading comprehension question.

Inference questions can be the most difficult to answer because they require you to draw meaning from the text when that meaning is implied rather than directly stated. Inferences are conclusions that we draw based on the clues the writer has given us. When you draw inferences, you have to be something of a detective, looking for clues such as word choice, tone, and specific details that suggest a certain conclusion, attitude, or point of view. You have to read between the lines in order to make a judgment about what an author was implying in the passage.

A good way to test whether you've drawn an acceptable inference is to ask, "What evidence do I have for this inference?" If you can't find any, you probably have the wrong answer. You need to be sure that your inference is logical and that it is based on something that is suggested or implied in the passage itself—not by what you or others might think. Like a good detective, you need to base your conclusions on evidence—facts, details, and other information—not on random hunches or guesses.

Vocabulary Definition

Questions designed to test vocabulary are really trying to measure how well you can figure out the meaning of an unfamiliar word from its context. *Context* refers to the words and ideas surrounding a vocabulary word. If the context is clear enough, you should be able to substitute a nonsense word for the one being sought, and you would still make the correct choice because you could determine meaning strictly from the sentence. For example, you should be able to determine the meaning of the following italicized nonsense word based on its context:

> The speaker noted that it gave him great *terivinix* to announce the winner of the Outstanding Leadership Award.

In this sentence, *terivinix* most likely means

> **a.** pain.
> **b.** sympathy.
> **c.** pleasure.
> **d.** anxiety.

Clearly, the context of an award makes choice **c**, *pleasure*, the best choice. Awards don't usually bring pain, sympathy, or anxiety.

When confronted with an unfamiliar word, try substituting a nonsense word and see if the context gives you the clue. If you're familiar with prefixes, suffixes, and word roots, you can also use this knowledge to help you determine the meaning of an unfamiliar word.

You should be careful not to guess at the answer to vocabulary questions based on how you may have seen the word used before or what you think it means. Many words have more than one possible meaning, depending on the context in which they're used, and a word you've seen used one way may mean something else in a test passage. Also, if you don't look at the context carefully, you may make the mistake of confusing the vocabulary word with a similar word. For example, the vocabulary word may be *taut* (meaning *tight*), but if you read too quickly or don't check the context, you might think the word is *taunt* (meaning *tease*). Always make sure you read carefully and that what you think the word means fits into the context of the passage you're being tested on.

Now it is time to practice answering the four types of reading comprehension questions.

Practice Passage 1

The following is a sample test passage, followed by four questions. Read the passage carefully, and then answer the questions, based on your reading of the text, by circling your choice. Note under your answer which type of question has been asked. Correct answers appear immediately after the questions.

> In the last decade, community policing has been frequently touted as the best way to reform urban law enforcement. The idea of putting more officers on foot patrol in high crime areas, where relations with police have frequently been strained, was initiated in Houston in 1983 under the leadership of then-Commissioner Lee Brown. He believed that officers should be accessible to the community at the street level. If officers were assigned to the same area over a period of time, those officers would eventually build a network of trust with neighborhood residents. That trust would mean that

Tips for Improving Your Reading Comprehension Score

Before the test:

- Practice, practice, practice!
- Working with a friend or family member, select paragraphs from an article in the newspaper and have your partner create questions to ask you about it.
- Read short passages from articles or books and make up questions for yourself.

During the test:

- Read the questions first, before you read the passage, so you will know what words and ideas to look out for.
- Focus your attention; don't let your mind wander during the reading of the test passages.
- If one part of a passage confuses you, just read on until you are finished. Then go back and look at the confusing part again.
- Look at each one of the multiple-choice answers, then compare each with the passage to see which ones can be eliminated.
- Focus on the main idea of the text. What is the passage mostly about?
- Don't skip any sentences when reading the passage.
- Don't let your own knowledge of the subject matter interfere with your answer selection. Stick with the information that is given in the passage.
- Read the passage actively, asking yourself questions about the main idea and jotting down notes in the margin.

---

merchants and residents in the community would let officers know about criminal activities in the area and would support police intervention. Since then, many large cities have experimented with community-oriented policing (COP) with mixed results. Some have found that police and citizens are grateful for the opportunity to work together. Others have found that unrealistic expectations by citizens and resistance from officers have combined to hinder the effectiveness of COP. It seems possible, therefore, that a good idea may need improvement before it can truly be considered a reform.

1. Community policing has been used in law enforcement since
   a. the late 1970s.
   b. the early 1980s.
   c. the Carter administration.
   d. Lee Brown was New York City police commissioner.

   Question type: _____

2. The phrase *a network of trust* in this passage suggests that
   a. police officers can rely only on each other for support.
   b. community members rely on the police to protect them.
   c. police and community members rely on each other.
   d. community members trust only each other.

   Question type: _____

3. The best title for this passage would be
   a. Community Policing: The Solution to the Drug Problem.
   b. Houston Sets the Pace in Community Policing.
   c. Communities and Cops: Partners for Peace.
   d. Community Policing: An Uncertain Future?

   Question type: _____

4. The word *touted* in the first sentence of the passage most nearly means
   a. praised.
   b. denied.
   c. exposed.
   d. criticized.

Question type: _____

Answers

Don't just look at the correct answers and move on. The explanations are the most important part, so read them carefully. Use these explanations to help you understand how to tackle each kind of question the next time you come across it.

1. b. Question type: 1, fact or detail. The passage says, "The idea of putting more officers on foot patrol in high crime areas, where relations with police have frequently been strained, was initiated in Houston in 1983 under the leadership of then-Commissioner Lee Brown." Do not be confused by the opening phrase, *In the last decade* because the passage does not include the current date, so you have no way of knowing which decade the passage is referring to. This information doesn't help you even if you know that a decade is a period of ten years. Don't be misled by trying to figure out when Carter was president. Also, if you happen to know that Lee Brown was New York City's police commissioner at one time, don't let that information lead you away from the information contained in the passage alone. Brown was commissioner in Houston when he initiated community policing.

2. c. Question type: 3, inference. The *network of trust* referred to in this passage is between the community and the police, as you can see from the sentence where the phrase appears. The key phrase in the question is *in this passage*. You may think that police can rely only on each other, or one of the other answer choices may appear equally plausible to you. But your choice of answers must be limited to the one suggested in this passage. Another tip for questions like this: Beware of absolutes! Be suspicious of any answer containing words like *only*, *always*, or *never*.

3. d. Question type: 2, main idea. A good title usually expresses the main idea. In this passage, the main idea comes at the end. The sum of all the details in the passage suggests that community policing is not without its critics and that therefore its future is uncertain. Another key phrase is *mixed results*, which means that some communities haven't had full success with community policing.

4. a. Question type: 4, vocabulary. The word *touted* is linked in this passage with the phrase *the best way to reform*. Most people would think that a good way to reform something is praiseworthy. In addition, the next few sentences in the passage describe the benefits of community policing. Criticism or a negative response to the subject doesn't come until later in the passage.

Practice Passage 2

Answer the questions that follow this passage. Circle the answers to the questions, and note under your answer which type of question has been asked. Then check your answers against the key that appears immediately after the questions.

There is some evidence that crime rates are linked to social trends, such as demographic and socio-economic changes. Crime statistics showed a decline in the post-World War II era of the 1940s and '50s. Following the Vietnam War in the 1970s, however, reported crimes were on the rise again, only to be followed by lower numbers of such reports in the 1980s. One of the reasons for these fluctuations appears to be age. When the population is younger, as in the 1960s when the baby boomers came of age, there is a greater incidence of crime nationwide. A second cause for the rise and fall of crime rates appears to be economic. Rising crime rates appear to follow falling economies. A third cause cited for the cyclical nature of crime statistics appears to be the ebb and flow of public policy decisions, which sometimes protect personal freedoms at the expense of government control. A youthful, economically disadvantaged population that is not secured by social controls of family and community or by government authority is likely to see an upswing in reported crimes.

1. Crime statistics seem to rise when populations are
   a. younger.
   b. older.
   c. veterans.
   d. richer.

Question type: _____

2. The main idea of the passage is that
   a. times of prosperity show lower crime statistics.
   b. when the economy slows, crime statistics rise.
   c. incidence of reported crime is related to several social and economic variables.
   d. secure families are less likely to be involved in crime.

Question type: _____

3. The best title for this passage would be
   a. Wars and Crime Statistics.
   b. Why Crime Statistics Rise and Fall.
   c. Youth and Crime Statistics.
   d. Poverty and Crime Statistics.

Question type: _____

4. Crime statistics show that crime is
   a. random.
   b. cyclical.
   c. demographic.
   d. social.

Question type: _____

Answers

1. a. Question type: 1, detail. This is a fairly clear example of how you can look quickly through a passage and locate a clearly stated detail. The word *young* appears in relation to the baby boomers; the idea is also suggested in the last sentence by the word *youthful.*

2. c. Question type: 2, main idea. The other answer choices are details—they're all in the passage, but they're not what the passage is *mostly* about. Choice **c** is the only one that combines several details into a statement that reflects the first sentence, which is also the topic sentence, of the paragraph.

3. b. Question type: 2, main idea. Each of the other choices expresses a detail, one of the reasons listed in the passage for fluctuation in crime rates. Choice **b** is the only one that expresses the sum of those details.

4. b. Question type: 1, detail. The passage mentions *the cyclical nature of crime statistics.* Other phrases that suggest this answer include *fluctuations, rise and fall,* and *ebb and flow.*

Practice Passage 3

Answer the questions that follow this passage. Circle the answers to the questions, and note under your answer which type of question has been asked. Then check your answers against the key that appears immediately after the questions.

In recent years, issues of public and personal safety have become a major concern to many Americans.

Violent incidents in fast-food restaurants, libraries, hospitals, schools, and offices have led many to seek greater security inside and outside of their homes. Sales of burglar alarms and high-tech security devices such as motion detectors and video monitors have skyrocketed in the last decade. Convenience stores and post offices have joined banks and jewelry stores in barricading staff behind iron bars and safety glass enclosures. Communities employ private security forces and encourage homeowners to keep trained attack dogs on their premises. While some people have sympathy for the impetus behind these efforts, there is also some concern that these measures will create a siege mentality leading to general distrust among people that could foster a dangerous isolationism within neighborhoods and among neighbors.

1. The passage suggests which of the following about community security?
   a. Communities are more dangerous today than they were ten years ago.
   b. Too much concern for security can destroy trust among neighbors.
   c. Poor security has led to an increase in public violence.
   d. Isolated neighborhoods are safe neighborhoods.

   Question type: _____

2. The word *foster* in the last sentence of the passage most nearly means
   a. adopt.
   b. encourage.
   c. prevent.
   d. secure.

   Question type: _____

3. The author believes that
   a. more security is needed to make neighborhoods safer.
   b. people should spend more on home security.
   c. people should not ignore the problems created by excessive safety concerns.
   d. attack dogs and high-tech devices are the best protection against violent crime.

   Question type: _____

4. In the last sentence, the phrase *siege mentality* means
   a. hostility.
   b. defensiveness.
   c. fear.
   d. corruption.

   Question type: _____

Answers
1. b. Question type: 4, inference. The key word here is *distrust*, which implies that neighbors become suspicious of each other if they are too worried about safety.
2. b. Question type: 3, vocabulary. The first answer choice is meant to confuse you if you associate the word *foster* with foster care and, by extension, with adoption. *Foster* means *nurture* or *help to grow*. Look again at the sentence. What could *a general distrust* (the thing that fosters) do to *a dangerous isolationism* (the thing being fostered)? A general distrust could *encourage* a dangerous isolationism.
3. c. Question type: 4, inference. By using phrases like *dangerous isolationism*, the author suggests that he or she doesn't approve of the shift toward heavier use of security devices. The other answer choices all indicate the author's approval of the trend being discussed.

4. b. Question type: 3, vocabulary. The key word here is *siege*. People who perceive themselves to be under attack tend to stick together in the face of a common enemy. They become quick to defend themselves against that enemy.

Create Your Own Questions

A good way to solidify what you've learned about reading comprehension questions is for you to write the questions. Here's a passage, followed by space for you to create your own questions. Write one question of each of the four types: fact or detail, main idea or title, inference or interpretation, and vocabulary definition.

As you create your own questions and answers, you will have the chance to understand how multiple-choice questions work. Typically, incorrect answers are incorrect because the reader has misunderstood, has a predisposition, uses unsound reasoning, or is only casually reading the passage. Knowing how multiple-choice questions work gives you a definite advantage when taking your written exam.

In recent years, law enforcement officers have welcomed the advent of a number of new technologies that have aided them greatly in their work. These include long-range eavesdropping devices and computer scanners that allow police to identify possible suspects by merely typing a license number into a computer in the patrol car. The scanner allows instant access to motor vehicle and criminal records and gives officers the opportunity to snare wrongdoers, even when they are not involved in criminal activity at the time. Police departments have praised the use of the computers, which they say help them get criminals off the streets and out of the way of honest citizens. Not all of those citizens agree with this attitude, however; some believe that arrests made solely on the basis of scanner iden-

tification constitute an invasion of privacy. They regard the accessing of records as illegal search and seizure. In New Jersey, Florida, and Arizona, lawsuits have been filed by citizens who believe that their constitutional rights have been violated. They believe that much computer-generated information is inaccurate and vulnerable to hackers who invade computer databases. Some believe that such information from scanners could be used to charge innocent citizens with crimes, or to target particular neighborhoods for harassment.

1. Detail question: _____

_____

    a.

    b.

    c.

    d.

2. Main idea question: _____

_____

    a.

    b.

    c.

    d.

3. Inference question: _____

_____

    a.

    b.

    c.

    d.

4. Vocabulary question: _____

_____

    a.

    b.

    c.

    d.

Possible Questions

Following is one question of each type, based on the passage. Your questions may be very different, but these will give you an idea of the kinds of questions that could be asked.

  1. *Detail question:* Computer scanners allow police to

    a. identify suspects.

    b. access computer databases.

    c. locate wrongdoers.

    d. all of the above

  2. *Main idea question:* Which of the following best expresses the main idea of the passage?

    a. New technologies are available to police officers.

    b. Police are skeptical of new policing technologies.

    c. New technologies raise questions of privacy.

    d. New technologies may be discriminatory.

  3. *Inference question:* The writer implies, but does not directly state, that

    a. computer technologies must be used with care.

    b. high-tech policing is the wave of the future.

    c. most citizens believe that high-tech policing is beneficial.

    d. most police officers prefer using the new technologies.

  4. *Vocabulary question:* In this passage, the word *snare* means

    a. question.

    b. interrupt.

    c. capture.

    d. free.

Answers

  1. d.

  2. c.

  3. d.

  4. c.

Reading Tables, Graphs, and Charts

Court officer exams may also include a section testing your ability to read tables, charts, and graphs. These sections are really quite similar to regular reading comprehension sections, but instead of pulling information from a passage of text, you will need to answer questions about a graphic representation of data. The types of questions asked about tables, charts, and graphs are actually quite similar to those about reading passages, though there usually aren't any questions on vocabulary. The main difference in reading tables, charts, or graphs is that you're reading or interpreting data represented in tabular (table) or graphic (picture) form rather than textual (sentence and paragraph) form.

Tables

Tables present data in rows and columns. The table on page 86 is a very simple table that shows the number of accidents reported in one county over a 24-hour period. Use it to answer question 1.

If English Isn't Your First Language

When nonnative speakers of English have trouble with reading comprehension tests, it's often because they lack the cultural, linguistic, and historical frame of reference that native speakers enjoy. People who have not lived in or been educated in the United States often don't have the background information that comes from reading American newspapers, magazines, and textbooks.

A second problem for nonnative English speakers is the difficulty in recognizing vocabulary and idioms (expressions like *chewing the fat*) that assist comprehension. In order to read with good understanding, it's important to have an immediate grasp of as many words as possible in the text. Test takers need to be able to recognize vocabulary and idioms immediately so that the ideas those words express are clear.

The Long View

Read newspapers, magazines, and other periodicals that deal with current events and matters of local, state, and national importance. Pay special attention to articles that are related to law enforcement.

Be alert to new or unfamiliar vocabulary or terms that occur frequently in the popular press. Use a highlighter pen to mark new or unfamiliar words as you read. Keep a list of those words and their definitions. Review them for 15 minutes each day. Though at first you may find yourself looking up a lot of words, don't be frustrated—you will look up fewer and fewer words as your vocabulary expands.

During the Test

When you are taking your written exam, make a picture in your mind of the situation being described in the passage. Ask yourself, "What did the writer mostly want me to think about this subject?"

Locate and underline the topic sentence that carries the main idea of the passage. Remember that the topic sentence—if there is one—may not always be the first sentence. If there doesn't seem to be one, try to determine what idea summarizes the whole passage.

TIME OF DAY	NUMBER OF ACCIDENTS
6:00 A.M.–9:00 A.M.	11
9:00 A.M.–12:00 P.M.	3
12:00 P.M.–3:00 P.M.	5
3:00 P.M.–6:00 P.M.	7
6:00 P.M.–9:00 P.M.	9
9:00 P.M.–12:00 A.M.	6
12:00 A.M.–3:00 A.M.	5
3:00 A.M.–6:00 A.M.	3

1. Based on the information provided in this table, at what time of day do the most accidents occur?
a. noon
b. morning rush hour
c. evening rush hour
d. midnight

The correct answer is **b**, morning rush hour. You can clearly see that the highest number of accidents (11) occurred between 6:00 A.M. and 9:00 A.M.

Graphs

Now, here's the same information presented as a graph. A graph uses two axes rather than columns and rows to create a visual picture of the data.

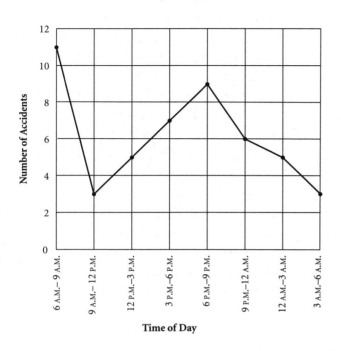

Here you can actually see the time of the greatest number of accidents represented by a line that corresponds to the time of day and number. These numbers can also be represented by a box in a bar graph, as follows.

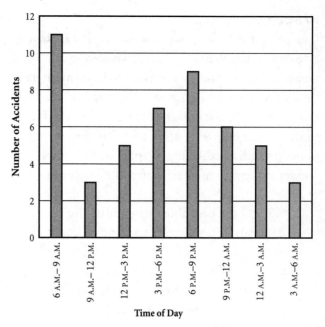

When reading graphs, the key is to be sure that you know exactly what the numbers on each axis represent. Otherwise, you're likely to misinterpret the information. On the bar graph, you see that the horizontal axis represents the time of day, and the vertical axis represents the number of accidents that occurred. Thus, the tallest box shows the time of day with the most accidents.

Practice

Like regular reading comprehension questions, questions on tables, charts, and graphs may also ask you to make inferences and maybe even do basic math using the information and numbers presented on the table, chart, or graph. For example, you may be asked questions like the following on the information presented in the preceding table, line graph, and bar graph. The answers follow immediately after the questions.

2. What is the probable cause for the high accident rate between 6:00 A.M. and 9:00 A.M.?
   a. People haven't had their coffee yet.
   b. A lot of drivers are rushing to work.
   c. There is a glare from the morning sun.
   d. Highway construction is heaviest during those hours.

3. What is the total number of accidents?
   a. 48
   b. 51
   c. 49
   d. 53

Answers

2. b. A question like this tests your common sense as well as your ability to read the graph. Though there may indeed be sun glare and many drivers may have not yet had their coffee, these items are too variable to account for the high number of accidents. In addition, choice d is not logical because construction generally slows traffic down. Choice b is the best answer, because from 6:00 A.M. to 9:00 A.M. there is consistently a lot of rush-hour traffic. In addition, many people do rush, and this increases the likelihood of accidents.

3. c. This question, of course, tests your basic ability to add. To answer this question correctly, you need to determine the value of each bar and then add those numbers together if you are given the bar graph. If you are given the table, you merely add up the column of numbers to find the total.

Charts

Finally, you may be presented information in the form of a chart like the one that follows. Here, the accident figures have been converted to percentages. In this figure, you don't see the exact number of accidents, but you see how accidents for each time period compare to the others.

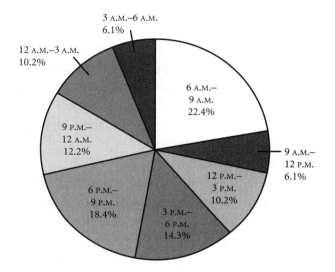

Practice

Try the following questions to hone your skill at reading tables, graphs, and charts.

Answer questions 1 and 2 on the basis of the following pie chart.

Causes of household fires

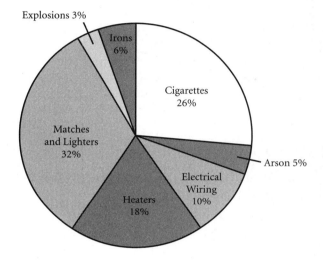

1. What is the percentage of smoking-related fires?
   a. 26%
   b. 32%
   c. 58%
   d. 26–58%

2. Based on the information provided in the chart, which of the following reasons applies to the majority of these fires?
   a. malicious intent to harm
   b. violation of fire safety codes
   c. carelessness
   d. faulty products

Answer questions 3 and 4 on the basis of the following graph.

Number of paid sick days per year of employment

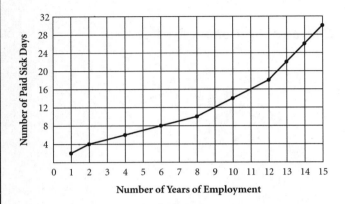

3. At what point does the rate of increase of sick days change?
  a. one year of employment
  b. four years of employment
  c. three years of employment
  d. nine years of employment

4. During what years of employment is the number of sick days equal to double the number of years of employment?
  a. 1, 4, and 12
  b. 13, 14, and 15
  c. 1, 2, and 15
  d. 2, 4, and 10

Answers

1. d. Of the causes presented in the chart, both cigarettes (26%) and matches and lighters (32%) are related to smoking. But not all match fires are necessarily smoking related. Thus, the best answer allows for a range between 26% and 58%.

2. c. Fires from cigarettes, heaters, irons, and matches and lighters—82% in total—are generally the result of carelessness. Only 5% of fires are arsons, so choice **a** cannot be correct. Electrical, heater, and explosion fires may be the result of fire safety code violations, but even so, they total only 31%. Finally, there's no indication in this chart that faulty products were involved.

3. c. In the first two years of employment, employees gain an additional two sick days. In the third year, employees gain only one additional day, that is, from four to five days.

4. c. In the first year, the number of sick days is two; in the second, four; and not until the 15th year does the number of sick days (30) again double the number of years of employment.

7 ▶ LEGAL DEFINITIONS

Although extensive legal knowledge is not required, all court officers should be familiar with common legal definitions, particularly those that will be used in their daily activities as court officers.

To prepare for the court officer exam, it is a good idea to build your bank of words. The greater your base of word knowledge, the easier it will be for you to answer any legal vocabulary question that comes your way. Each night, target ten words that you do not know. Study the definitions. Try to use the words in conversation, in your reports or memos, or in an e-mail. The more you use a word, the more familiar it will become to you. When words are familiar, you can count on them to help you with all forms of communication—or to pass any kind of test.

Additional Resources

A legal dictionary should be part of every court officer's reading list. Many Internet sites offer free legal definitions.

Books

Ellis Wild, Susan, ed. *Webster's New World Law Dictionary* (Springfield, MA: Webster's New World, 2006).

Garner, Bryan A., ed. *Black's Law Dictionary, Ninth Edition* (Eagan, MN: Thomson West, 2009).

Law, Jonathan, and Martin, & Elizabeth A., eds. *A Dictionary of Law, Seventh Edition* (Oxford: Oxford University Press, 2009).

Sperry, Len. *Dictionary of Legal and Ethical Terms and Issues* (New York: Brunner-Routledge, 2006).

Websites

Duhaime's Legal Dictionary
http://www.duhaime.org/legaldictionary.aspx

FindLaw for Legal Professionals
http://dictionary.lp.findlaw.com

The Free Dictionary
http://legal-dictionary.thefreedictionary.com

Jurist Legal Intelligence
http://jurist.law.pitt.edu/dictionary.htm

Law.com
http://dictionary.law.com

Nolo's Plain English Law Dictionary
http://www.nolo.com/dictionary/

WWLIA Legal Information Services
http://www.wwlia.org/Legal Dictionary.aspx

Prefixes, Suffixes, and Word Roots

A familiarity with common prefixes, suffixes, and word roots can dramatically improve your ability to determine the meaning of unfamiliar vocabulary words. The following tables list common prefixes, suffixes, and word roots; their meanings; an example of a word with that prefix, suffix, or word root; the meaning of that word; and a sentence that demonstrates the usage of the word. Refer to this list often to refresh your memory and improve your vocabulary.

Prefixes

Prefixes are syllables added to the *beginnings* of words to change or add to their meanings. This table lists some of the most common prefixes in the English language.

Prefix	Meaning	Example	Definition	Sentence
a	without	atheist *n.*	to be without	My friend, John, is an **atheist** and did not want to attend the wedding church ceremony
ab	away from	abnormal *adj.*	unusual	He has very **abnormal** hair.
ante	before	anticipate *v.*	to give advance thought to	His decades of experience allowed him to **anticipate** the problem.
anti	against	antipode *n.*	exact or direct opposite	North is the **antipode** of south.
auto	by oneself	automaton *n.*	a robot; a person who seems to a act mechanically without thinking.	The workers on the assembly line looked like **automatons**.
be	all over	believe *v.*	to have faith	My daughter **believes** in Santa Claus.
bi	two	bisect *v.*	to divide into two equal parts	If you **bisect** a square, you will get two rectangles of equal size.
circum	around	circumscribe *v.*	to draw a line	She carefully **circumscribed** the space that yould become her office.

Prefix	Meaning	Example	Definition	Sentence
co	together	cohesive adj.	united	Although they come from different backgrounds, they have a **cohesive** team.
con	with	consensus n.	general agreement	After hours of debate, the group finally reached a **consensus** and selected a candidate.
contra	against	contradict v.	to state the opposite	Why do you need to **contradict** everything I say?
counter	against	counterproductive adj.	going against the goal	Complaining is **counterproductive.**
de	down	descend v.	to move downward	The airplane will **descend** prior to landing.
dis	away	dispel v.	to drive away	To **dispel** rumors that I was quitting, I scheduled a series of meetings for the net three months.
dis	not	disorderly adv.	messy	He has a **disorderly** room.
duo	two	duality n.	having two sides or parts	The novel explores the quality of good and evil in human beings, also known as our **duality**.
ex	out from	expel v.	to drive out or away	Let's **expel** the invaders!
in	not	invariable adj.	not changing	The weather here is **invariable**.
inter	together	interact v.	to act upon or influence	The psychologist took notes while watching the kids **interact**.
intra	within	intravenous adj.	within or into	The nurses always administered his medication **intravenously**.
intro	into, within	introvert n.	a shy or withdrawn person	Unlike his sister, Zak was a real **introvert** and rarely left the house.

Prefix	Meaning	Example	Definition	Sentence
in	in, into	induct v.	to bring in (to group)	He was **inducted** into the Baseball Hall of Fame.
macro	large	macrocosm n.	the large-scale world	Any great **macrocosm** will eventually affect the microcosm.
mal	bad, wrong	maltreat v.	to treat badly	After the dog saved his life, Philip swore he would never **maltreat** another animal.
mal	ill	malaise n.	discomfort or illness	The **malaise** many women feel during the first few months of pregnancy is called "morning sickness."
micro	small	microcosm n.	little or miniature version of a whole	Brooklyn Heights, directly across the East River, is a **microcosm** of Manhattan.
mini	small	minority, n.	small group within a larger group	John lost the election because he only had the **minority** vote.
mis	wrong	misuse v.	to use wrongly	He likes to **misuse** his authority by asking his employees to pick up his dry cleaning.
mono	one	monologue n.	a long speech by one person	I was very moved by the **monologue** in scene III.
multi	many	multifaceted adj.	having many sides	This problem is **multifaceted** and we should make sur we examine all sides carefully.
non	not	nonviable adj.	not able to live or survive	Starting a new business is **nonviable** in today's economy.
op	against	oppose v.	to go against	She wants to **oppose** me in the election.
pent	five	pentameter n.	a line of verse (poetry) with five metrical feet	Most of Shakespeare's sonnets are written in iambic **pentameter**.

Prefix	Meaning	Example	Definition	Sentence
per	very	persuade *v.*	to push one in a certain direction	He tried to **persuade** me to go on the trip even though I said I have an exam guide to write.
poly	many	polyglot *n.*	one who speaks or understands several languages	It's no wonder she's a **polyglot**; she's lived in eight different countries.
port	carry	portable *n.*	capable of being moved or carried	This playpen is **portable** for families on the go.
post	after	postscript *n.*	message added after the close of a letter	His **postscript** was almost as long as his letter.
pre	before	precede *v.*	to come before	The appetizers **precede** the dinner.
pro	forward	protect *v.*	to watch over	I will always **protect** my child from danger.
pseudo	false	pseudonym *n.*	false or fake name	Mark Twain is a **pseudonym** for Samuel Clemens.
quad	four	quadruped *n.*	an animal with four	Some **quadrupeds** evolved into bipeds.
quint	five	quintuplets *n.*	five offspring born at one time	Each **quintuplet** weighed three pounds.
re	back	remember *v.*	to have a memory of	Do you **remember** all the crazy times we had in high school?
sub	under	subvert *v.*	to bring about the destruction of	His attempt to **subvert** his boss cost him his job.
super	above, over	supervisor *n.*	one who watches over	Alex refused the promotion because he didn't feel comfortable being his friend's **supervisor**.
term	end	terminate *v.*	to end	The budget cuts led the committee to **terminate** his position.

Prefix	Meaning	Example	Definition	Sentence
tetra	four	tetralogy n.	artistic works	Series of four related "Time Zone" was fourth and final work in Classman's **tetralogy**.
trans	change	transform n.	the act or process of undergoing change	Your **transformation** to adulthood was incredible.
tri	three	triangle n.	a figure having three angles	In an isosceles **triangle**, two of the three angles are the same size.
un	not, against	unmindful adj.	unaware	He is **unmindful** of his wife's feelings.
uni	one	unify v.	to form into a single unit; to unite	The new leader was able to **unify** the three factions into one strong political party.
voc	to call	vocation n.	one's profession	I am proud to be a part of the teaching **vocation**.

Suffixes

Suffixes are syllables added to the *ends* of words to change or add to their meanings. This table lists some of the most common prefixes in the English language.

Suffix	Meaning	Example	Definition	Sentence
acy	quality or state of	indeterminacy n.	state or quality of being undetermined	The **indeterminacy** of his statement made it impossible to tell which side he supported.
al	capable of	practical adj.	suitable for use	He has years of **practical**, on-the-job experience.
ance, ence	quality	tolerance n.	ability to tolerate	She has a high level of **tolerance** for rudeness.
ant, ent	performs an action	applicant n.	one who applies	There were many **applicants** to consider, but Kim had the highest GPA.

Suffix	Meaning	Example	Definition	Sentence
ary	place for	sanctuary *n.*	a sacred place	With three noisy roommates, Ellen frequently sought the quiet **sanctuary** of the library.
ate	to cause	esuscitate *v.*	to bring back to life	Thanks to a generous gift, we were able to **resuscitate** the study-abroad program.
atrium, anorium	place for	arboretum *n.*	a garden devoted primarily to trees	They built a deck with an **arboretum** for their bonsai tree collection.
cide	kill	pesticide *n.*	Substance for killing insects	The **pesticide** is also dangerous for humans.
dom	state of	wisdom *n.*	having knowledge	His old age has given him many years of **wisdom**.
en	to cause	broaden *v.*	to widen	Traveling around the world will **broaden** your understanding of other cultures.
er, or	one who does something	director *n.*	a person who provides guidance	The work of this **director** was really outstanding in this play.
ful	full of	meaningful *adj.*	significant	When Robert walked into the room, Annette gave him a **meaningful** glance.
ia	diseases	anorexia *n.*	an eating disorder	She has been hospitalized for **anorexia** twice before.
ial	pertaining to	commercial *adj.*	of or engaged in commerce	**Commercial** vehicles must have special license plates.
ian, an	related to	human *n.*	of human species	It is **human** to cry.
ic	pertaining to	aristocratic *adj.*	of or pertaining to the aristocracy	Although she was never rich or powerful, she has a very **aristocratic** manners.
ify, fy	to make	electrify *v.*	to charge	The singer will **electrify** the audience with her performance.

Suffix	Meaning	Example	Definition	Sentence
ile	capability	fragile *adj.*	breakable	Be very careful, that box is **fragile**; my china is inside.
ing	action	singing *v.*	to sing	The chorus was **singing** all day.
ion	action	selection *n.*	choice	The **selection** process was very difficult because each candidate had excellent qualifications.
ish	having the quality of	childish *adj.*	like a child	He didn't get the job because of his **childish** behavior during the interview.
ism	quality, state or condition of	optimism *n.*	belief that things will work out for the best	Her **optimism** makes people want to be around her.
itis	inflammation	tonsillitis *n.*	inflammation of the tonsils	Her **tonsillitis** was so severe that doctors had to remove her tonsils immediately.
ity	quality or state of	morality *n.*	state of being moral	He argued that the basic **morality** of civilized societies hasn't changed much over the centuries.
ive	having the quality of	descriptive *adj.*	giving a description	The letter was so **descriptive** that I could picture every place she'd been.
ize	to make	alphabetize *v.*	to put in alphabetical order	Please **alphabetize** these files for me.
less	lacking	painless *adj.*	without pain	The doctor assured me that it is a **painless** procedure.
ly	in the manner of	boldly *adv.*	in a bold manner	Despite his fear, he stepped **boldly** onto the stage.
ment	act or condition of	judgment *n.*	ability to judge or make wise decisions	He exercised good **judgment** by remaining silent during the meeting.

Suffix	Meaning	Example	Definition	Sentence
ness	state of	happiness *n.*	to be happy	Your **happiness** means the world to me.
ology	the study of	zoology *n.*	the scientific study of animal life	She took a summer job at the zoo because of her strong interest in **zoology**.
or, er	one who performs	narrator *n.*	one who tells the an account	A first-person **narrator** is usually not objective.
orus, ose	full of	humorous *adj.*	full of humor	His **humorous** speech made the evening go by quickly.
otic	process	hypnotic *adj.*	mesmerizing	He was so handsome, I fell into a **hypnotic** state.
ship	status	friendship *n.*	act of being friends	She ended our 11-year **friendship** for no reason.
tion	act, state, or condition of	completion *n.*	the act of	The second siren signaled the **completion** of the fire drill.
ty	state	anonymity *n.*	state of being anonymous	Your **anonymity** is guaranteed when you make a report to the Fairfield Crime Hotline.
ure	act	assure *v.*	to promise	I can **assure** you that your job is safe.
y	inclination	dreamy *adj.*	dream like	I have been in a **dreamy** state all day.

Common Latin Word Roots

Many words in the English language have their origins in Latin. The following table shows the original Latin words that we have used to create various English words. The Latin words serve as roots, providing the core meanings of the words; prefixes, suffixes, and other alterations give each word its distinct meaning. The word roots are listed in alphabetical order.

Root	Meaning	Example	Definition	Sentence
amare	to love	amorous *adj.*	readily showing or feeling love	She told him to stop his **amorous** advances, as she was already engaged.
audire	to hear	audience *n.*	assembled group of listeners or spectators; people within hearing	The **audience** was stunned when the game show host slapped the contestant.
bellum	war	belligerent *adj.*	inclined to fight; hostile, aggressive	The citizens feared that their **belligerent** leader would start an unjust war.
capere	to take	captivate *v.*	to capture the fancy of	The story **captivated** me from the beginning; I couldn't put the book down.
dicere	to say, speak	dictate *v.*	to state or order; to say what needs to be written down	She began to **dictate** her notes into the microphone.
ducere	to lead	conduct *v.*	to lead or guide (through)	He **conducted** a detailed tour of the building.
facere	to make or do	manufacture *v.*	to make or produce	The clothes are **manufactured** here in this factory.

Root	Meaning	Example	Definition	Sentence
lucere	to light	lucid *adj.*	very clear	No one could possibly have misunderstood such a **lucid**
manus	hand	manicure *n.*	cosmetic treatment of the finger nails	To maintain her long finger-nails, she gets a **manicure** every week.
medius	middle	median *adj.*	middle point; middle in a set of numbers	The **median** household income in this wealthy neighborhood is $89,000.
mittere	to send	transmit *v.*	to send across	The message was **transmitted** over the intercom.
omnis	all, every	omnipresent *adj.*	present everywhere	That top-40 song is **omnipresent**; everywhere I go, I hear it playing.
plicare	to fold	application *n.*	putting one thing on another; making a formal request	His loan **application** was denied because of his poor credit history.
ponerel, positum	to place	position *n.*	the place a person or thing occupies	Although he is only 22, he holds a very powerful **position** in the company.
portare	to carry	transport *v.*	to carry across	The goods will be **transported** by boat.

Root	Meaning	Example	Definition	Sentence
quarere	to ask,	inquiry *n.*	act of inquiry, investigation, or questioning	The **inquiry** lasted several months but yielded no new information.
scribere	to write	scribe *n.*	person who makes copies of writing	The **scribe** had developed thick calluses on his fingers from years of writing.
sentire	to feel	sentient *adj.*	capable of feeling	No **sentient** beings should be used for medical research.
specere	to look at	spectacle *n.*	striking or impressive sight	The debate was quite a **spectacle**—you should have seen the candidates attack one another.
spirare	to breathe	respiration *n.*	the act of breathing	His **respiration** was steady, but he remained unconscious.
tendere	to stretch	extend *v.*	to make longer, stretch out	Please **extend** the deadline by two weeks so we can complete the project properly.
verbum	word	verbatim *adv.*	word for word	The student failed because she had copied an article **verbatim** instead of writing her own essay.

Common Greek Word Roots

Many other English words have their origins in the ancient Greek language. The following table shows the Greek words that we have used to create various English words. The Greek words serve as roots, providing the core meanings of the words; prefixes, suffixes, and other alterations give each word its distinct meaning. The word roots are listed in alphabetical order.

Root	Meaning	Example	Definition	Sentence
bios	life	biology *n.*	the science of living organisms	He is majoring in **biology** and plans to go to medical school.
chronos	time	chronological *adj.*	arranged in the order in which things occurred	The story is confusing because she did not put the events in **chronological** order.
derma	skin	dermatology *n.*	branch of medical science dealing with the skin and its diseases	She has decided to study **dermatology** because she has always been plagued by rashes.
gamos	marriage, union	polygamy *n.*	the practice or custom of having more than one spouse or mate at a time	Throughtout history, certain cultures have practice **polygamy**, but it is uncommon today.
genos	race, sex, kind	genocide *n.*	deliberate extermination of one race of people	The **genocide** in Bosnia in the 1990s created a generation of orphaned children.
geo	earth	geography *n.*	the study of earth's surface; the surface or topographical features of a place	The **geography** of this region made it difficult for the different tribes to interact.
graphein	to write	calligraphy *n.*	beautiful or elegant handwriting	She used **calligraphy** when she addressed the wedding invitations.

Root	Meaning	Example	Definition	Sentence
krates	member of a group	democrat *n.*	one who believes in or advocates democracy as a principle of government	I have always been a **democrat**, but I refuse to join the Democratic Party.
kryptos	hidden, secret	cryptic *adj.*	concealing meaning; puzzling	He left such a **cryptic** message on my answering machine that I don't know what he wanted.
metron	to measure	metronome *n.*	device with a pendulum that beats at a determined rate to measure time or rhythm	She used **a metronome** to help her keep the proper pace as she played the song.
morphe	form	polymorphous *adj.*	having many forms	Most mythologies have a **polymorphous** figure, a "shape shifter" who can be both animal and human.
pathos	suffering, feeling	pathetic *adj.*	arousing feelings of pity or sadness	Willy Loman is a complex character who is both **pathetic** and heroic.
philos	loving	xenophile *n.*	a person who is attracted to foreign peoples, cultures, or customs	Alex is a **xenophile**; I doubt he'll ever come back to the States.
phobos	fear	xenophobe *n.*	person who fears foreigners or different cultures or customs	Don't expect Len to go on the trip; he's a **xenophobe**.
photos	light	photobiotic *adj.*	living or thriving only in the presence of light	Plants are **photobiotic** and will die without light.

Root	Meaning	Example	Definition	Sentence
podos	foot	podiatrist n.	an expert in the diagnosis and treatment of ailments of the human foot	The **podiatrist** saw that the ingrown toenail had become infected.
psuedein	to deceive	pseudonym n.	false name	Was George Eliot a **pseudonym** for Mary Ann Evans?
pyr	fire	pyromaniac n.	one who has a compulsion to set things on fire	The warehouse **fire** was not an accident; it was set by a **pyromaniac**.
soma	body	psychosomatic adj.	of or involving both the mind and body	In a **psychosomatic** illness, physical symptoms are caused by emotional distress.
tele	distant	telescope n.	optical instrument for making distant objects appear larger and nearer when viewed through the lens	While Galileo did not invent the **telescope**, he was the first to use it to study the planets and stars.
therme	heat	thermos n.	insulated jug or bottle that keeps liquids hot or cold	The **thermos** kept my coffee hot all afternoon.

Legal Definitions

As you become more comfortable with prefixes, suffixes, and root words, you will inevitably become more comfortable with legal terminology. Nevertheless, there are certain legal terms that are utilized quite often in a courtroom setting. Legal terminology can be difficult and confusing for the novice, especially since most words are rooted in Latin. The following is a list of 100 common legal definitions and terms. This is not an exhaustive list, but it will help to familiarize you with some legal jargon. If you should need additional terms or definitions, please refer back to the resources listed on page xx of this chapter.

Accomplice: One who assists and/or partakes in the commission of a crime.

Acquittal: a judgment from the court that finds the defendant not guilty of the crime he or she allegedly committed.

Actus reas: A Latin term meaning the "guilty act." This element of the crime must be proven beyond a reasonable doubt.

Administrative law: A government agency, such as the Health Department, the FDA, or the parole board, that has the authority to make and enforce law in a specific area.

Affidavit: A written statement sworn to under oath.

Affirmative defense: A defense in which the defendant admits to committing the crime but states that it was done for a legitimate reason, such as self defense, duress, or necessity.

Aggravating circumstances: A factor presented during sentencing that is unfavorable toward the defendant and makes the crime appear worse.

Alibi: Evidence for a person's whereabouts on a particular date and time in a specific location.

Allocution: When a defendant admits to his or her crime in open court; this is often done as part of the plea bargaining process.

Appeal: An application to an appellate/intermediary court, also known as the Court of Appeals, to review the decision or judgment of a lower court.

Appellate jurisdiction: The authority of a higher court to review a lower court's decision.

Arraignment: A critical stage of the criminal justice process when a defendant is brought to court and notified of the charges against him or her; the defendant is also read his or her constitutional rights. A defendant may enter a plea of guilty, not guilty or no contest at this time. A judge will determine the defendant's eligibility for bail.

Arrest: When a person is seized and in police custody because he or she is accused of committing a specific crime.

Bailee/bailor: A bailee is someone who is in lawful possession of another's property. The bailor is the legal owner of that property. This differs from *bail*, which is a tangible guarantee that a defendant will appear in court on a specific date.

Bill of Rights: The first ten amendments to the U.S. Constitution which outline our freedoms and liberties, such as the right to religious expression, the right to assemble peacefully, and the right to privacy.

Burden of proof: Proof that is needed to lawfully establish an invasion or intrusion of one's privacy and/or one's liberty (e.g., a stop and frisk requires reasonable suspicion, an arrest requires probable cause, and a guilty verdict in a criminal trial requires guilt beyond a reasonable doubt).

Castle Doctrine: An element of self defense (depending on one's jurisdiction) which does not require a homeowner to retreat from the home when he or she is assaulted. The homeowner can use reasonable force to defend his or her "castle."

Certiorari: A writ asking a higher court to review a lower court's decision.

Civil commitment: A court process where one is involuntarily admitted into a psychiatric hospital based on clear and convincing evidence.

Clear and present danger: The test used by the Supreme Court to determine if one's speech can be restricted.

Common law: The system of judge-made law that originated in England and was used in early America. Today, all common law is codified (i.e., written or statutory law).

Competency to stand trial: A person's ability to aid a lawyer in his or her own defense and to understand the basic nature of the court proceedings.

Concurrent jurisdiction: When more than one court, or state has jurisdiction (legal authority) over a criminal or civil matter.

Confession: When one admits to their guilt.

Corpus delecti: These are all of the elements of the crime. It is a Latin phrase that means the "body of the crime."

Corrections: The components of our penal system that are responsible for making sure that the court-appointed punishment is enforced for convicted defendants. This includes jails, prisons, probation, and parole.

Corroborate: To present additional information to strengthen or support evidence or testimony.

Courts of general jurisdictions: A court that has the legal authority to overhear all types of cases.

Courts of limited jurisdiction: A court that has the legal authority to overhear specialized cases, such as traffic court, drug court, or family court.

Criminal contempt: A criminal charge based on one's misbehavior in court.

Cross examination: The questioning of a witness by the opposing party.

Curtilage: The property that immediately surrounds one's home and is used for domestic purposes. This area is protected from unreasonable searches and seizures via the Fourth Amendment.

Defamation: Ruining the character or reputation of another with false rumors in written (libel) or spoken (slander) form.

Delinquent offender: A juvenile who engages in behavior that violates the criminal penal code, such as kidnapping, rape, or robbery.

Deposition: The out-of-court recorded testimony of a witness. It may be used to preserve testimony, to gain information about a case (i.e., discovery), or to impeach one's statements later on.

Determinate sentence: A fixed sentence, such as 15 years or 50 years.

Direct examination: The questioning of a lawyer's own witness.

Discovery: The process by which one party is compelled to turn over its evidence to the other party. In criminal trials, the process of discovery requires the prosecutor to submit all evidence to the defense, even if such evidence is exculpatory (i.e., proves the defendant's innocence).

Double jeopardy: A legal rule found in the Fifth Amendment which prohibits a person from being tried for the same case twice.

Due process: One's guarantee of his or her constitutional rights during arrest, trial and the judicial process.

Duress: An affirmative defense to a criminal charge in which the defendant states that he or she committed the crime but was forced or coerced to do so.

Evidence: Anything offered as proof during a case. Evidence can be testimonial (witness statements), real (weapon or signed contract), or demonstrative (maps, graphs).

Exclusionary rule: A rule developed by the Supreme Court which maintains that all evidence obtained in violation of the Bill of Rights will have to be excluded at trial.

Exculpatory evidence: Evidence that favors the defendant's innocence.

Exigent circumstances: Emergency situations that require immediate action.

Extradition: Making an accused individual who has fled the state forcibly return to the area of original jurisdiction.

Ex post facto: Retroactive laws, which are unconstitutional; literally "after the fact."

Federalism: The division of power between the federal government and state government.

Felony: A serious criminal charge that can result in imprisonment for a year or more; in some jurisdictions, felonious behavior can result in a death sentence.

Felony murder: Any death committed during the commission of a felony; intent is not a required element.

Foreign Intelligence Surveillance Act (FISA): The passage of this law increased the government's ability to obtain wiretaps and search warrants for national defense purposes.

Forfeiture: Money or items linked to criminal activity can be confiscated by the government as part of one's sentence.

Frame up: When a law enforcement officer manipulates evidence to convict a particular defendant.

Fraud: Taking someone's money or property through deceitful means.

Frisk: A limited pat down of a person to search for weapons.

Fruit of poisonous tree doctrine: The exclusion of all evidence obtained through prior unconstitutional police conduct.

Good faith exception: An exception to the exclusionary rule if the prosecution can show that the officer in question was acting in "good faith" (e.g., acting upon a search warrant later found to be invalid).

Grand jury: Composed of 16 to 24 people and used in half of the states to obtain an indictment in a criminal case. In the other half of the states, an information (formal criminal charge) is filed with a judge; the judge determines probable cause during this preliminary hearing.

Habeus corpus: The Latin phrase meaning "to produce the body." This is a writ asking the detaining body (jail or prison) to justify the continued incarceration of a particular defendant.

Hearsay evidence: Testimonial evidence that is based on a third party's knowledge. This is typically inadmissible in criminal court.

Immunity: An exemption from prosecution for possible criminal activity when a witness agrees to cooperate with the prosecutor's office.

Incarceration: Imprisonment in a secure correctional facility.

Inciting: Urging another person to commit an illegal act.

Indeterminate sentencing: A sentence of indeterminate duration. Such sentences have a minimum and a maximum length, such as 5 to 15 years, 50 to life, and so on.

Inevitable discovery: Allows the admission of unconstitutionally obtained evidence, in spite of the exclusionary rule, if the prosecutor can prove that such evidence would inevitably have been discovered by police in the near future.

Informant: A person who secretly gives information to the police regarding criminal matters.

Intermediate sanctions: Criminal sanctions that are halfway between an offender being free in the community or being in a secure correctional establishment. Examples of intermediate sanctions, also known as extra-institutional punishments or community-based sanctions, include probation, parole, electronic monitoring, house arrest, and halfway houses.

Interrogation: The process of police questioning.

Judgment: A court's final determination.

Jury nullification: When a jury ignores the law and bases its verdict on feelings and emotions rather than fact.

Magistrate: A judicial officer that has limited jurisdiction, such as issuing warrants, conducting bail hearings and arraignments, or ruling on child support.

Manslaughter: When the unlawful killing of a human being occurs with provocation.

Mens rea: A Latin phrase meaning "guilty mind." This is one's mental intent and is typically an element of the crime that needs to be proven beyond a reasonable doubt.

Misdemeanor: A criminal act that can be punishable only through a fine and/or less than one year in jail.

Mitigating circumstances: A factor presented during sentencing that is favorable toward the defendant and lessens his or her criminal responsibility.

Nolo contendere or no contest: The defendant does not admit or deny guilt but refuses to contest the charge. In Latin, this means "I do not wish to contend."

Obstruction of justice: Intentional acts that preclude the police or the courts from seeking the truth.

Overbreadth doctrine: The doctrine maintained by the Supreme Court that prohibits laws that broadly regulate and restrict constitutional freedoms.

Parole: The early conditional release of a criminal offender with an indeterminate sentence based on good behavior.

Plain view doctrine: If police see contraband in a place they are legally authorized to be, they may seize the contraband as evidence of a crime.

Pre-sentence investigation (PSI): A report that is typically completed by a probation officer and includes background information on the defendant and the crime, in addition to sentencing and/or treatment recommendations.

Probable cause: The standard of proof necessary to make an arrest; it means that there is sufficient evidence that the defendant committed the alleged crime of which he or she is suspected.

Probation: A conditional release into the community, in lieu of incarceration, under the supervision of a probation officer. Probation is the most common form of correctional supervision.

Reasonable doubt: If there is reasonable doubt in the minds of a jury or in the mind of a judge during a criminal trial, the jury or the judge must find the defendant not guilty. Guilt must be established beyond a reasonable doubt.

Recidivist: A repeat criminal offender.

Search warrant: A legal document authorized by a judge that allows law enforcement to search for particular items in a particular place.

Solicitation: Unlawfully attempting to get another to commit a crime act.

Standing: The legal right to challenge a violation of one's constitutional rights (also known as legal standing).

Statue of limitations: Legislatively imposed restrictions on how long a prosecution can occur after a crime has taken place.

Strict liability crimes: Crimes that require proof of only the actus reus, not the mens rea. Such crimes include felony murder and statutory rape.

Status offender: A juvenile who commits a law violating behavior as a result of his or her underage status, such as truancy or running away.

Stop and frisk: The Supreme Court standard that was established in the case of *Terry v. Ohio*; if officers have "mere suspicion" that a suspect may be armed, they can perform a "Terry stop and frisk." This includes a pat down of a suspect's outer garments to search for weapons.

Subpoena: A court order requiring one's presence in court on a specific date and time to testify or present evidence.

Summons: A court order requiring a defendant's presence in court on a specific date and time to face charges.

Transferred intent: The doctrine that allows the legal system to prosecute a defendant for a crime if he or she had the intention of harming one person but mistakenly harmed someone else.

Trial de novo: A new trial that ignores the previous trial.

Venire: The process of selecting candidates for the jury pool.

Voir dire: The process of asking potential jurors questions to determine their eligibility for jury duty. It is a French phrase that translates to "to tell the truth."

Warrant: A court order that allows law enforcement to arrest a specific individual and/or search for evidence.

Venue: The proper location for a trial.

Practice Questions

Color of law: The appearance of an act being performed based on legal rights and/or enforcement of a code or statute when, in reality, no legal rights exist.

1. Based on this information, which of the following is an example of a violation of acting under color of law?
   a. A police department arrests demonstrators for trespassing when the demonstrators have obtained a local authority permit for their protest march.
   b. An off-duty police officer who is out of his jurisdiction makes an arrest after witnessing a crime.
   c. A judge signs a warrant at her home instead of at the courthouse.
   d. A parking enforcement officer tickets his neighbor's abandoned vehicle.

Diligence: Reasonable care or attention to a matter that is sufficient to avoid a claim of negligence, or is a fair attempt.

2. A court officer must exercise diligence when attempting to service civil process. Which of the following is an example of diligence?
   a. A court officer drives past the service address three times before returning the process as unserved.
   b. A court officer discovers the intended party has moved. He interviews neighbors, and effects a postal search and a public record search to locate the party.
   c. A court officer leaves a contact card at the service address on the first service attempt and waits ten days for a call from the intended party.
   d. A court officer hands the process off to a civilian process server who lives closer to the service address.

3. What is another example of diligence?
   a. A woman hires a private detective to determine whether her husband is an adulterer.
   b. A couple asks for references from a potential housekeeper.
   c. A woman hires a private house inspector to evaluate a house she has contingently purchased.
   d. A man checks the engine oil level in a used car he is considering buying.

Reasonable wear and tear: A provision that limits an obligor's liability upon termination of a contract.

4. A reasonable wear and tear clause would NOT be found in which type of contract?
   a. a commercial equipment lease
   b. a consumer auto lease
   c. an apartment lease
   d. a sales contract for a used car

Loiter: To hang around a public location or business where there is no legitimate purpose.

5. Based on this definition, what is an example of loitering?
   a. A homeless man reads the newspaper daily in the public library from 9 A.M. to 6 P.M.
   b. An elderly woman sits in the park for five hours and feeds the birds.
   c. A prostitute occupies a bar stool for four hours after paying for one soft drink.
   d. A group of teenagers sit in front of a sporting goods store for two days in anticipation of the store's grand opening sales event.

Answers

1. a. If the demonstrators have obtained a legal permit to protest, no trespass has occurred. The Civil Rights Act of 1964 cites similar incidents against the peaceful protests and the Freedom Riders. Choice **b** is incorrect because an officer who witnesses a crime outside his or her bailiwick has arrest authority of a similarly situated citizen. Choice **c** is incorrect because a judge may sign a warrant anywhere in his or her jurisdiction. Choice **d** is incorrect if the parking enforcement officer is empowered within his jurisdiction to cite abandoned vehicles.

2. b. The court officer sought information from three different sources. This is a reasonable effort to locate the party for service. Choice **a** is incorrect because no attempts at service or discovering information have been made. Choice **c** is incorrect because one attempt and a ten-day wait does not constitute diligent effort. Choice **d** is incorrect because the court officer has abandoned the assignment by passing it off to a civilian process server.

3. c. This is an example of due diligence that is carried out pursuant to a contract over a specified time. Choice **a** is incorrect because this function is self-serving. Choices **b** and **d** are incorrect because they are not conclusive.

4. d. A used car is *purchased;* the other three answers involve *rentals* of property that will be returned to the owner.

5. c. Prostitution is illegal and it is clear from this scenario that the prostitute is attempting to solicit trade by taking four hours to consume a soft drink. Choice **a** is incorrect because reading in the library is a legitimate purpose. Choice **b** is incorrect because the woman is utilizing the park for a purpose. Choice **d** is incorrect because the teenagers are planning to frequent the store and partake in a sales event.

CHAPTER

8 ▶ APPLYING COURT OFFICER PROCEDURES

There is nothing more paramount to career success than the ability to understand and apply established court officer procedures into regular practice. Procedures are established by court rules, statutes, memorandums, and orders.

Many courts provide a handbook of established procedures and acceptable practice. Others leave it to the individual court officer to gather his or her own information and compile it into a workbook. When the procedures are well drafted and provide a means to an end, they are executed flawlessly or with minimal difficulty.

The court officer exam might contain questions that deal with court officer procedures and their applications. Some questions will provide a procedure and a mock situation. Test takers are then asked how to respond to the situation based on the procedure. Other procedure questions supply a procedure and then ask test takers to identify the true or false statement based on that procedure.

For both types of questions, test takers may refer back to the procedure as needed. No outside knowledge is necessary; you should base your answer solely on the procedure as it is written. For questions based on court officer procedures, make sure to closely read and understand the procedure before you examine the question and answer choices.

To succeed on court officer procedure questions, you must possess common sense, problem-solving skills, good reasoning ability, good judgment, and sensitivity to human and cultural conditions. Training, practice, and experience can help you develop good problem-solving skills, but natural common sense is the indispensable ingredient.

Train yourself to play the "what if?" game. Do it in various public places. Ask yourself, "If I were a court officer, what would I do if . . ." This simple game could program your brain to respond promptly to these types of questions.

Tips for Answering Court Officer Procedure Questions

- Read carefully, but don t read anything into the situation that isn t there.
- Read all the options before you choose an answer.
- If possible, find information that supports your answer.
- Think like a court officer. Safety first; use the least possible force.
- Use your common sense.
- Stay calm and work methodically.

Practice Questions

Use the following court officer document to answer questions 1 through 5.

Administrative Memorandum #05-01
Investiture of Judges
FROM: CHIEF JUDGE ABIGAIL ADAMS
DATE: December 2, 2010
TO: All Court Personnel
On December 8, 2010, the court will hold an investiture ceremony for two newly seated judges, Judge Thomas Ricks and Judge Geraldine Koch.

The ceremony will be held at the Commissioner's Auditorium and will commence at 4 P.M. The court will be dark. The warrant judge will be Judge Quinn Rogers, who will attend the ceremony and will be available by direct pager. Bailiff Elaine Amos will assist Judge Rogers as needed.

The court is expecting 17 visiting judges in addition to our nine judges and two magistrates who will attend the ceremony. Seventy-two people have responded to invitations. There is adequate seating. Guests will be admitted beginning at 3:30 P.M.

ASSIGNMENTS: Security will be managed by Captain Tasha Desmond. Judicial security will be managed by Lieutenant Steven McDowell and Sergeant Carla Austin. The floor security will be supervised by Sergeant Harold Norman. There will be four court security officers at the main entrance for screening. Standard screening protocol will be in effect. The uniform of the day will be Class A dress. All civilian court personnel will wear appropriate business attire. All judges will be robed.

At the conclusion of the ceremony, a reception will be held in the Garden Room. The event is being catered by Gourmet Catering

Company, who will enter at the south entrance at 4:30 P.M. One CSO from Sergeant Norman's detail will admit the vendor. All activities are expected to be concluded by 8 P.M. Exit security will be managed by Sergeant Norman and a roving parking lot detail of two CSOs.

1. The bailiff assigned to assist the warrant judge is
   a. Evelyn Maxwell.
   b. Ellen Carpenter.
   c. Elaine Amos.
   d. Edie Dorman.

2. The Gourmet Catering Company will arrive at
   a. 2:30 P.M.
   b. 3:30 P.M.
   c. 4:00 P.M.
   d. 4:30 P.M.

3. What is the number of court security officers handling main entrance screening?
   a. three
   b. four
   c. five
   d. six

4. The uniform of the day for this event is
   a. Class A.
   b. Class B.
   c. business attire.
   d. not mentioned in the order.

5. The parking lot security detail is being managed by
   a. Lieutenant McDowell.
   b. Sergeant Austin.
   c. Sergeant Norman.
   d. Sergeant Koch.

Use the following court officer procedure to answer questions 6 and 7.

Civil process that cannot be served will be returned to the civil clerk within three days after the process is labeled as non-service. The court officer who attempted service will complete Form CPNS-01 in triplicate. The original will be placed in the court file, the first copy mailed to the plaintiff or plaintiff attorney with the returned process, and the second copy returned to the court officer to support log entry. The court officer will retain the form for one year.

6. Civil process that cannot be served will be returned by the court officer to the
   a. plaintiff.
   b. attorney for the plaintiff.
   c. civil clerk.
   d. judge's clerk.

7. Which form will the court officer complete?
   a. CPNS-01
   b. CVNS-01
   c. NSC-001
   d. CC/NS01

Use the following memorandum, which pertains to a particular court officer procedure, to answer questions 8 through 10.

Memorandum

To: **All Court Officers**
From: **Tom Cox, Court Services Supervisor**
RE: **Security**
Date: **September 1, 2010**

In lieu of the recent security breach, the following will serve as a reminder of Court Procedure 32, subsection 53A—Court Admittance.

Visitors enter and proceed through the security turnstile located to the right of the main entrance. Employees enter and proceed through the security turnstile located to the left of the main entrance.

As per county directive, all those who pass through the court's main entrance must be screened for contraband. Bags, briefcases, etc, are to pass through the scanning machine. Everyone must clear the metal detector. If someone is unable to clear a metal detector, a wand detector will be utilized. If this individual is unable to clear the wand detector, you are to contact your supervisor. The individual must be asked to stand aside until your supervisor arrives.

All employees must have visible court identification for admittance. All visitors must have picture identification and be able to identify a clear purpose for their visit.

All court officers will remain at their designated posts unless directed otherwise by their immediate supervisor.

Any exceptions to this policy must be made by a supervisor. Failure to adhere to the policy will result in disciplinary action.

8. Joan, a court clerk who has faithfully served the county court for the last 17 years, cannot clear the metal detector. She is late for Judge Foreman's court and she is afraid that she is going to be fired. Based on the memorandum, you should

   a. call your supervisor.

   b. use the wand detector.

   c. allow Joan to enter to avoid time delays.

   d. tell Joan she must return in one hour.

9. It is 12 P.M. and it is time for your lunch break. Your supervisor has been detained upstairs on another issue. Mark Conkling, another court officer, tells you that he will cover your post while you take your break. Based on the memorandum, you should

   a. thank him and tell him you will take only 15 minutes.

   b. tell him not to worry because your post does not need coverage in your absence.

   c. wait for your supervisor.

   d. call the court clerk for permission.

10. Nory Padilla, a family court law advocate, has been working for the juvenile court system for ten years. As she rushes into court, she realizes that she left her county ID in the car, which is ten blocks away. You have known Nory for years and you know that she is scheduled to appear in court in a few minutes. Based on this information you

   a. ask her to leave and retrieve her identification.

   b. let her in; she is on the court's docket.

   c. tell her to wait while you call your supervisor.

   d. tell her to enter through the visitors' turnstile. If she has a driver's license, she can come in.

Answers

1. c. Bailiff Elaine Amos is assigned to assist Judge Quinn Rogers.

2. d. The order states that the caterer will arrive at 4:30 P.M.

3. b. The order requires four CSOs to perform screening duties.

4. a. Class A uniforms for court officers is the uniform of the day. Choice **c** is required for civilian court personnel.

5. c. Sergeant Norman is in charge of the parking lot detail. Choices **a** and **b** are assigned to judicial security. Choice **d**, Sergeant Koch, is not mentioned.

6. c. The court rule requires that the process be returned to the civil clerk by the court officer.

7. a. Form CPNS-01 is identified in the court rule. The other answers are incorrect because these forms are not mentioned in the court rule.

8. b. When one cannot clear the metal detector, the next step is to use the handheld wand. If Joan was unable to clear the wand, you would then contact a supervisor. You have no authority to let her in the courthouse or to tell her to return in one hour.

9. c. The memorandum clearly states that you should not leave your designated post unless you are directed to do so by your immediate supervisor. Doing so could result in disciplinary action.

10. a. Employees cannot enter without court ID. Her ID is in the car and she should be instructed to retrieve it. Even though you are certain of her identity, allowing her to enter violates policy. All IDs must be visible for entrance. Allowing her to enter through the visitors' turnstile is another policy violation.

9 ▶ CLERICAL ABILITY

Court officers are required to maintain thorough records, including a daily activity log, a record of money collected, and narrative incident reports. Court officers also complete court-approved forms that document service of civil process, evictions, and writs of execution.

With advances in technology, many forms have become available in software formats or over the Internet at state court sites. The results are professional-looking forms with legible content.

Documentation is vital in court proceedings. Excellent clerical ability produces solid documentation.

Court officers in supervisory or management positions are required to schedule personnel, prepare employment evaluations, complete equipment service schedules, and oversee and approve submitted forms and reports.

Once you begin your position as a court officer, it is important that you are able to read, understand, and integrate several data sources simultaneously. To see if you can perform this job duty, there will be questions on the exam that relate to tables and charts. They may contain specific information such as names, codes, and dates; it is your responsibility to be able to explain what the data represents. The exam will challenge you to do this through specific questions directly related to the chart or table presented.

There is no need to worry if reading charts and tables is not your best skill—remember, practice makes perfect. Here are some tips for helping you along:

1. Read the chart very carefully. Determine the nature of the information that is being presented.

2. Read the question carefully to determine what to look for in the chart or table. If you read the question too quickly, you may misinterpret the information the question wishes to ascertain.

   For example—"Which one of the following is least true?" If you read this too quickly, you might miss "least" and just pick the first answer you see that is true. These are common mistakes test takers make —your ability to read carefully and do well on these types of questions will prove to your future employer that you are diligent, dedicated and meticulous, imperative qualities for the court officer position.

3. Make notes on the table or graph to help you. Even if a question appears to be really simple, take your time and jot down some notes. It may not be as simple as you originally thought. Take note of "keys" or "legends" which may provide additional information about the data.

4. If you are completely stumped on a question, try using the process of elimination. If you know the answer has to be around 10%, but the four choices given are 5%, 15%, 30%, and 50%, you can eliminate the last two answers. Now your chances of picking the right choice are 50% rather than 25%. Remember, there is no penalty for guessing. It is better to answer the question than to leave it blank.

Practice Questions

Record Keeping

Study the following form and answer questions 1 through 5 based on the form content and its use. Carefully examine numbers that are aligned in the grid. Numbers that appear similar can throw your focus and result in errors.

Court Officer Pistol Qualifications Results
Rangemaster: Walton
Group 1
Date: July 6, 2010
Stage Score

Officer	1	2	3	Total	Rating
Amos	68	75	81	224	Qualified
Baker	87	84	94	265	Marksman
Carter	78	89	98	265	Marksman
Cullen	85	98	89	272	Expert
Daniels	85	87	95	267	Marksman
Edwards	89	75	75	232	Sharpshooter
Ford	68	88	88	231	Sharpshooter
Hanley	87	85	85	259	Marksman
Henderson	98	97	97	290	Distinguished Expert
Howard	86	67	67	237	Sharpshooter

1. How many court officers are rated Sharpshooter?
  a. two
  b. three
  c. four
  d. five

2. The court officer with the lowest score in Stage 3 was
  a. Amos.
  b. Baker.
  c. Edwards.
  d. Howard.

3. What is the number of court officers whose score increased between Stage 1 and Stage 2?
  a. five
  b. six
  c. seven
  d. eight

4. What is the number of court officers whose score decreased between Stage 2 and Stage 3?
  a. two
  b. three
  c. four
  d. five

5. The rangemaster is
  a. Walton.
  b. Watson.
  c. Williams.
  d. Winston.

Answer questions 6 through 10 based on the following charts.

Arraignments Completed by Judge Forman from 1300 hrs to 1400 hrs on Friday			
Defendant's Name	Charge	Bail	Time
Jones, Jim	Larceny	Yes	1300 hrs to 1305 hrs
Smith, Joy	Burglary*	No	1306 hrs to1315 hrs
Long, Sam	Larceny	Yes	1316 hrs to 1321 hrs
Small, Richie	Larceny	Yes	1321 hrs to 1335 hrs
Big, Lloyd	Assault*	No	1326 hrs to 1335 hrs
Little, Rick	Attempted Murder*	No	1335 hrs to 1355 hrs
*violent Crime			

Arraignments Completed by Judge Forman from 1300 hrs to 1400 hrs on Monday			
Defendant's Name	Charge	Bail	Time
Fields, Jim	Manslaughter* 1st Degree*	No	1300 hrs to 1320 hrs
Jordon, Jill	Assault*	No	1321 hrs to 1329 hrs
Hox, Dan	Possession with Intent to Sell	Yes	1330 hrs to 1335 hrs
Moore, Clinton	Possession with Intent to Sell	Yes	1336 hrs to 1340 hrs
Appel, Ellie	Assault*	No	1341 hrs to 1350 hrs
Josephs, Anthony	Possession with Intent to Sell	No	1351 hrs to 1356 hrs
*violent Crime			

6. In which types of cases does Judge Forman spend the most time conducting her arraignments?
   a. manslaughter
   b. possession with intent to sell
   c. assault
   d. burglary

7. Which cases are most likely to receive bail?
   a. burglary
   b. larceny
   c. assault
   d. possession with intent to sell

8. Which day did Judge Forman appear to conduct more arraignments for violent crimes?
   a. Monday
   b. Friday
   c. Wednesday
   d. Monday and Friday had the same number of violent crime arraignments.

9. Which charge below did Judge Forman see on Monday for arraignment that she did not see on Friday?
   a. larceny
   b. assault
   c. possession with intent to sell
   d. burglary and larceny

10. In descending order, which arraignment takes the most time?
   a. Manslaughter, assault, possession with intent to sell
   b. Possession with intent to sell, larceny, burglary
   c. Manslaughter, assault, larceny
   d. They all took approximately the same time.

Clerical Recording

Look at the following sets of numbers and answer question 11 based entirely on the information presented.

Docket No:			
543262626	**5432562626**	**543262626**	**543262626**
Barbara Walters	Barbara Walters	Barbara	Barbara Walters
Larceny/E Felony	Larceny/E Felony	Larceny/E Felony	Larceny/E Felony

11. In the data presented here,
   a. all the columns are the same.
   b. only three columns are the same.
   c. column 1 and Column 4 are the same.
   d. all of the columns are different.

Look at the following addresses and answer question 12 based entirely on the information presented.

Pina Caso	Pina Caso	Pina Coso
554 West 59th Street	554 West 59th Street	554 West 59th Street
New York, NY 10019	New York, NY 10011	New York, NY 10019

12. In the data presented here,
   a. all the columns are the same.
   b. only two columns are the same.
   c. column 1 and column 3 are the same.
   d. all of the columns are different.

Answers

1. **b.** Court Officers Edwards, Ford, and Howard are rated Sharpshooters.

2. **d.** Howard shot 67 in Stage 3, Amos 81, Baker 94, and Edwards 75.

3. **a.** Five court officers had scores that increased between Stage 1 and Stage 2.

4. **b.** Three court officers had scores that decreased between Stage 2 and Stage 3.

5. **a.** Walton is identified on the first line as the rangemaster. The other names are not mentioned.

6. **a.** Out of the options given, the manslaughter arraignment took 20 minutes, which was more time than any of the others.

7. **b.** Larceny is the answer: Judge Forman granted bail to every defendant charged with larceny.

8. **d.** On both days during the designated time slot, there were an equal number of violent offenders arraigned. Look at the key under the second chart—the * indicates whether a crime is categorized as being violent.

9. **c.** "Possession with the intent to sell" was the only charge listed that was in Forman's courtroom on Monday but not on Friday. Larceny and burglary were both on Friday and assault was seen on Friday and Monday.

10. **a.** In this question, you are looking for the answer that goes from the highest amount of time to the lowest amount of time. Choice **a** is the correct answer—manslaughter (20 minutes), assault (nine minutes) and possession with intent to sell (five minutes)

11. **c.** Column 1 and Column 4 have exactly the same information. Column 2 has a different docket number and Column 3 has a different last name.

12. **d.** All of the columns are different. Column number 2 has a different zip code and Column 1 and Column 3 spell the individual's last name differently.

10 ▶ PRACTICE TEST 2

This is the second practice test in this book and is based on the most commonly tested areas on the court officer exam. The skills tested on the exam that follows are the ones that have been tested on previous court officer exams that focus on job-related skills. The exam you take may look somewhat different from this exam, but you'll find that this exam provides vital practice in the skills you need to pass a court officer exam.

The practice test consists of 100 multiple-choice questions in the following areas: memory; reading text, tables, charts, and graphs; legal definitions; court officer procedures; and clerical ability. You should give yourself three hours to take this practice test. The question number and time limit of the actual court officer exam can vary from region to region.

1.	ⓐ	ⓑ	ⓒ	ⓓ
2.	ⓐ	ⓑ	ⓒ	ⓓ
3.	ⓐ	ⓑ	ⓒ	ⓓ
4.	ⓐ	ⓑ	ⓒ	ⓓ
5.	ⓐ	ⓑ	ⓒ	ⓓ
6.	ⓐ	ⓑ	ⓒ	ⓓ
7.	ⓐ	ⓑ	ⓒ	ⓓ
8.	ⓐ	ⓑ	ⓒ	ⓓ
9.	ⓐ	ⓑ	ⓒ	ⓓ
10.	ⓐ	ⓑ	ⓒ	ⓓ
11.	ⓐ	ⓑ	ⓒ	ⓓ
12.	ⓐ	ⓑ	ⓒ	ⓓ
13.	ⓐ	ⓑ	ⓒ	ⓓ
14.	ⓐ	ⓑ	ⓒ	ⓓ
15.	ⓐ	ⓑ	ⓒ	ⓓ
16.	ⓐ	ⓑ	ⓒ	ⓓ
17.	ⓐ	ⓑ	ⓒ	ⓓ
18.	ⓐ	ⓑ	ⓒ	ⓓ
19.	ⓐ	ⓑ	ⓒ	ⓓ
20.	ⓐ	ⓑ	ⓒ	ⓓ
21.	ⓐ	ⓑ	ⓒ	ⓓ
22.	ⓐ	ⓑ	ⓒ	ⓓ
23.	ⓐ	ⓑ	ⓒ	ⓓ
24.	ⓐ	ⓑ	ⓒ	ⓓ
25.	ⓐ	ⓑ	ⓒ	ⓓ
26.	ⓐ	ⓑ	ⓒ	ⓓ
27.	ⓐ	ⓑ	ⓒ	ⓓ
28.	ⓐ	ⓑ	ⓒ	ⓓ
29.	ⓐ	ⓑ	ⓒ	ⓓ
30.	ⓐ	ⓑ	ⓒ	ⓓ
31.	ⓐ	ⓑ	ⓒ	ⓓ
32.	ⓐ	ⓑ	ⓒ	ⓓ
33.	ⓐ	ⓑ	ⓒ	ⓓ
34.	ⓐ	ⓑ	ⓒ	ⓓ
35.	ⓐ	ⓑ	ⓒ	ⓓ

36.	ⓐ	ⓑ	ⓒ	ⓓ
37.	ⓐ	ⓑ	ⓒ	ⓓ
38.	ⓐ	ⓑ	ⓒ	ⓓ
39.	ⓐ	ⓑ	ⓒ	ⓓ
40.	ⓐ	ⓑ	ⓒ	ⓓ
41.	ⓐ	ⓑ	ⓒ	ⓓ
42.	ⓐ	ⓑ	ⓒ	ⓓ
43.	ⓐ	ⓑ	ⓒ	ⓓ
44.	ⓐ	ⓑ	ⓒ	ⓓ
45.	ⓐ	ⓑ	ⓒ	ⓓ
46.	ⓐ	ⓑ	ⓒ	ⓓ
47.	ⓐ	ⓑ	ⓒ	ⓓ
48.	ⓐ	ⓑ	ⓒ	ⓓ
49.	ⓐ	ⓑ	ⓒ	ⓓ
50.	ⓐ	ⓑ	ⓒ	ⓓ
51.	ⓐ	ⓑ	ⓒ	ⓓ
52.	ⓐ	ⓑ	ⓒ	ⓓ
53.	ⓐ	ⓑ		
54.	ⓐ	ⓑ	ⓒ	ⓓ
55.	ⓐ	ⓑ	ⓒ	ⓓ
56.	ⓐ	ⓑ	ⓒ	ⓓ
57.	ⓐ	ⓑ	ⓒ	ⓓ
58.	ⓐ	ⓑ	ⓒ	ⓓ
59.	ⓐ	ⓑ	ⓒ	ⓓ
60.	ⓐ	ⓑ	ⓒ	ⓓ
61.	ⓐ	ⓑ	ⓒ	ⓓ
62.	ⓐ	ⓑ		
63.	ⓐ	ⓑ	ⓒ	ⓓ
64.	ⓐ	ⓑ	ⓒ	ⓓ
65.	ⓐ	ⓑ	ⓒ	ⓓ
66.	ⓐ	ⓑ	ⓒ	ⓓ
67.	ⓐ	ⓑ	ⓒ	ⓓ
68.	ⓐ	ⓑ	ⓒ	ⓓ
69.	ⓐ	ⓑ	ⓒ	ⓓ
70.	ⓐ	ⓑ	ⓒ	ⓓ

71.	ⓐ	ⓑ	ⓒ	ⓓ
72.	ⓐ	ⓑ	ⓒ	ⓓ
73.	ⓐ	ⓑ	ⓒ	ⓓ
74.	ⓐ	ⓑ		
75.	ⓐ	ⓑ		
76.	ⓐ	ⓑ		
77.	ⓐ	ⓑ	ⓒ	ⓓ
78.	ⓐ	ⓑ	ⓒ	ⓓ
79.	ⓐ	ⓑ		
80.	ⓐ	ⓑ	ⓒ	ⓓ
81.	ⓐ	ⓑ	ⓒ	ⓓ
82.	ⓐ	ⓑ	ⓒ	ⓓ
83.	ⓐ	ⓑ	ⓒ	ⓓ
84.	ⓐ	ⓑ	ⓒ	ⓓ
85.	ⓐ	ⓑ	ⓒ	ⓓ
86.	ⓐ	ⓑ	ⓒ	ⓓ
87.	ⓐ	ⓑ	ⓒ	ⓓ
88.	ⓐ	ⓑ	ⓒ	ⓓ
89.	ⓐ	ⓑ		
90.	ⓐ	ⓑ	ⓒ	ⓓ
91.	ⓐ	ⓑ	ⓒ	ⓓ
92.	ⓐ	ⓑ	ⓒ	ⓓ
93.	ⓐ	ⓑ	ⓒ	ⓓ
94.	ⓐ	ⓑ	ⓒ	ⓓ
95.	ⓐ	ⓑ		
96.	ⓐ	ⓑ	ⓒ	ⓓ
97.	ⓐ	ⓑ		
98.	ⓐ	ⓑ		
99.	ⓐ	ⓑ	ⓒ	ⓓ
100.	ⓐ	ⓑ	ⓒ	ⓓ

Memory and Observation

Carefully study the following scene for five minutes. After this time, answer questions 1 through 5 based on what you've seen without referring back to the image.

1. What is the woman in front of the National Bank doing?

   a. going into the bank

   b. holding a large bag

   c. holding a child's hand

   d. walking toward the Bait Shop

2. What is the number directly in front of the bakery sign?

   a. 20th

   b. 23rd

   c. 26th

   d. 30th

3. Which business is directly to the right of the bakery?

   a. the karate studio

   b. the bank

   c. the post office

   d. the bait shop

4. How many adults can you see in the picture?

   a. 6

   b. 7

   c. 8

   d. 9

5. What street corner did the accident occur?

   a. 22nd Street and 3rd Avenue

   b. 23rd Street and 2nd Avenue

   c. 23rd Street and 3rd Avenue

   d. 3rd Street and 2nd Avenue

Read the following passage carefully for five minutes. After this time, answer questions 6 through 15 based on what you've read without referring back to the passage.

Terry Stops

Often in the course of routine patrol, a police officer needs to detain a person briefly for questioning without an arrest warrant or even probable cause. The officer may also feel that it is necessary to frisk this person for weapons. This type of detention is known as a Terry Stop, after the U.S. Supreme Court case *Terry v. State of Ohio*. In that case, the court determined that a Terry Stop does not violate a citizen's right to be free from unreasonable search and seizure, as long as certain procedures are followed. First, the person must be behaving in some manner that arouses the police officer's suspicion. Second, the officer must believe that swift action is necessary to prevent a crime from being committed or a suspect from escaping. Finally, to frisk the individual, the officer must reasonably believe that the person is armed and dangerous. We will now look at each of these elements in more detail.

In determining whether an individual is acting in a suspicious manner, a police officer must rely on his or her training and experience. Circumstances in each case will be different, but an officer must be able to articulate what it was about a person's behavior that aroused suspicion, whether it was one particular action or a series of actions taken together. For example, it may not be unusual for shoppers in a store to wander up and down the aisles looking at merchandise. However, it may be suspicious if a person does this for an inordinate period, seems to be checking the locations of surveillance equipment, and is wearing loose clothing that would facilitate shoplifting. Similarly, it is not unusual for a person wearing gym shorts and a T-shirt to be running through a residential neighborhood; however, a person running while dressed in regular clothes might legitimately be suspect. It is important to note that a person who simply appears out of place based on the manner in which he or she is dressed is not alone cause for suspicion on the part of a police officer.

In addition to the behavior that arouses an officer's attention, the officer must believe that immediate action must be taken to prevent the commission of a crime or a suspect from escaping. In some situations, it may be better to wait to develop probable cause and arrest the person. One important element of this decision is the safety of any other people in the area. In addition, a police officer may determine that his or her immediate action is necessary to avert the commission of a crime, even if no people are in danger. If the suspect appears, for example, to be checking out parked cars for the possibility of stealing one, an officer may well be able to wait until the crime is in progress (thereby having probable cause for an arrest) or even until the crime is actually committed, when patrol cars can be dispatched to arrest the individual. On the other hand, a person who appears to be planning a carjacking should be stopped before the occupants of a car can be hurt. Again, an officer must make a quick decision based on all the circumstances.

Once an officer has detained a suspicious person, the officer must determine if he or she feels it is necessary to frisk the individual for weapons. Again, an officer should rely on his or her training and experience. If the officer feels that the detainee poses a threat to the officer's safety, the suspect should be frisked. For example, although there may certainly be exceptions, a person suspected of shoplifting is not likely to be armed. On the other hand, a person suspected of breaking and entering may very well be carrying a weapon. In addition, the officer should be aware of the behavior of the person once the stop is made. Certain behavior indicates the person is waiting for an opportunity to produce a weapon and threaten the officer's safety. The safety of the officer and any civilians in the area is the most important consideration.

6. According to the reading passage, a Terry Stop is
   a. an arrest for shoplifting.
   b. the brief detention and questioning of a suspicious person.
   c. an officer's frisking a suspect for weapons.
   d. the development of a case that results in an arrest warrant.

7. According to the passage, a Terry Stop includes the frisking of a suspect if
   a. the officer sees evidence of a weapon.
   b. the person is suspected of breaking and entering.
   c. there are civilians in the area.
   d. the officer or others are in danger.

8. An officer on foot patrol notices two people standing on a street corner. The officer observes the two, and after a moment, one of the people walks slowly down the street, looks in the window of a store called McFadden's, walks forward a few feet, and then turns around and returns to the other person. They speak briefly, and then the other person walks down the street, performing the same series of motions. They repeat this ritual five or six times each. The officer would be justified in performing a Terry Stop based on the suspicion that the people
   a. appeared to be carrying weapons.
   b. looked out of place.
   c. might be planning to rob McFadden's.
   d. were obstructing the sidewalk.

9. According to the passage, an officer may choose to conduct a Terry Stop to
   a. discourage loitering.
   b. prevent a crime from being committed or a suspect from escaping.
   c. find out if a person is carrying a concealed weapon.
   d. rule out suspects after a crime has been committed.

10. According to the passage, the determination that a person is suspicious
   a. depends on the circumstances of each situation.
   b. means someone looks out of place.
   c. usually means someone is guilty of planning a crime.
   d. usually indicates that a person is carrying a concealed weapon.

11. An officer has stopped a suspicious individual. The suspect seems to be trying to reach for something under her coat. The officer should
   a. call for backup.
   b. arrest the suspect.
   c. frisk the suspect.
   d. handcuff the suspect.

12. An officer observes a person sitting on a bench outside a bank at 4:30 P.M. The officer knows the bank closes at 5:00 P.M. The person checks his watch several times and watches customers come and go through the door of the bank. He also makes eye contact with a person driving a blue sedan that appears to be circling the block. Finally, a parking space in front of the bank becomes vacant, and the sedan pulls in. The driver and the man on the bench nod to each other. The officer believes the two are planning to rob the bank just before it closes. What is the first thing the officer should do?
   a. Begin questioning the man on the bench because it appears he's going to rob the bank.
   b. Begin questioning the driver of the sedan because it appears she's driving the get-away car.
   c. Go into the bank, warn the employees, and ask all the customers to leave for their own safety.
   d. Call for backup because it appears the potential robbers are waiting for the bank to close.

13. According to the U.S. Supreme Court, a Terry Stop
  a. is permissible search and seizure.
  b. often occurs in the course of police work.
  c. should be undertaken only when two officers are present.
  d. requires probable cause.

14. According to the passage, persons suspected of shoplifting
  a. should never be frisked, as shoplifters rarely carry weapons.
  b. may legitimately be the subjects of a Terry Stop.
  c. always wear loose clothing and wander in the store a long time.
  d. may be handcuffed immediately for the safety of the civilians in the area.

15. An officer in a squad car is patrolling a wealthy residential neighborhood. She notices one house in which a light will come on in one part of the house for a few minutes, and then go off. A moment later, a light will come on in another part of the house, and then go off. This happens several times in different parts of the house. The officer also notes that the garage door is standing open and that there are no cars parked there or in the driveway. The officer believes there may be a burglary in progress, and pulls over to observe the house. While she is watching the house, a man wearing torn jeans and a dirty T-shirt walks by the house. According to the passage, the officer should NOT
  a. allow the man to see her, as he may be dangerous.
  b. involve the neighbors by asking them if they have information.
  c. stop the man because there is no indication he is involved in criminal activity.
  d. radio headquarters until she is absolutely sure a crime is being committed.

Reading Text, Tables, Charts, and Graphs

Read the following passage, then answer questions 16 through 20 based solely on information from the passage.

On Saturday, March 27, at approximately 12:20 P.M., two officers arrived at the corner of Fordham and Jerome Avenue, directly under the #4 train. The officers received a call from Isa Torres, the police dispatcher, at 12:15 P.M.; the owner of the Spanish restaurant on the corner registered a complaint against two unruly patrons. Upon entering the restaurant, Jose Rodriguez, the restaurant owner, told Officers Thomas Cox and Mark Conkling that the two men sitting in the far right-hand corner of the restaurant refused to pay their bill and were verbally abusive to the waitress. Officer Conkling spoke to the waitress, Carol Mendoza, who stated that the patron in the red shirt grabbed her leg, cursed at her, and told her that he was not paying his bill. Officer Cox approached the two gentlemen: the first man, whose back was to the entrance, was Caucasian, approximately 6 feet 7 inches tall, 200 pounds, and wearing a blue shirt. The other patron was of Latino descent, approximately 5 feet 10 inches tall, 175 pounds, and wearing a red shirt. The two men began screaming at Officer Cox; they stated that they would not pay their bill because their food was terrible and their waitress was rude. After the officer asked them to lower their voices, the patron in the red shirt stood up in front of Officer Cox in a threatening manner. Officer Cox twisted the patron's right hand behind his back, handcuffed him, and arrested him for public disorder. The man smelled of alcohol and was visibly intoxicated. The other patron, also intoxicated, agreed to pay the bill. He was taken down to the station but no charges were filed against him.

16. The "public disorder" occurred
  a. outside the restaurant.
  b. outside the #4 train.
  c. outside on the corner of Fordham and Jerome.
  d. inside the Spanish restaurant.

17. Who initially informed the two officers about the complaint?
  a. Isa Torres
  b. Jose Rodriguez
  c. Carol Mendoza
  d. Mark Conkling

18. Which of the following describes the patron who was arrested?
  a. 200 pounds
  b. 6 feet 7 inches
  c. 175 pounds
  d. blue shirt

19. One of the patrons started to scream at Officer Cox because
  a. he did not want to pay his bill.
  b. his food was of poor quality.
  c. Carol was rude.
  d. all of the above.

20. When did the officers received the complaint?
  a. 12:15 P.M.
  b. 12:20 P.M.
  c. 12:15 A.M.
  d. 12:20 A.M.

Read the following passage, then answer questions 21 through 24 based solely on information from the passage.

DNA is a powerful investigative tool because, with the exception of identical twins, no two people have the same DNA. In other words, the sequence, or order of the DNA building blocks, is different in particular regions of the cell, making each person's DNA unique. Therefore, DNA evidence collected from a crime scene can link a suspect to a crime or eliminate one from suspicion in the same way that fingerprints are used. DNA can also identify evidence from a victim through the DNA of relatives if a victim's body cannot be found. For example, if technicians have a biological sample from the victim, such as a bloodstain left at a crime scene, the DNA taken from that evidence can be compared with DNA from the victim's biological relatives to determine if the bloodstain belongs to the victim. When a DNA profile developed from evidence at one crime scene is compared with a DNA profile developed from evidence found at another crime scene, they can be linked to each other or to the same perpetrator, whether the crime was committed locally or in another state.

21. What is the primary purpose of this paragraph?
  a. to show how DNA is a powerful investigative tool
  b. to illustrate how the unique characteristics of DNA make different types of comparisons and eliminations possible
  c. to teach the reader that identical twins have the same DNA
  d. to show how laboratory technicians develop DNA profiles

22. All of the following are true EXCEPT
    a. everyone, except for identical twins, has different DNA.
    b. the sequence of DNA building blocks is the same in particular regions of the cell, making comparisons possible.
    c. DNA can be used for comparisons or eliminations of offenders from different states.
    d. DNA from relatives can be used to identify victims.

23. According to the passage, DNA should be collected from a crime scene because
    a. it is better than fingerprints.
    b. there is DNA left at every crime scene.
    c. it can be used to eliminate potential suspects.
    d. DNA is a new investigative tool.

24. Which of the following conclusions can be drawn from the paragraph?
    a. DNA can be collected from sources other than blood.
    b. DNA can be collected from bloodstains only.
    c. DNA cannot be collected from bloodstains.
    d. DNA can connect crime scenes only if it is taken from bloodstains.

Read the following passage, then answer questions 25 through 27 based solely on information from the passage.

Police officers, researchers, and other criminal-justice practitioners have been struggling to find a uniform definition for the term *gang*. It may be that the different forms and structures of street gangs complicate the difficulty in finding one all-purpose definition. For example, some researchers have drawn a distinction between street gangs and drug gangs. Drug gangs are seen as much more organized than street gangs, and are generally smaller, more cohesive, and hierarchical. They are organized for the sole purpose of selling drugs and protecting their individual members from discovery.

On the other hand, street gangs can be characterized as having organized themselves for the protection of their perceived territory and the gang membership itself. Because a street gang's mission is to protect its territory, a street gang by nature is more visible than a drug gang because it must mark the boundaries of that territory. To further complicate this issue, other types of gangs, like motorcycle gangs and prison gangs, share some characteristics with both street gangs and drug gangs, as well as characteristics unique to themselves.

25. What would be the best title for this passage?
    a. Drug Gangs and Street Gangs
    b. Defining Street Gangs
    c. Defining Gangs
    d. Problems for Gang Researchers

26. Based on the passage, which of the following sentences is true?
    a. Gangs are completely disorganized groups of criminals.
    b. Gangs are always highly organized.
    c. Motorcycle gangs are more organized than prison gangs.
    d. Street gangs are less organized than drug gangs.

27. Based on the passage, which of the following is NOT true?
    a. Street gangs are organized to protect the identities of individual members.
    b. A street gang's mission is to protect its territory.
    c. Prison gangs share some characteristics with street gangs.
    d. Drug gangs tend to be smaller than street gangs.

Read the following passage, then answer questions 28 through 33 based solely on information from the passage.

Many public safety officials, especially police officers, have certain restrictions on the protections provided by the Bill of Rights. While most Americans can express themselves freely thanks to the First Amendment, police officers, due to the nature of their employment, cannot. Clearly, police officers on duty and especially in uniform are generally restricted from making political speeches and especially from endorsing political candidates. A police officer's diminished First Amendment right extends to his or her off-duty hours; if the officer's conduct would tend to reflect negatively on his or her department or the profession, freedom of speech is limited.

If a police officer questions a suspect about an incident, the Fifth Amendment—sometimes referred to the *right to avoid self-incrimination*—allows the suspect the right to not answer those questions. On the other hand, a police officer under suspicion of wrongdoing does not have the right to refuse to answer questions. An excessive force complaint against a police officer could result in any number of criminal filings. While police officer statements made in conjunction with an incident cannot generally be used against officers in court, they still cannot refuse to answer questions.

According to the Fourth Amendment, the government can neither search nor seize a police officer's property except with probable cause. Police officers daily use areas and containers that are not protected in the same manner as the public. A police officer's supervisor can, within certain limits, search a police officer's locker, police vehicle, and perhaps an equipment bag without the probable cause necessary to search similar areas belonging to the public.

28. Which constitutional amendment generally covers issues surrounding freedom of speech?
    a. First
    b. Second
    c. Fourth
    d. Fifth

29. According to the passage, which of the following is true?
    a. The Constitution provides that police officers can carry firearms.
    b. An excessive force complaint violates the Fifth Amendment.
    c. A police officer's freedom of speech can be limited during his or her off-duty hours.
    d. A police officer can always refuse to answer questions.

30. Which of the following is the best title for the passage?
    a. An Overview of the Constitution
    b. Drug Use and the Police Department
    c. The Powers of the Police
    d. The Bill of Rights and Public Safety Officials

31. According to the passage, the Fifth Amendment generally covers which of the following?
    a. self-incrimination
    b. search and seizure
    c. free association
    d. freedom of speech

32. According to the passage, all of the following are areas wherein police officers might have diminished Fourth Amendment rights EXCEPT their
    a. homes.
    b. lockers.
    c. squad cars.
    d. equipment bags.

33. Based on information the passage, you can assume that a police officer should refrain from the use of racial slurs because
a. he or she can be arrested.
b. it reflects poorly on the officer and the department.
c. he or she is completely unprotected by the First Amendment.
d. it might lead to a search and seizure of the officer's personal belongings.

Read the following passage, then answer questions 34 through 37 based solely on information from the passage.

Police administrators have had an interest in trying to professionalize the police, but researchers and administrators have argued as to whether higher education can achieve this goal. The interest on the effects of police education dates back to the early 1900s. Many believed that higher education would curtail the abuses of police power and put an end to illegal police practices such as corruption, grafting, and violations of civil rights. In England, during the 1820s, Sir Robert Peel understood many of the problems that were inherent in the field and formally established the London Metropolitan Police in an attempt to professionalize this occupation. By the early 1900s, August Vollmer, a police administrator in Berkeley, California, was the first administrator to advocate for college educated officers, and he was also the first police administrator to hire part-time college students as police officers. He believed that college-educated officers could perform their roles more skillfully and more professionally than their uneducated counterparts. Due to his efforts, the University of California at Berkeley began offering criminal justice courses. Despite Vollmer's call for more educated officers and the findings of the Wickersham Commission in 1931, which hinted at the benefits of requiring college degrees for officers, their requests were ignored; the issue of education and policing would have to wait until the 1960s before the topic would generate a discussion of any magnitude.

34. All of the following are cited as reasons for requiring higher education for police officers EXCEPT
a. corruption.
b. graffiti.
c. civil rights violations.
d. abuse of power.

35. The University of California at Berkeley began to offer criminal justice courses due to the efforts of
a. Vollmer.
b. Peel.
c. Wickersham.
d. Robert.

36. All the following statements are true EXCEPT
a. Peele was the first police administrator to hire college students as police officers.
b. Peele attempted to professionalize the police department.
c. most officers in Berkeley in the early 1900s were college educated.
d. the topic of higher education and policing has been of interest since the 1900s.

37. The issue of policing and higher education had to wait until the _____ in order for a significant discussion to commence.
a. 1820s
b. 1900s
c. 1930s
d. 1960s

Read the following passage, then answer questions 38 through 41 based solely on information from the passage.

In order for evidence to be admissible and, therefore, introduced into court, it must conform to many rules and restrictions. A court can rule that evidence is inadmissible if it is irrelevant, confusing, unfairly prejudicial, or cumulative. For police officers, another key element of introducing evidence at a trial is maintaining the chain of custody.

By ensuring the chain of custody, the judge is trying to ensure that evidence presented in court is in nearly the same condition as it was found at the crime scene. Typically, the chain of custody begins with the person who found the evidence and culminates with the person who brings the evidence before the court. Moreover, chain of custody is proven by people testifying as to where and how evidence was maintained from its first finding until its ultimate presentation in court.

38. Which of the following is a reason a judge may not allow evidence into court?
   a. It may prove the defendant guilty.
   b. It may prove the defendant not guilty.
   c. The witness knows the defendant.
   d. It doesn't prove any facts related to the case.

39. It can be inferred that the chain of custody probably ends with the
   a. judge presiding over the trial.
   b. defendant.
   c. defendant or plaintiff's trial attorney.
   d. jury.

40. When does the chain of custody begin?
   a. when the crime is committed
   b. when the trial begins
   c. when the jury returns a verdict
   d. when the evidence is found

41. Which of the following is NOT true?
   a. Evidence must be relevant.
   b. Evidence must be prejudicial.
   c. Judges and juries use evidence.
   d. Evidence must be admissible.

Read the following passage, then answer questions 42 through 46 based solely on information from the passage.

Around 1880, it was suspected, and later confirmed, that no two individuals' fingerprints are alike. While the basic pattern for human fingerprints comes from their genetic encoding, the fingerprints are also affected during development by the conditions in the womb. The position of the fetus, the condition of the amniotic fluid in the womb, and other environmental factors affect the formation of the fingerprints. The combination of the vast number of possible genetic combinations and the unpredictable and endless combinations of the environmental factors mean that no two individuals are going to have the same fingerprints, not even twins.

Once found to be a positive way to identify individuals, fingerprints had a number of uses in the police service. Fingerprints can be visible, plastic, or latent. Visible prints would be those left by touching a substance before touching a surface, like a bloody fingerprint. Plastic would be prints left in a soft substance, such as wood putty or clay. Latent means hidden. Latent fingerprints are left behind by the natural oils from our hands. These oils stay on an object in the pattern of the fingerprint.

42. According to the passage, which of the following is true?
  a. Identical twins have identical fingerprints.
  b. An individual's genetic code provides the basic pattern.
  c. Environmental conditions have no impact on the development of fingerprints.
  d. Few genetic combinations of fingerprints are possible.

43. Which of the following is an example of plastic fingerprints?
  a. an ink thumbprint left on a piece of paper
  b. fingerprints on a doorknob
  c. fingerprints found in tar
  d. fingerprints found on a glass door

44. According to the passage, which of the following is NOT a type of fingerprint?
  a. latent
  b. visible
  c. amniotic
  d. plastic

45. What causes latent fingerprints when a suspect touches an object?
  a. the suspect's genetic code
  b. the wet objects the suspect touched earlier
  c. the secretion of amniotic fluid
  d. the oil on the suspect's fingers

46. According to the passage, which of the following is NOT true?
  a. Amniotic fluid can affect the formation of fingerprints.
  b. In the early 1900s, no one acknowledged that each individual's fingerprints were distinct.
  c. Law enforcement agencies have multiple uses for fingerprinting.
  d. Muddy fingerprints are considered visible prints.

Read the following passage, then answer questions 47 through 52 based solely on information from the passage.

Have computers made our lives easier or more difficult? Computer technology or information technology (IT) has allowed criminal justice agencies to keep better records (such as records of criminal offenders and parking tickets), share information between agencies, and start newer and more sophisticated programs (such as 911 emergency). Most law enforcement agencies rely heavily on computer technology, and most agency officials admit that their jobs would be difficult without computers. Moreover, recent studies show that most criminal justice agencies are relying more and more on computer technology. However, this new technology has not come without its share of problems. There has been great difficulty in keeping abreast of new technology. Some criminal justice agencies have been very slow in implementing IT. Even though IT can assist with efficiency and productivity, the formidable task of implementing and maintaining such systems can overshadow its benefits. IT also opens up a huge area for criminal activity. Overall, computer crime is relatively new to the criminal justice system. It arose as a serious problem in the 1980s and law enforcement officials have had to figure out appropriate ways to deal with such behavior. This "new crime" has severely impacted law enforcement policies. Legislative bodies have had to pass laws and acts to deal with computer fraud, while many state and federal agencies have had to develop specialized departments. Computers can be the target of a crime (i.e. theft), they can be targeted when they are used to "disable" (as in the transmission of viruses), or they can be used as a device to commit crime (such as fraud, embezzlement, and child pornography). Furthermore, the growth of IT has produced constitutional debates over people's right to privacy. The amendment of the Freedom of Information Act and passage of the Fair Credit Reporting Act sparked the passing of the Federal Privacy Act, which prevents agencies from using collected data differently than initially intended. Civil rights can be violated when agencies keep personal and confidential files on their computers and that information is subsequently accessed by a "hacker" and used in an inappropriate manner. Computers have made the jobs of law enforcement officials easier in some ways, but so much harder in other ways. They must not only keep up with new technology but attempt to develop new ways to combat this new type of crime.

47. Based on the information given, the best title for this passage would be
   a. Computer Technology: A Necessity for Criminal Justice Agencies
   b. Computer Technology: Strengths vs. Weaknesses
   c. Computer Technology: The Growth of IT
   d. Computer Technology: Aiding Crime in the 21st Century

48. One of the ways to describe computer crime is that
   a. it is a relatively new problem for law enforcement.
   b. it can lead to civil rights violations.
   c. both **a** and **b**
   d. neither **a** nor **b**

49. The growth of IT has produced constitutional debates over
   a. privacy rights.
   b. freedom of speech.
   c. the Fair Credit Reporting Act.
   d. the Freedom of Information Act.

50. IT has forced law enforcement agencies to do all of the following EXCEPT
   a. keep up with new technology.
   b. develop new ways to combat crime.
   c. develop specialized departments.
   d. hire more specialized officers.

51. Computer technology or information technology (IT) has allowed criminal justice agencies to
   a. keep better records.
   b. share information between agencies.
   c. start newer and more sophisticated programs.
   d. all of the above.

52. Based on the information in the passage, which of the following is true?
   a. The Federal Privacy Act resulted in the Fair Credit Reporting Act.
   b. The Fair Credit Reporting Act resulted in the Freedom of Information Act.
   c. The Freedom of Information Act resulted in the Federal Privacy Act.
   d. The Federal Privacy Act resulted in the Fair Credit Reporting Act.

Legal Definitions

The following are legal terms court officers regularly use in the performance of their official duties. Answer questions 53 through 59 based on the definitions.

Affirmative action—a policy of action as opposed to *inaction*. It is often used to balance working environments along lines of gender and race by granting hiring preferences to underrepresented candidates.

Arbitration—a commonly used form of alternate dispute resolution that can be binding or nonbinding. Arbitration is conducted by a single arbitrator or by a three-person panel. Widely used in resolving unionized labor disputes.

Employment at will—a common law rule that an employment contract of indefinite duration can be terminated by either the employer or the employee at any time for any lawful reason.

Equal Employment Opportunity Commission (EEOC)—a federal agency created pursuant to the Civil Rights Act of 1964 to administer and enforce prohibitions against discrimination in the workforce.

Fair Credit Reporting Act (FCRA)—a federal law that requires obsolete or incorrect credit information be removed from an individual's credit profile. The law allows adverse information, such as charged off debts and civil judgments, to remain for seven years and bankruptcy to remain for ten years.

Fair Labor Standards Act (FLSA)—a federal law that established the minimum wage, standard of equal and fair pay, and 40-hour workweek, and serves as a guideline for states to follow.

The Family and Medical Leave Act of 1993 (FMLA)—an act established by Congress that allows employees in companies of 50 or more employees to take an unpaid leave of up to 12 weeks in any 12-month period. The act covers the birth or adoption of a child, and serious illness of a family member or the employee.

Workers' compensation—an exclusive remedy under law that provides for wage continuation, medical treatment, and rehabilitation for employees who sustain job-related injuries at the workplace regardless of fault.

Yellow dog contract—an employment contract that prevents an employee from joining a labor union. These contracts are not legal and not enforceable.

53. Affirmative action is a federal law that requires employers to racially balance workplaces. This statement is
   a. true.
   b. false.

54. A job candidate who feels that he or she was denied employment based on race, gender, or ethnicity would file a complaint through the
   a. National Labor Relations Board.
   b. State Labor Department.
   c. Equal Employment Opportunity Commission.
   d. Office of the Attorney General.

55. Henry Jones filed bankruptcy in 1992 and was discharged in 1993. In 2005, Jones applies for a job and his prospective employer obtains a credit report. The report shows a debt that was discharged in bankruptcy. The creditor refuses to remove the incorrect information. This is a violation of the
   a. Fair Credit Reporting Act.
   b. Fair Debt Collection Practices Act.
   c. RICO statute.
   d. bankruptcy code.

56. Colin Yen is a member of a labor union. He files a grievance after he is docked five days' pay for destruction of company property. The matter is referred to binding arbitration pursuant to the master labor agreement. The decision of the arbitrator is
   a. a guideline for settlement between the parties.
   b. a recommendation that can be used in civil court by either party.
   c. a final decision that holds both parties to the decision.
   d. one step in the grievance process.

57. Joan Armstrong has been employed with the same company for 13 years. In February, her mother is diagnosed with liver cancer. Joan has no accumulated vacation time, but must take time off to care for her mother. She applies for
   a. extended leave of absence.
   b. family and medical leave.
   c. sabbatical.
   d. bereavement leave.

58. Edward Norris is employed with the water department of a large city. While he is working in the sewer, he is struck in the head by a falling manhole cover and suffers a skull fracture. He is entitled to
   a. workers' compensation.
   b. pain and suffering damages.
   c. punitive damages.
   d. exemplary damages.

59. Luisa Santos is offered employment with a company that has recently terminated its union affiliation. As a condition of employment, Santos must sign an agreement that she will not join a labor union. The agreement is called a
   a. blue sky agreement.
   b. covenant not to compete.
   c. yellow dog contract.
   d. black cat contract.

60. The "Whistleblowers Act" is a state law that prohibits retaliation against public employees who report official wrongdoing. In many states, the law has been extended to include private sector employees. Based on this information, which incident is the most accurate example of a protected action under the act?
   a. An administrative assistant complains to the state labor department because her supervisor is having sexual relations with a subordinate employee.
   b. A police officer provides evidence of payoffs between drug dealers and police to the FBI instead of his own police department.
   c. A court clerk complains to the state judicial conduct board because a judge takes a daily three-hour lunch.
   d. A public health nurse complains to the state board of health because his supervisor continually assigns him to treat Asian patients.

61. The Employee Retirement Income Security Act (ERISA) was enacted in 1974. It is a federal law that sets minimum standards for most voluntary established pension and health plans in private industry to provide protection for individuals covered in the plans. A fiduciary duty is placed upon plan administrators and trustees to act prudently and to minimize risk of losses to plan assets, as well as avoid conflicts of interests in the placement of investments. Based on this information, a breach of fiduciary duty would be
   a. disclosing information to a prospective bank that will manage fund assets.
   b. a plan administrator accepting free travel from an investment banker.
   c. a plan trustee never attending meetings, and instead voting by proxy.
   d. a plan administrator placing investments with a brokerage firm that employs his cousin as a commissioned sales representative.

62. Nepotism is a practice of favoring relatives with preferred employment to candidates who are more qualified. Many public agencies have enacted anti-nepotism policies. While the policy has eliminated favoritism and preferential hiring, it has also discouraged family members from following career paths of their parents and siblings. Based on this definition, claims of nepotism would be investigated by the EEOC. This statement is
a. true.
b. false.

63. What agency regulates workplace health and safety?
a. Department of Labor
b. Occupational Safety and Health Administration
c. Workers Compensation Bureau
d. Federal Emergency Management Agency

64. Occupational disease is caused by direct long-term exposure to a workplace hazard. An example of occupational disease is
a. black lung disease.
b. contact dermatitis.
c. chronic fatigue syndrome.
d. deviated septum.

65. Employers may furnish fringe benefits to their employees as an incentive to attract qualified workers. Of the following, which is NOT a fringe benefit?
a. vacation
b. tuition reimbursement
c. workers' compensation insurance
d. health insurance

Court Officer Procedures

Use the following court officer procedure to answer questions 66 through 71.

Background Investigations
All applicants' employment applications will be verified for accuracy pertaining to:

- professional licenses or college degrees
- drivers' records
- criminal records check

If a professional license or college degree cannot be confirmed, the applicant may produce official verification/confirmation from an accredited source. If the provided source is counterfeit, the applicant will be disqualified.

Drivers' records will be checked with the Department of Motor Vehicles. A certified copy of the applicants' driving record will be reviewed for driving under the influence, driving while license suspended, and moving violations.

In the event the criminal records check produces a "hit" and the information is confirmed as the applicant, the following will be considered before the applicant is disqualified:

1. the nature of the offense, when the offense was committed, and the disposition of the offense
2. if the offense was an isolated incident or culmination of prior bad acts

The applicant will be allowed an opportunity to explain the offense as well as the circumstances and disposition. The applicant may reduce the explanation to writing, or the investigator may note the explanation at his or her discretion.

All matters will be considered on a case-by-case basis. If the investigator, in his or her discretion, believes that a further review is warranted, the applicant may be required to appear before a review panel and present his or her case prior to any final disposition. Investigators are well advised to use sound judgment and to keep an open mind in the review process.

66. Based on policy, an applicant is automatically disqualified for
   a. a criminal conviction.
   b. a poor driving record.
   c. an unverifiable college degree.
   d. any prior bad conduct.

67. The results of a criminal records check must be verified to determine if the records are in fact those of the applicant
   a. always.
   b. when any crimes have been committed.
   c. when major crimes have been committed.
   d. never.

68. Investigators are advised to use sound judgment and keep an open mind. What factors are NOT listed as considerations in review of an applicant's criminal record?
   a. the age of the applicant at the time of the offense
   b. the date of the offense
   c. the applicant's employment status at the time of the offense
   d. the disposition of the offense

69. The DMV must provide a copy of the applicant's driving record, but pursuant to the policy, the record need not be certified. This statement is
   a. always true.
   b. never true.
   c. true, when the applicant has a clean driving record.
   d. true, when the applicant has only minor moving violations.

70. An applicant may be required to present further information in support to
   a. the EEOC.
   b. a review panel.
   c. a court of competent jurisdiction.
   d. the background investigator.

71. Sergeant Winters receives a hit on Matthew Crawford: In 2002, he was arrested in Indianapolis, Indiana, for disorderly conduct. Crawford was fined $75 and ordered to attend a court-sponsored class on good citizenship. Sergeant Winters reviews Crawford's employment application. Crawford has answered "no" to the employment application question: Have you ever been arrested and convicted of a misdemeanor offense? Based on this policy, Sergeant Winters's first course of action is to
   a. contact Crawford and ask if wants to change his employment application.
   b. contact the court in Indianapolis and obtain the file to verify the subject's identity.
   c. disqualify Crawford from further consideration and close the file.
   d. continue with the background investigation and revisit this matter.

Use the following situation to answer question 72.

Sergeant Winters verifies that the party convicted of the offense is Crawford. Crawford is contacted and offers in writing the following information. In October 2002, Crawford was attending an Indianapolis Colts professional football game. He admits to having consumed three 16-ounce lite beers. After the game ended and he left the stadium, he needed to urinate and there were no public bathroom facilities in or around the area where he and his two friends had parked, approximately one-half mile from the stadium. The three found what they believed was an isolated area (an alley) and, by a garage, relieved themselves. They were observed by a passing Indianapolis Police Department cruiser and were stopped and questioned. Freely admitting to the incident, Crawford was written a misdemeanor citation for disorderly conduct, by what he termed an overly aggressive female officer. He appeared in municipal court on the charge and plead guilty, with the understanding that the case would be dismissed upon completion of a court-ordered class on good citizenship and payment of a $75 fine. Crawford stated that he paid the fine and attended the class. Crawford was further informed by his court-appointed attorney that there would be no formal record of the arrest and that if asked in the future if he ever was arrested, he should answer "no."

72. Sergeant Winters's review of the court record verifies Crawford's truthfulness, with the exception of Crawford's final statement regarding the nonpublic record of the arrest. Sergeant Winters should
   a. contact Crawford's court-appointed attorney for further information.
   b. contact the court to determine if this is a clerical error.
   c. contact Crawford and advise him to clear up this discrepancy immediately.
   d. input his determination of the findings for further review.

Use the following court officer procedure to answer questions 73 through 75.

Interviewing Former and Current Employers
The investigator will contact the former and current employees of all applicants without exception. The investigator will first inform the interviewed party that the applicant is not the subject of a criminal investigation. The investigator will next present a signed copy of the release of information to the interviewed company or employer.

Even with the signed release of information, which contains a save harmless provision, the interviewed company/employer may be hesitant to provide a complete employment file, citing privacy concerns. If this situation arises, the investigator is to obtain the following:

1. dates of employment
2. job title(s)
3. reason for leaving (may not be furnished)
4. would they rehire this employee?

The investigator may allow the employer to redact certain sensitive information prior to allowing file review. The investigator will not consider the withholding of the employment file or lack of provided information in the negative. Only confirmed negative information may be used in disqualification of the applicant.

Situation: Sergeant Garcia has not received a reply to his inquiry from the former employer of court officer candidate Joseph Peyton. Peyton lists on his application for employment that he was a private police officer with Farm Brooke General Hospital Security Police Authority for two years. On April 7, Garcia visits the hospital's personnel office. The director of the Private Police Authority, William Gerard, informs Garcia that it is the hospital's policy not to provide copies of employment files for review unless subpoenaed for a court proceeding. He will confirm only limited information Garcia furnishes to the hospital about Peyton. Gerard's attitude toward Peyton does not appear positive.

73. Based on policy, Garcia should
   a. furnish the information to the hospital and complete the interview.
   b. request a subpoena and obtain the employment file.
   c. question others at the hospital who worked with Peyton.
   d. make notes regarding Gerard's negative attitude about Peyton.

74. Furnished information that is redacted cannot be considered in a negative fashion in considering an applicant for employment. This statement is
   a. true.
   b. false.

75. A *save harmless* provision indemnifies the court from liability from the applicant for any damages the applicant may suffer because of the background investigation. This statement is
   a. true.
   b. false.

Use the following court officer procedure to answer questions 76 and 77.

No employment shall be offered to any relative of any employee by blood or marriage as follows:

   1. spouse
   2. child or stepchild
   3. sibling or stepsibling
   4. uncle or aunt
   5. grandparent or grandchild
   6. in-law
   7. cousin removed to the fourth degree of kinship

This policy applies to all new hires as of 1/1/2008. All employees hired prior to 1/1/2008 who meet these criteria are grandfathered until there is a change in their status (e.g., divorce).

Situation: Sergeant Kozorez discovers that Rachael Burns's sister is the daughter-in-law of Judge Stanford Rebar of the First District Court of Appeals. It is possible that Burns could be assigned to the Court of Appeals as a court security officer or a bailiff.

76. Based on policy, Burns is not disqualified from employment. This statement is
   a. true.
   b. false.

77. The Eighth Superior Court offers a three-month unpaid internship to first-year law students as an alternative to working as a law clerk in the private sector. Issac Levine applies for one of the four internships. Levine is the son of Judge Morris Levine of the Court's Domestic Law Division. Based on policy, Issac Levine is

a. exempt from policy because the internship is unpaid.

b. eligible on the condition he is not assigned to the Domestic Law Division.

c. disqualified pursuant to the court's anti-nepotism policy.

d. disqualified in the Eighth Superior Court, but eligible in another court.

Use the following court officer procedure to answer questions 78 through 80.

Outside Employment

Employees may not hold outside employment that conflicts with the interests of the court or with the employees' official duties. All outside employment requests must be submitted on Form OE-041 and will be reviewed by the chief judge. If outside employment is approved, it is subject to review on a six-month basis. Approval may be revoked at will.

78. Based on policy, an example of prohibited outside employment is a

a. court reporter who transcribes medical records for a doctor's office.

b. staff attorney who teaches paralegal studies at the college level.

c. court officer who works for a bail bonds company tracking bail jumpers.

d. court clerk who performs secretarial service for a tax attorney.

79. Based on policy, once outside employment is approved, an employee is free to change jobs without further approval of the court. This statement is

a. true.

b. false.

80. Bailiff Melanie Snyder asks Staff Attorney Daniel Davis to represent her in a real estate transaction. The work entails review of the purchase agreement and appearing at the closing. Davis agrees to represent Snyder for a nominal fee. Based on the policy, Davis should

a. refer the work to a private practice attorney.

b. proceed; this one-time transaction does not qualify as outside employment.

c. memo the chief judge for this one-time transaction.

d. complete Form OE-041 and wait for approval from the chief judge.

Use the following court officer procedure to answer questions 81 through 83.

Injury Claims

Employees who are the subject of Form 100 reporting work-related injuries will be interviewed within 48 hours of the date of loss by the investigator. Standard investigation procedures will be implemented. All *sub-rosa* investigations will be approved by the Office of Court Administration on request from the chief judge prior to commencement of activities.

Situation: Sergeant Tejani is assigned the investigation of CSO Bernard Donaldson, a seven-year employee assigned to the First District Court of Appeals. On Monday, January 17, at 9:10 A.M., Donaldson files an injury report claiming that he slipped and fell on the floor of a public bathroom in the courthouse. The fall was caused by standing water on the floor. He complains of a sore back and left ankle pain and is sent to the clinic for examination. The clinic confirms a lower lumbar strain and a bone chip below the ankle. Donaldson is placed off work.

81. Based on policy, Tejani's first interview with Donaldson must occur by
   a. January 18.
   b. January 19
   c. January 20.
   d. January 21.

82. Sergeant Tejani interviews Donaldson at his home. Donaldson provides a sworn statement detailing the slip and fall. Donaldson stated he was alone in the bathroom. In legal terms, based on his injury status, Donaldson is referred to as the
   a. claimant.
   b. plaintiff.
   c. disabled.
   d. petitioner.

83. Sergeant Tejani proceeds to the courthouse and interviews CSO Lisa Seretsky, who was assigned with Donaldson at the main entrance security station on the date of loss. Donaldson reported for his shift at 8 a.m., attended roll call, and operated his post. Seretsky states that Donaldson left his post shortly after 9 A.M., stating that he was going to "check out two suspicious men by the men's room" on the main floor. Seretsky did not observe the subjects and remained at the security station. Several minutes later, Donaldson returned, limping, informing Seretsky that he had fallen in the bathroom and was in

great pain. Donaldson radioed for a supervisor. After being relieved, he was conveyed to the clinic for examination by CSO Bernadette Gladwin at 9:25 A.M. Following basic investigations procedure, Tejani's next interview is with
   a. the CSO supervisor.
   b. the attending physician at the clinic.
   c. CSO Bernadette Gladwin.
   d. the relief CSO who replaced Donaldson.

Use the following information to answer questions 84 through 90.

Situation: Tejani reviews the medical file and finds nothing extraordinary. In reviewing Donaldson's past medical history, on February 16, 2008, Donaldson reported for work with a full bandage on his left hand. He reported that he had sustained a deep laceration on the palm from a snow blower blade and required nine sutures. The injury occurred on his day off on February 15 at his home. The injury was not investigated by Court Professional Standards Bureau. Further review of Donaldson's personnel file shows an irregular pattern of vacation days in winter months, but a consistent two-week vacation every August since 2007. Using the Internet, Tejani matches the weather reports to Donaldson's winter vacation days.

There was significant snowfall on every vacation day. There were 2.5 inches of snow on January 16.

Tejani reviews state business records and discovers that Donaldson's brother, Henry, owns a landscape business that provides snow removal services. Donaldson does not have a request for outside employment on file.

84. Following basic investigation procedure, Tejani should
   a. interview Henry Donaldson.
   b. recommend *sub-rosa* investigation activities pertaining to Bernard Donaldson.
   c. recommend *sub-rosa* investigation activities pertaining to Henry Donaldson.
   d. reinterview Bernard Donaldson.

85. An invaluable investigation tool in this case has been
   a. Donaldson's personnel file.
   b. the Internet.
   c. Donaldson's medical records.
   d. state business records.

86. Based on policy, *sub-rosa* investigations
   a. may be commenced at any time by the investigator.
   b. are approved by the Supreme Court.
   c. are approved by the Office of Court Administration.
   d. are prohibited by court policy.

87. The term *sub-rosa investigation* is defined as an inquiry conducted in a secret or private way. A procedure not used in effectuating a *sub-rosa* investigation is
   a. directly interviewing the subject of the investigation.
   b. contacting knowledgeable parties under a pretext.
   c. surveillance of the subject.
   d. use of confidential informants.

88. What is the form that documents an employee's work-related injury?
   a. Form 1
   b. Form 100
   c. Form 1000
   d. Form EINJ

89. Regardless of where the injury occurred, Donaldson's claim will be adjudicated through the state Workers' Compensation Bureau. This statement is
   a. true.
   b. false.

90. Donaldson's alleged work-related injury occurred at the First District Court of Appeals Courthouse. Pursuant to the policy, a civilian who suffers a slip and fall injury at the courthouse is investigated by the
   a. Court Professional Standards Bureau.
   b. state police.
   c. Office of the Attorney General.
   d. Office of Court Administration.

Clerical Ability

Study the following forms and answer questions 91 through 100 based on the form content and use.

Court Officer Trainee Examination Eligibility List

The following candidates have successfully completed the examination process for the position of court officer trainee. The eligibility list is ranked by performance on all completed tests.

RANK	NAME	SCORE
1	RACHAEL BURNS	95
2	GEORGE JACKSON	94
3	MATTHEW CRAWFORD	94
4	ALICIA ORLOWSKI	91
5	CARL DURHAM	90
6	ROLAND FUHRMAN	90
7	WILLIAM REGAN	90
8	MARCIA McPHERSON	89
9	RAYMOND KRAMER	88
10	MILLICENT PARR	88
11	RANDOLPH TENNETT	88
12	NATHAN WALTERS	88
13	DORIS WASHINGTON	88
14	HENRY MOON	86
15	MAUREEN HOOPER	85
16	SALVATORE VITELLO	84
17	JOHN WELKEY	84
18	JOAN MEREDITH	82
19	LAWRENCE PARKS	82
20	FRANCIS ALBERTSON	80

CERTIFICATION DATE: October 1, 2010

EXPIRATION DATE: October 1, 2011

NOTE: THIS LIST IS NOT SUBJECT TO AFFIRMATIVE ACTION OR VETERANS PREFERENCE HIRING.

L. MARTIN BURR, Court Administrator

SAMUEL FINCH, Senior Examiner

DOROTHY HYATT, Director of Court Personnel

Court Officer Trainee Examination Summary
TOTAL APPLICANTS TESTED: 82

WRITTEN EXAMINATION TOTAL POSSIBLE POINTS: 50
PASSED: 56

ORAL INTERVIEW TOTAL POSSIBLE POINTS: 25
PASSED: 47

MEDICAL & PSYCHOLOGICAL TOTAL POSSIBLE POINTS: 15
PASSED: 44

BACKGROUND INVESTIGATION TOTAL POSSIBLE POINTS: 10
PASSED: 40

TOTAL POSSIBLE EXAMINATION POINTS: 100

PASSING SCORE FOR ELIGIBILITY LIST: 80

91. What is the number of eligible candidates with identical scores?
  a. 12
  b. 13
  c. 14
  d. 15

92. How many candidates failed the written examination?
  a. 25
  b. 26
  c. 30
  d. 32

93. The total possible points for the written examination and oral interview are 75. For a candidate to qualify for the third phase of testing, what is the minimum point total?
  a. 60
  b. 65
  c. 70
  d. 80

94. The average score for the 20 eligible candidates is 87.8. If only above-average scores were accepted, how many candidates would be eliminated from the list?
  a. five
  b. six
  c. seven
  d. eight

95. The eligibility list is valid for two years. This statement is
a. true.
b. false.

96. The senior examiner who certified the eligibility list is
a. Seth Maxwell.
b. Dorothy Hyatt.
c. L. Martin Burr.
d. Samuel Finch.

97. The chief judge of the court certified the eligibility list. This statement is
a. true.
b. false.

98. The eligibility list is not subject to affirmative action hiring preferences. This statement is
a. true.
b. false.

99. What is the percentage of female candidates in the first ten positions?
a. 30%
b. 40%
c. 50%
d. 60%

100. The 20th position on the eligibility list is held by
a. Lawrence Parks.
b. Millicent Parr.
c. Francis Albertson.
d. Carl Durham.

Answers

1. **c.** The woman in front of the bank is holding a small boy's hand.
2. **b.** The sign on the bakery shop reads "23rd Bakery."
3. **d.** The Bait Shop is the only store located directly next to the Bakery.
4. **d.** There are a total of nine adults in this picture: There are three people standing by the fire hydrant; there are two police officers in the street; there is one woman in front of the bank; there are two people fighting in the Karate window; and there is one person looking out of the window next to the Karate studio.
5. **c.** The accident is on the corner of 23rd Street and 3rd Avenue.
6. **b.** A Terry Stop is described in the first three sentences of the first paragraph of the passage.
7. **d.** See the fourth paragraph. If the officer feels that the suspect poses a threat to the officer's safety, the suspect should be frisked.
8. **c.** Based on the actions described, an officer's training and experience would indicate that the people were planning a robbery.
9. **b.** See the first paragraph.
10. **a.** See the second paragraph.
11. **c.** See the fourth paragraph.
12. **d.** See the third paragraph.
13. **a.** See the first paragraph.
14. **b.** Refer to the second paragraph.
15. **c.** See the second paragraph.
16. **d.** The public disorder happened in the location described in **a**, **b**, and **c**; however, the disorder was inside the restaurant, not outside. Therefore, the only logical choice would be choice **d**.
17. **a.** AThe officers were initially informed about Jose Rodriguez's complaint through police dispatcher Isa Torres.

18. **c.** The man in the red shirt was the one that was arrested by Officer Cox. He was described as being 175 pounds. The other patron, in the blue shirt, was described as being 6 feet 7 inches tall and 200 pounds.
19. **d.** All of the answers presented were given by the patron when he was approached by Officer Cox.
20. **a.** The officers received the complaint at 12:15 P.M. and arrived 5 minutes later at 12:20 P.M.
21. **b.** This choice most completely summarizes the primary purpose of the paragraph. The other choices are all supporting details in the passage.
22. **b.** See the second sentence of the passage: "The sequence or order of the DNA building blocks is *different* in particular regions of the cell . . . ."
23. **c.** The passage states that DNA collected from crime scenes can either incriminate or eliminate a suspect.
24. **a.** The passage states, "If technicians have a biological sample from the victim, such as a bloodstain . . . ." From this statement, you can infer that DNA is collected from biological samples, of which bloodstains are one example.
25. **c.** The primary purpose of the passage is to discuss the struggle "to find a uniform definition for the term *gang*."
26. **d.** The fourth sentence of the passage states, "Drug gangs are seen as much more organized than street gangs . . . ."
27. **a.** The passage states that drug gangs are organized to protect their members' identities, whereas street gangs are organized to protect territory. This statement directly contradicts choice **a**, which makes that choice the correct answer.

28. a. The first paragraph outlines the connection between the First Amendment and freedom of speech.

29. c. According to the passage, a police officer's off-duty speech can be limited if it reflects negatively on his or her department or profession. No information regarding choice **a** is provided. The third paragraph uses an excessive force complaint as an example of how the Fifth Amendment is diminished, and choice **d** states the opposite of information provided in the passage.

30. d. The passage is about how some amendments found in the Bill of Rights do not necessarily apply to public safety officials, of which (as stated in the passage's first sentence) police officers are a subset.

31. a. The third paragraph relates self-incrimination with the Fifth Amendment.

32. a. The passage never states that an officer's Fourth Amendment rights may be diminished in his or her home.

33. b. The passage states that an officer's First Amendment rights may be diminished, not eradicated; therefore, choices **a** and **c** are incorrect. Choice **d** relates to the Fourth Amendment and makes no sense.

34. b. Graffiti was not cited as a problem; grafting was cited as an issue. Grafting is using one's power in a way it was not intended to be used.

35. a. It was the efforts of August Vollmer, specifically, that led to criminal justice courses at the University of California at Berkeley.

36. a. Vollmer was the first police administrator to hire part-time college students as police officers.

37. d. It wasn't until the 1960s that the topic of higher education for police officers would generate a discussion of any magnitude.

38. d. The passage states, "A court can rule that evidence is inadmissible if it is irrelevant." If evidence doesn't prove any facts related to the case, it may not be relevant to the matter before the court and the judge may not allow the evidence.

39. c. The passage states that typically the chain of custody "culminates with the person who brings the evidence before the court." It makes sense that this would be a trial attorney for either the defendant or the plaintiff.

40. d. The passage states that the "chain of custody begins with the person who found the evidence."

41. b. The paragraph states that evidence may be excluded if it is unfairly prejudicial. All evidence that would tend to convict a person of a crime would be prejudicial against that person; however, unfair evidence could be excluded.

42. b. The passage states, "The basic pattern for human fingerprints comes from their genetic encoding."

43. c. According to the passage, plastic fingerprints "would be prints left in a soft substance, such as wood putty or clay." Tar would also fit the bill. You could also answer this question by eliminating the other choices.

44. c. The types of fingerprints are stated in the last paragraph.

45. d. The last sentence in the passage states, "Latent fingerprints are left behind by the natural oils from our hands."

46. b. The opening of the passage says that around 1880, this idea was suspected. Choice **a** can be confirmed by the third sentence in the passage. Choices **c** and **d** are true according to information in paragraph 2.

47. b. "Computer Technology: Strengths vs. Weaknesses" would be the best title for this passage because the author is weighing the advantages and disadvantages of computer technology.

48. c. Both **a** and **b** are correct because the author describes computer crime as a relatively new problem for law enforcement and a crime that can result in the violation of one's civil rights.

49. a. The growth of IT has produced constitutional debates over the right to privacy.

50. d. The passage states that many departments have had to create specialized units, but there is no mention of hiring more specialized officers.

51. d. The beginning of the passage discusses the fact that IT has allowed criminal justice agencies to keep better records (records of criminal offenders, parking tickets, etc.), share information between agencies, and start newer and more sophisticated programs (such as 911 emergency). Hence, "all of the above" is the answer.

52. c. The passing of the Freedom of Information Act and the Fair Credit Reporting Act resulted in the passage of the Federal Privacy Act.

53. b. Affirmative action is not a federal *law* but a recommended course of action to grant hiring preferences to underrepresented classes in certain industries.

54. c. EEOC investigates complaints of job discrimination.

55. a. The Fair Credit Reporting Act prohibits this type of creditor conduct.

56. c. Binding arbitration is a final decision incumbent on both parties.

57. b. The Family and Medical Leave Act of 1993 allows 12 weeks of unpaid leave in any 12-month period to care for a family member.

58. a. The injury sustained was work related and is covered by workers' compensation benefits.

59. c. This is an illegal condition of employment and is unenforceable as a matter of law.

60. b. The reporting of a crime is a protected action under the act. The other examples all are subjective behavior incidents that do not rise to official misconduct.

61. b. Accepting free travel is likely illegal as well as a breach of fiduciary duty. Choice **d** is not a breach of duty if the purchases do not constitute a significant percentage of the plan's assets and are low risk. Choices **a** and **c** are not breaches of duty because prospective banks can review plan assets to determine costs and fees, and trustees can vote by proxy under most board bylaws.

62. b. Unless there was an element of discrimination attached to nepotism hiring, the EEOC has no jurisdiction in this type of incident.

63. b. OSHA is a federal agency with state equivalents that regulate workplace safety.

64. a. Coal miners with continued exposure to asbestos and mine gases are known to suffer black lung disease, which is a common occupational disease.

65. c. Workers' compensation insurance is required by states with payroll employees.

66. c. Policy dictates that a presented counterfeit college degree or professional license is automatic grounds for disqualification.

67. a. Many factors such as common names or transposed identification information can produce incorrect results.

68. c. The applicant's employment status was not listed as a consideration.

69. b. The policy requires a certified driving record from the DMV.

70. b. A review panel may require an appearance by the applicant before taking any action on the pending application.

71. b. Court files contain pertinent background information, and this information will verify the identity of the convicted party.

72. c. This is the best course of action in this situation. Crawford is likely being truthful, but the responsibility for correction falls to him, *not* Sergeant Winters. Choice **a** is incorrect because the attorney cannot discuss the case unless privilege is waived by Crawford.

Choice **b** is incorrect because correcting the court file is not Winters's purpose. Choice **d** is incorrect even if Winters suggests ignoring the conviction, the ultimate hiring authority could disqualify Crawford.

73. a. Policy dictates that Garcia obtain what information he can about Peyton from the hospital and respect their protocol. Choice **b** is incorrect because there is no pending court action. Choice **c** is not an admissible method of reference checking per policy, and choice **d**, Gerard's negative attitude, is also inadmissible.

74. a. Information that is redacted is often done so due to privacy concerns.

75. b. The *save harmless* provision indemnifies the *employer or party who furnishes information* from any potential liability from the applicant.

76. a. By law, there is no kinship between Judge Rebar and Burns.

77. c. An internship is employment, and the policy does not distinguish between paid and unpaid positions, making choice **a** incorrect. Choice **d** is incorrect because state courts are constitutionally established as one court of justice. Superior courts are a branch of the one court, disqualifying Levine at any superior or subordinate level court.

78. c. Court officers serve bench warrants and search for defendants who fail to appear in court. This similar private sector work conflicts with the official duties of the court officer. The other examples listed have no direct conflict with those positions' official duties.

79. b. All outside employment requests must be submitted to the chief judge for approval.

80. d. Policy requires Form OE-041 be submitted to the chief judge. Davis would likely modify the form informing the chief judge of the one-time transaction.

81. b. January 19 is 48 hours from the date of loss.

82. a. A work-related injured party is classified as the claimant. Choices **b** and **d** are incorrect because those terms relate to parties who bring litigation. Choice **c** is a generic term.

83. c. Gladwin conveyed Donaldson to the clinic, spending time with him before and after the incident. Logically, Gladwin is the next person to be interviewed.

84. a. Henry Donaldson should be interviewed to determine if Bernard is working for his company. All other choices are post-interview recommendations if there is evidence that Bernard Donaldson may have been injured working for his brother and the work-related injury claim is fraudulent.

85. b. The Internet has proved an undeniably useful investigative tool. The weather reports for 2008 could be obtained from local newspaper archives or the U.S. Weather Bureau website. Being able to access the data from a computer saves countless hours of drive time and physical research.

86. c. The Office of Court Administration, upon request from the chief judge, approves *sub-rosa* activities.

87. a. All other methods are designed to obtain information without the subject's knowledge.

88. b. The form that documents an employee's work-related injury is Form 100.

89. a. The work-related injury allegation will be subject to the state workers compensation statute. If proved the injury is not work related, the claim is dismissed.

90. d. A premises liability claim is investigated by the Office of Court Administration. Choice **a** is incorrect because the Court Professional Standards Bureau investigates employee-related matters.

91. c. There are two at 94, three at 90, five at 88, two at 84, and two at 82.

92. b. Of the 82 candidates, 56 passed the written examination (82 − 56 = 26).

93. a. 80% of 75 points is 60.

94. c. Starting with candidate #14, Henry Moon, all candidates who scored below 87.8 would be eliminated.

95. b. The list is valid for one year, from October 1, 2006 to October 1, 2007.

96. d. The senior examiner who certified the eligibility list is Samuel Finch.

97. b. The chief judge does not appear on the list of certifying officials.

98. a. There are no hiring preferences attached to this eligibility list.

99. b. Four female candidates (#1, #4, #8, and #10) are ranked in the first ten positions.

100. c. The 20th position on the eligibility list is held by Francis Albertson.

11 ▶ PRACTICE TEST 3

T his is the third practice test in this book and is based on the most commonly tested areas on the court officer exam. The practice test consists of 100 multiple-choice questions in the following areas: memory; reading text, tables, charts, and graphs; legal definitions; court officer procedures; and clerical ability. Allow yourself three hours to take this practice test.

1. (a) (b) (c) (d)
2. (a) (b) (c) (d)
3. (a) (b) (c) (d)
4. (a) (b) (c) (d)
5. (a) (b) (c) (d)
6. (a) (b) (c) (d)
7. (a) (b) (c) (d)
8. (a) (b) (c) (d)
9. (a) (b) (c) (d)
10. (a) (b) (c) (d)
11. (a) (b) (c) (d)
12. (a) (b) (c) (d)
13. (a) (b) (c) (d)
14. (a) (b) (c) (d)
15. (a) (b)
16. (a) (b) (c) (d)
17. (a) (b) (c) (d)
18. (a) (b) (c) (d)
19. (a) (b) (c) (d)
20. (a) (b) (c) (d)
21. (a) (b) (c) (d)
22. (a) (b) (c) (d)
23. (a) (b) (c) (d)
24. (a) (b) (c) (d)
25. (a) (b) (c) (d)
26. (a) (b) (c) (d)
27. (a) (b) (c) (d)
28. (a) (b) (c) (d)
29. (a) (b) (c) (d)
30. (a) (b) (c) (d)
31. (a) (b) (c) (d)
32. (a) (b) (c) (d)
33. (a) (b) (c) (d)
34. (a) (b) (c) (d)
35. (a) (b) (c) (d)

36. (a) (b) (c) (d)
37. (a) (b) (c) (d)
38. (a) (b) (c) (d)
39. (a) (b) (c) (d)
40. (a) (b) (c) (d)
41. (a) (b) (c) (d)
42. (a) (b) (c) (d)
43. (a) (b) (c) (d)
44. (a) (b) (c) (d)
45. (a) (b) (c) (d)
46. (a) (b) (c) (d)
47. (a) (b) (c) (d)
48. (a) (b) (c) (d)
49. (a) (b) (c) (d)
50. (a) (b) (c) (d)
51. (a) (b) (c) (d)
52. (a) (b) (c) (d)
53. (a) (b) (c) (d)
54. (a) (b) (c) (d)
55. (a) (b) (c) (d)
56. (a) (b) (c) (d)
57. (a) (b) (c) (d)
58. (a) (b) (c) (d)
59. (a) (b) (c) (d)
60. (a) (b) (c) (d)
61. (a) (b) (c) (d)
62. (a) (b) (c) (d)
63. (a) (b) (c) (d)
64. (a) (b) (c) (d)
65. (a) (b) (c) (d)
66. (a) (b) (c) (d)
67. (a) (b) (c) (d)
68. (a) (b) (c) (d)
69. (a) (b) (c) (d)
70. (a) (b) (c) (d)

71. (a) (b) (c) (d)
72. (a) (b) (c) (d)
73. (a) (b) (c) (d)
74. (a) (b) (c) (d)
75. (a) (b) (c) (d)
76. (a) (b) (c) (d)
77. (a) (b) (c) (d)
78. (a) (b) (c) (d)
79. (a) (b) (c) (d)
80. (a) (b) (c) (d)
81. (a) (b) (c) (d)
82. (a) (b) (c) (d)
83. (a) (b) (c) (d)
84. (a) (b) (c) (d)
85. (a) (b) (c) (d)
86. (a) (b) (c) (d)
87. (a) (b) (c) (d)
88. (a) (b) (c) (d)
89. (a) (b) (c) (d)
90. (a) (b) (c) (d)
91. (a) (b) (c) (d)
92. (a) (b) (c) (d)
93. (a) (b) (c) (d)
94. (a) (b) (c) (d)
95. (a) (b) (c) (d)
96. (a) (b) (c) (d)
97. (a) (b) (c) (d)
98. (a) (b) (c) (d)
99. (a) (b) (c) (d)
100. (a) (b) (c) (d)

Memory and Observation

You will be given ten minutes to study the following four wanted posters. Try to remember as many details as you can. You may not take any notes at this time. Then, answer questions 1 through 10 without referring back to the wanted posters.

Wanted for Assault

Name: James Beckham
Age: 31
Height: 5'11"
Weight: 215
Race: Caucasian
Hair color: blond
Eye color: green

Identifying marks: piercing in left ear; tattoo of woman's face on left shoulder
Note: carries a gun and must be considered dangerous; has a heroin habit

Wanted for Armed Robbery

Name: Manuel Martinez
Age: 34
Height: 5'8"
Weight: 198
Race: Hispanic
Hair color: black
Eye color: brown

Identifying marks: tattoo on left shoulder that says "Mother"; scar on right shoulder from previous gunshot wound
Note: has family in the Dominican Republic

Wanted for Rape

Name: David Torsiello
Age: 43
Height: 5'9"
Weight: 180
Race: Caucasian
Hair color: brown
Eye color: brown

Identifying marks: missing right eye from industrial accident; often wears a patch over right eye
Note: carries a hunting knife; tends to confront victims outside their residences and force them inside

Wanted for Murder

Name: Fernando Gomez
Age: 32
Height: 5'7"
Weight: 178
Race: Hispanic
Hair color: brown
Eye color: brown

Identifying marks: scar on upper thigh; tattoo of Mexican flag on upper right arm; lost thumb in a car accident
Note: last seen in a stolen black 1998 Nissan Altima

1. Which suspect was involved in an industrial accident?

a.

b.

c.

d.

2. Which suspect might flee the country for the Dominican Republic?

a.

b.

c.

d.

3. Which suspect has green eyes?

a.

b.

c.

d.

4. An officer observes one suspect lurking outside an apartment building as a woman returns home from her night shift. Which suspect has a history of such behavior?

a.

b.

c.

d.

5. Which suspect is NOT in his thirties?

a.

b.

c.

d.

6. Which suspect can you assume is of Mexican heritage?

a.

b.

c.

d.

7. What is an identifiable mark of this suspect?
    a. a tattoo of a woman's face on his left shoulder
    b. a scar on his upper thigh
    c. a tattoo on his left shoulder that says "Mother"
    d. a scar on his right shoulder

8. The suspect wanted for _____ is missing a finger.
    a. rape
    b. assault
    c. armed robbery
    d. murder

9. Which suspect has a drug habit?

a.

b.

c.

d.

10. Suspect Fernando Gomez was last seen in what kind of stolen car?
    a. black 1999 Nissan Altima
    b. black 1998 Nissan Altima
    c. black 1998 Nissan Pathfinder
    d. blue 1998 Nissan Altima

You will be given ten minutes to study the following map. Try to remember as many details as you can. You may not take any notes at this time. Then, answer questions 11 through 15 without referring back to the wanted posters.

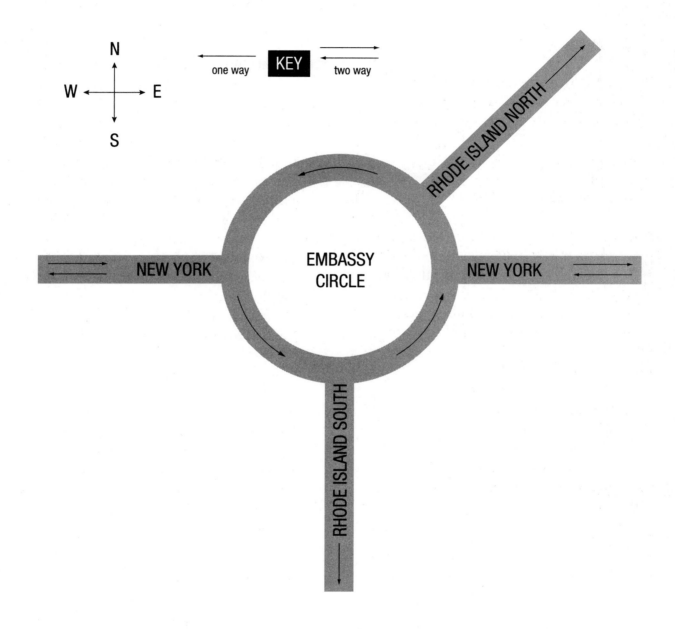

11. If a vehicle traveling from the east wanted to go west on New York Avenue, it would need to travel around the circle
   a. north and east.
   b. north and west.
   c. south and east.
   d. south and west.

12. You are driving east on New York Avenue and need to enter Rhode Island Avenue South. You should travel
   a. northeast.
   b. northwest.
   c. southeast.
   d. southwest.

13. If Court Officer William Gates is traveling from east to west in the traffic circle, he must
   a. drive completely around the traffic circle.
   b. drive north around the traffic circle.
   c. drive south around the traffic circle.
   d. none of the above.

14. Rhode Island Avenue runs
   a. from north to south.
   b. from south to north.
   c. south and northeast.
   d. south to northeast.

15. New York Avenue is a two-way street. This statement is
   a. true.
   b. false.

Reading Text, Tables, Charts, and Graphs

Read the following passage, then answer questions 16 through 21 based solely on information from the passage.

The late 1980s and early 1990s brought concerns across America about the rise in gang violence. It is estimated that between 30,000 and 50,000 gang members live in Chicago, America's third largest city. As a result, the City Council of Chicago passed an anti-loitering ordinance; they concluded that public loitering by gang members led to an increase in the murder rate, an increase in other violent and drug-related crimes, and an inability for police, under existing law, to curb gang presence and criminal activity. Loitering also allowed gang members to establish areas of control in certain neighborhoods that enabled them to intimidate residents. Their presence produced a legitimate fear for the safety of people and property in those areas. This ordinance was passed to protect the public, to prevent intimidation of residents, to prevent gang-related crime, and to deter others from associating with gang members. Anti-loitering statues helped residents believe that they (not the gang members) were in control of their neighborhoods. Unfortunately, very few studies that provided empirical support for the effectiveness of such laws. Nevertheless, Chicago's City Council attributed the decreasing crime rates to the implementation of the ordinance, but others believed that the drop in crime rates simply reflected a national trend. During the three years of the ordinance's enforcement, more than 89,000 dispersal orders were issued and over 42,000 individuals were arrested for noncompliance. The law was later held unconstitutional by Chicago's appellate court, the state supreme court, and the U.S. Supreme Court. Essentially, the law was deemed "vague on its face" and it was held to be in violation of the 14th Amendment's due process clause. Justice Stevens, writing for the plurality, held that the ordinance violated the *void for vagueness doctrine*. According to the court in *Morales*, vagueness may nullify a law for two reasons: 1) "It may fail to provide the kind of notice that will enable ordinary people to understand what conduct it prohibits," and 2) "It may authorize and even encourage arbitrary and discriminatory enforcement." The decision in *Morales* created much controversy. The dissenting opinion, led by Justice Thomas in conjunction with the Chief Justice and Justice Scalia, criticized the majority's decision, stating that "there is no fundamental right to loiter." The *Morales* ruling will severely impact urban areas and minority communities in a devastating way. The court has ignored the rights of residents in favor of the rights of gang members.

16. Based on the following passage, which of the following is NOT a reason why the anti-gang loitering statute was passed?
   a. public safety
   b. to ameliorate resident fears
   c. to appease public opinion
   d. to dissuade others seeking gang initiation

17. Which of the following reasons were given by the Court to determine the unconstitutionality of the ordinance?
   a. The language of the statute lacked clarity.
   b. There were few studies to provide evidence for its impact on gang crime.
   c. The statue could be capriciously implemented.
   d. Both a and c are correct.

18. Based on the passage, what is the position of the author on the legislation?
   a. The author is supportive of anti-loitering statutes.
   b. The author is against anti-loitering statutes.
   c. The author's view cannot be clearly determined from the information presented.
   d. The author supports the passage of anti-loitering statutes in urban areas only.

19. Loitering enabled gang members to
   a. institute territorial boundaries.
   b. terrorize police officers on foot patrol.
   c. monopolize the drug trade.
   d. appear inconspicuous to residents passing by.

20. According to the passage, why did three of the justices dissent from the majority's opinion?
   a. There is no evidence to show that such laws decrease gang-related crime.
   b. The right to linger on the street is not a right that is protected by the Constitution.
   c. Too many residents are in fear of their safety.
   d. The cops cannot control gang-related crime in any other viable way.

21. Which of the following would be the best title for this passage?
   a. Chicago—America's Third Largest City—Riddled with Gangs
   b. Loitering and the Vagueness Doctrine: Can the Court See the Fear on Our Faces?
   c. Arbitrary and Capricious: What is the Definition of Loitering?
   d. Anti-loitering Statues—The only Effective Way to Combat Gang Activity

Read the following passage, then answer questions 22 through 24 based solely on information from the passage.

If police officers want to stop a vehicle, they must have a valid reason for making the stop. All traffic stops must adhere to the guidelines set forth by the Fourth Amendment. As a result, police must have reasonable suspicion that a traffic violation has occurred.

What if an officer wants to stop a car because he or she believes that individuals in the car may be involved in illegal activity? Can the officer stop the car for a traffic violation when his or her real intent is to investigate possible criminal wrongdoings? The answer is "yes." This is known as a pretextual stop.

In *Whren v. United States* (1996), the Supreme Court legalized pretextual stops; the original intent of the officer is irrelevant as long as there is proof to show that an actual traffic violation occurred. If a traffic violation has occurred, the police may stop the car regardless of the initial reason for wanting to stop the car. For example, the police may pull over a vehicle for failing to signal while changing lanes, but they really want to see if there are drugs in the car. Remember, a broken taillight, items hanging from the rearview mirror, failure to signal when changing lanes, speeding, failure to wear a seatbelt, or talking on a cell phone while driving without a hands-free device are all valid reasons for making a stop. However, it is important to remember that random stops based on "hunches" are not allowed and would not withstand constitutional muster.

22. Which of the following states one of the main points of this passage?
a. The police may stop a car for any reason.
b. The police may stop a car if they have a hunch that its occupants are involved in criminal activity.
c. The police may stop a car if they have reasonable suspicion that a traffic violation has occurred.
d. Officers may only stop a car if their suspicion reaches the level of probable cause.

23. The passage claims that pretextual stops
a. violate the Fourth Amendment.
b. do not violate the Fourth Amendment.
c. are allowed if there is probable cause.
d. are almost always based on an experienced officer's hunches.

24. The police can pull a vehicle over for
a. suspected criminal activity.
b. a broken taillight.
c. failure to signal.
d. both b and c.

Read the following passage, then answer questions 25 through 28 based solely on information from the passage.

At approximately 12:15 A.M. on Tuesday, Mark and Lisa Walters were driving their red Ford minivan Northbound on Colonial Drive. Peter and Debbie Gudio, their next door neighbors, were driving in the opposite direction, on their way to the local grocery store. Suddenly, Mrs. Kelleher's dog ran out into the street. Mrs. Kelleher owns a yellow lab/retriever mix named Max. Max is approximately ten years old and although he is very playful and friendly, he never listens to commands. Upon seeing the dog dart into the street, Mr. Walters jerked the wheel of his car to the left to avoid striking the animal but subsequently hit Mr. Gudio's 2010 gray Honda Civic on the driver's side door. The impact caused Mr. Gudio to lose control of his vehicle. The passenger side of Mr. Gudio's car struck the front of Mrs. Kelleher's car, which was parked at the end of her driveway. Mrs. Kelleher had just recently purchased the blue 2010 Toyota Corolla and was upset to see that her new car incurred substantial damage. Mr. Baxter, Mrs. Kelleher's next door neighbor, called 911. It did not appear that anyone was seriously injured.

25. Which car suffered front-end damage?
   a. the blue Toyota
   b. the red Ford
   c. the gray Honda
   d. none of these

26. Which car was on its way to the local grocery store?
   a. the blue Toyota
   b. the red Ford
   c. the gray Honda
   d. none of these

27. Which car swerved to avoid striking Max?
   a. the blue Toyota
   b. the red Ford
   c. the gray Honda
   d. none of these

28. Who contacted the authorities?
   a. Mr. Walters
   b. Mr. Kelleher
   c. Mr. Gudio
   d. Mr. Baxter

Read the following passage, then answer questions 29 through 34 based solely on information from the passage.

On Thursday, December 26, one month before her birthday, Antoinette Varrin heard a loud crashing noise. She could not tell where the noise originated from. As she jumped out of bed, she noticed the clock and the fact that it was 2:15 A.M. Scared, she awoke her husband, Robert, to investigate the cause of the noise. Believing there was a burglar, he told Antoinette to lock herself in the master bathroom. He walked down the hall and entered the second door on the right, which was his daughter's room. He told his daughter, Katherine, to also lock herself inside the master bathroom. Katherine ran out of the room, turned left down the hallway, and knocked on the bathroom door until Antoinette unlocked it, allowing her entry. After leaving Katherine's room, Robert proceeded down the hallway toward the kitchen area. Once he was near the refrigerator, he grabbed the phone and called for the police. As he hung up the phone, he heard noises coming from the garage area. Upon entering the garage, he saw that the garage window was broken and that Antoinette's birthday gift, a brand new flat-screen plasma television, was missing. He had purchased her gift early and hidden it in the garage to surprise her. As he looked out the window, he saw a black four-door sedan speed away. He opened the garage door, walked to the end of his driveway, and waited for the police.

29. From the passage, it can be inferred that when Antoinette heard the noise, she was most likely
   a. sleeping.
   b. watching TV.
   c. on her way to the bathroom.
   d. coming home from work.

30. The four-door sedan most likely contained
   a. the individuals who broke into the garage.
   b. Katherine's television.
   c. Antoinette's birthday gift.
   d. both a and c.

31. What is the most likely reason that Robert walked toward the kitchen area?
   a. He thought the noises came from the kitchen.
   b. He wanted to make sure no one was in the kitchen.
   c. It was late and after all of the commotion, he was probably hungry.
   d. The phone was located in the kitchen.

32. When Robert left Katherine's room, he made a
   a. right turn into the hallway toward the kitchen.
   b. left turn into the hallway toward the kitchen.
   c. right turn into the hallway toward the garage.
   d. left turn into the hallway toward the garage.

33. At the time of the burglary, how many people, in total, were in the house?
   a. one
   b. two
   c. three
   d. more than three

34. Why was this house targeted for a burglary?
   a. It was shortly after Christmas.
   b. The burglars knew that Robert was hiding Antoinette's birthday gift in the garage.
   c. It was part of a gang initiation.
   d. The reason is unknown.

Read the following passage, then answer questions 35 through 39 based solely on information from the passage.

In order for our society to make decisions about the kinds of punishments we will impose on convicted criminals, we must understand why we punish criminals. Some people argue that retribution is the purpose of punishment and that, therefore, the punishment must in some direct way fit the crime. This view is based on the belief that a person who commits a crime deserves to be punished. Because the punishment must fit the specific crime, the theory of retribution allows a sentencing judge to consider the circumstances of each crime, criminal, and victim in imposing a sentence.

Another view, the deterrence theory, promotes punishment in order to discourage commission of future crimes. In this view, punishment need not relate directly to the crime committed, because the point is to deter both a specific criminal and the general public from committing crimes in the future. However, punishment must necessarily be applied uniformly and consistently in order for the members of the public to understand how they would be punished if they committed a crime. Laws setting sentencing guidelines are based on the deterrence theory and do not allow a judge to consider the specifics of a particular crime in sentencing a convicted criminal.

35. According to the passage, punishment
   a. is rarely an effective deterrent to future crimes.
   b. must fit the crime in question.
   c. is imposed solely at the discretion of a judge.
   d. may be imposed for differing reasons.

36. The retribution theory of punishment
   a. is no longer considered valid.
   b. holds that punishment must fit the crime committed.
   c. applies only to violent crimes.
   d. allows a jury to recommend the sentence that should be imposed.

37. The passage suggests that a person who believes that the death penalty results in fewer murders most likely also believes in
   a. the deterrence theory.
   b. the retribution theory.
   c. giving judges considerable discretion in imposing sentences.
   d. the integrity of the criminal justice system.

38. Which of the following would be a good title for this passage?
   a. Sentencing Reform: A Modest Proposal
   b. More Criminals Are Doing Time
   c. Punishment: Deterrent or Retribution?
   d. Why I Favor Uniform Sentencing Guidelines

39. A person who believes in the deterrence theory would probably also support
   a. nonunanimous jury verdicts.
   b. early release of prisoners because of prison overcrowding.
   c. a broad definition of the insanity defense.
   d. allowing television broadcasts of court proceedings.

Read the following passage, then answer questions 40 through 43 based solely on information from the passage.

The rules for obtaining evidence, set down in state and federal law, usually come to our attention when they work to the advantage of defendants in court, but these laws were not created with the courtroom in mind. They were formulated with the pragmatic intent of shaping police procedure before the arrest, in order to ensure justice, thoroughness, and the preservation of civil liberties. A good police officer must be as well schooled in the rules for properly obtaining evidence as is a defense lawyer, or risk losing a conviction. When a case is thrown out of court or a defendant is released because of these evidentiary "technicalities," we are often angered and mystified, but we are not always aware of how these rules of evidence shape police procedure in positive ways every day.

40. The main idea of this passage are that
   a. the rules of evidence protect the rights of defendants at trial.
   b. police officers should know the rules of evidence.
   c. the rules of evidence help shape police procedure.
   d. the rules of evidence have more positive than negative effects.

41. According to the passage, rules of evidence are designed to ensure all the following EXCEPT
   a. meticulousness in gathering evidence.
   b. proof of guilt.
   c. protection of individual rights.
   d. fairness of treatment.

42. According to the passage, why should a police officer know the rules of evidence?
   a. The rules protect the rights of crime victims.
   b. The public does not appreciate the rules' importance.
   c. An officer must follow the rules to obtain a conviction.
   d. Following the rules protects officers from accusations of misconduct.

43. In saying that the intent of rules of evidence is pragmatic, the author most likely means that
   a. the focus of the rules is on police procedures in the field rather than on legal maneuvers in court.
   b. the practical nature of the rules enables lawyers to use them in court to protect defendants.
   c. the framers of these rules designed them to maintain idealistic standards of fairness.
   d. the rules are often misused in court because of their limited scope.

Read the following passage, then answer questions 44 and 45 based solely on information from the passage.

A lawful arrest must be based on probable cause, which is defined as facts and circumstances based on apparently reliable information that would lead a person of reasonable intelligence, experience, and common sense to conclude that an offense has been, is being, or will be committed by a particular person. Reasonable suspicion about a crime may be enough to stop and question a person, but without probable cause, it is not enough to make a lawful arrest.

44. A trooper could make a lawful arrest based on which of the following?

  a. A bank manager approaches the trooper, points to a man sitting in a car across the street from the bank, and tells the officer that the man appears to have been watching the entrance to the bank for more than an hour.

  b. A trooper observes a woman walk quickly out of a bank, enter a double-parked car, and drive away rapidly.

  c. An obviously intoxicated person approaches the trooper, points to a bank located across the street, and tells the officer to arrest the bank manager for stealing all the money out of his savings account.

  d. A bank manager approaches the trooper, points to an obviously intoxicated person, and tells the officer that the person reached over the bank counter and stole money from the bank teller.

45. A trooper could make a lawful arrest based on which of the following?

  a. reasonable suspicion by a trained trooper that a crime may have been committed

  b. an anonymous letter alleging a crime and who committed it

  c. hearsay information about a person with a reputation for criminal conduct

  d. the observation of a person who begins to run from the scene of crime as he sees the police approaching

Read the following passage, then answer questions 46 through 48.

A person is guilty of criminal trespass when he or she knowingly enters or remains unlawfully in a building. He or she enters or remains unlawfully when he or she does so without permission, license, or privilege. A person is guilty of burglary when he or she knowingly enters or remains unlawfully in a building with intent to commit a crime therein. A person is guilty of assault when, with intent to cause physical injury to another person, he or she causes such physical injury.

46. Charlotte Braverman received a call from her son's teacher, Mrs. Stoker, who told her that her son was going to fail his courses. Ms. Braverman immediately went to the school and entered the building through the front door and under the No Trespassing and All Persons Must Stop at Security signs. She passed the security desk without stopping and proceeded to Mrs. Stoker's classroom. Braverman asked for an explanation from Stoker, but an intense argument developed and Braverman grabbed Stoker by the neck, choked her for a few seconds, and pushed her into a chair. Stoker was not injured. The school principal filed a complaint, and Trooper Rook arrested Braverman. Regarding charges against Braverman, which of the following is correct?

  a. She is guilty of criminal trespass for unlawfully entering the building because she did not stop at the security desk.

  b. She is not guilty of criminal trespass because she was the parent of a student and had legitimate business in the school.

  c. She is guilty of assault because she choked Stoker.

  d. She is guilty of burglary for unlawfully entering the school with intent to commit a crime therein.

47. Assume the same facts as question 46, but in addition, as Braverman was leaving the classroom, she noticed the teacher's grade book on the desk. She went into the women's bathroom and hid there, waiting for Stoker to leave so that she could take the grade book and destroy it. When Stoker left, Braverman entered the classroom, took the grade book, ripped out the pages, and threw them into a trash can. Regarding charges against Braverman, which of the following is incorrect?
   a. She is guilty of criminal trespass for unlawfully entering or remaining in the building without license or privilege.
   b. She is not guilty of burglary because she did not have the intent to commit a crime when she first entered the school, and the intent to steal and destroy the grade book was formulated after she entered.
   c. She is guilty of burglary for unlawfully entering or remaining in the school with intent to commit a crime therein, i.e., the larceny and destruction of the grade book.
   d. She is guilty of both criminal trespass and burglary.

48. Assume the same facts as in questions 46 and 47, but in addition, as Braverman left her house to go to the school, she told her neighbor that she was going to beat the heck out of her son's teacher. Regarding charges against Braverman, which of the following is NOT true?
   a. She is guilty of criminal trespass for unlawfully entering or remaining in the school without license or privilege.
   b. She is guilty of assault because she entered the school with the intent to assault Mrs. Stoker.
   c. She is guilty of burglary for unlawfully entering or remaining in the school with intent to commit a crime therein, i.e., assault.
   d. She is guilty of both criminal trespass and burglary.

Read the following passage, then answer questions 49 and 50.

Traffic laws are enacted to enhance the orderly flow of traffic, regulate motor vehicles and drivers, and promote public safety. The number of vehicles, drivers, and roads far exceeds the number of law enforcement personnel available for regulatory duties.

49. To achieve the goals of traffic law, it is most effective for a police agency to enforce traffic laws in a manner to
   a. ensure that summonses are issued for all violations.
   b. concentrate only on the most serious violations.
   c. encourage the public's voluntary compliance with the traffic laws.
   d. raise as much revenue as possible.

50. A trooper observes a motorist pass a steady red light. The trooper should issue a summons in all of the following circumstances EXCEPT when the motorist
   a. did not intentionally drive through the light.
   b. appears to be an upstanding, law-abiding citizen.
   c. intentionally drove through the light but had looked both ways before proceeding.
   d. carefully drove through the light because of an extreme emergency.

Legal Definitions

Answer questions 51 through 65 based on common legal terms and definitions court officers might come across during their official duties.

51. A constructive eviction occurs when extraordinary circumstances forces a party to vacate property without notice. Which of the following is an example of a constructive eviction?
  a. The owner sells a rental property to a government agency that plans to demolish it in six months to build a roadway.
  b. The owner of a rental property fails to pay utilities, and the heat and power are shut off in February.
  c. The owner of a rental property wants his mother to occupy the property in two months.
  d. The neighboring house is raided by police.

52. A party who dies without a will dies "intestate." The court appoints an administrator to marshal and liquidate assets to legal heirs. If the appointed party is female, she is known as the
  a. administratrix.
  b. receiver.
  c. administrator.
  d. guardian *ad litem.*

53. A jury must deliberate dutifully and fairly. When a jury is deadlocked and cannot reach a verdict, it is given an instruction by the judge to deliberate harder. The instruction is known as an Allen charge, named for
  a. the judge who first ordered a jury to return and deliberate further.
  b. the Supreme Court case *Allen v. Gainer,* which challenged a state constitutional ban on coercive jury deliberations.
  c. football legend George Allen, who demanded grueling practices from his players.
  d. the jury foreman who asked if the jury could continue deliberations after court hours.

54. A deed that includes a restraint on alienation provision requires certain acts be performed in consideration of a conveyance of title. These provisions are unenforceable. Based on this information, which is an example of such a provision?
  a. A home is sold by a mother to her son with the provision that it never be sold to anyone outside the family.
  b. A home cannot be sold to a Hispanic family until 2019.
  c. A home cannot be sold and demolished by the purchaser.
  d. A home is sold provided it is never used for illegal purposes.

55. Redaction is when a document is examined for terms that are not advantageous to one party. It is also a method used to delete sensitive information from documents. Based on the latter, what information would require redaction?

a. the names and addresses of witnesses who will testify in a civil trial

b. the name of a minor who is a witness to a traffic accident

c. the Social Security number of a party who files an identity theft complaint

d. the home address of a film star who appears at a public meeting

56. Vertical privity is a relationship between companies in the chain of distribution of a product. The relationship creates responsibilities for the companies involved, including liability for product defects. Based on this information, an example of vertical privity is a(n)

a. wholesaler that buys discontinued goods from a manufacturer and resells to a chain of outlet stores that sells them to the public "as is."

b. oil refinery that processes crude oil into gasoline and sells to distributors for resale to independent retail sellers.

c. stockbroker that sells publicly traded securities to the public.

d. automobile manufacturer that sells vehicles through its own dealer network.

57. A party who knowingly participates in the furtherance of a criminal act but does not actually commit the crime is known as the

a. accessory after the fact.

b. accomplice.

c. alibi witness.

d. none of the above.

58. The number of cases a judge handles in a specific period of time is known as the

a. docket.

b. book of business.

c. caseload.

d. calendar.

59. When a party is convicted of multiple crimes in the same court, the court may sentence the party to serve the same amount of time for all convictions. The process is known as

a. concurrent sentencing.

b. consecutive sentencing.

c. delayed sentencing.

d. suspended sentencing.

60. Retail fraud is a criminal act that involves the theft of retail goods while the retail merchant is open for business to the general public. The common name for the crime is

a. conversion.

b. shoplifting.

c. absconding.

d. concealment.

61. The unauthorized taking and driving of an automobile without the intent to steal the vehicle is the difference between auto theft and
  a. operating while impaired.
  b. larceny.
  c. joy riding.
  d. reckless driving.

62. A series of acts with a common purpose or objective is known as
  a. *modus operandi.*
  b. pattern of activities.
  c. chain of evidence.
  d. scheme.

63. Entrapment occurs when a party is induced or persuaded by law enforcement to commit a crime when the party had no previous intent to commit a criminal act. The exception is when there is criminal activity afoot and law enforcement provides an opportunity for the criminal party to act. Based on this information, which of the following is an example of entrapment?
  a. Police officers pose as drug dealers in an area with high narcotics activities.
  b. A police officer poses as a drunk man with exposed money and jewelry at a bus stop.
  c. A police officer poses as a prostitute and solicits sex from a bank patron inside the bank.
  d. A police officer poses as a hit man to a woman who solicits the murder of her husband.

64. The crime of uttering and publishing involves the intentional presentation of false or altered documents for the purposes of receiving goods, money, or items of value. Based on this information, which of the following is NOT an example of uttering and publishing?
  a. A person presents a check to a utility company that is returned for nonsufficient funds.
  b. A person changes the amount on a payroll check from $100 to $1,000.
  c. A person changes the date on a retail store sales receipt to reflect a sale less than 90 days earlier to obtain a cash refund from the store.
  d. A man obtains a copy of a professional license and substitutes his name for the license holder's.

65. A prisoner in failing health often applies for a commutation of sentence, a legal process that empowers the governor of a state to reduce the sentence or release the prisoner based on time served. Based on this information, a commutation of sentence differs from a pardon because pardons
  a. do not apply to the sick or infirmed.
  b. nullify a conviction.
  c. are granted by the president of the United States on federal crimes.
  d. require that a prisoner serve his or her sentence in full.

Court Officer Procedures

Read the following court officer procedure, then answer questions 66 through 70 based solely on information from the passage.

Court Policy Firearms

By order of the State Supreme Court, all courts will mandate the following policies regarding firearms in the courthouse:

No persons shall possess a firearm inside the courtroom or on the courthouse grounds except for the following:

1) On-duty city, state, and county law enforcement officers who are attending matters before the court on behalf of their agencies, departments, or offices (does not apply to federal law enforcement agents who are required to carry firearms by their agencies);
2) Corrections officers who are transporting prisoners either to or from the court;
3) All others entitled by law to carry a firearm who have been authorized by the chief judge and who have registered with the court security desk.

Penalty: All persons found in violation of this policy shall be subject to contempt of the court, punishable by a jail term of not more than 93 days, a fine of $1,000, or both. The firearm will be confiscated and, upon conviction, disposed of as allowed by law.

66. On May 1, the Ninth District Court hears the matter of *People v. Janice Culver*. Culver is a rap star whose stage name is Hood Heiress. Present are her attorney, Samuel Lyman, and Jackson Henderson. Henderson identifies himself at the court security desk as a sergeant with a police department 35 miles west of the courthouse. He advises the court security officer that he is armed and employed as a security advisor with Culver Music Group, Inc., the defendant's employer. Based on the court's firearms policy, the court security officer should
   a. admit Henderson to the courthouse with his firearm intact.
   b. admit Henderson to the courthouse only after he locks the firearm in the truck of his car in the court parking lot.
   c. deny Henderson access to the courthouse.
   d. arrest Henderson and confiscate the firearm.

67. On August 17, Jana McKay is eating dinner at Franco's Pizza and Sub Shop, when Lewis Walker and Benito Ramirez attempt an armed robbery. Both are immediately apprehended by state police troopers, who happened to arrive at the restaurant at the time of the robbery. McKay identifies herself to the arresting officers as a deputy U.S. marshal, stating that she witnessed the crime. On September 1, McKay is subpoenaed to the preliminary examination of both defendants by the prosecuting attorney. McKay identifies herself at the court security desk and states that she is armed. The court security officer should
   a. admit McKay to the courthouse with her firearm intact.
   b. admit McKay to the courthouse, but have her check her weapon at the desk in a secured locker.
   c. deny McKay access to the courthouse.
   d. arrest McKay and confiscate the firearm.

68. Attorney R. Herbert Marx is the lead plaintiff counsel in the civil wrongful death case of *Estate of Robinson Fisher v. Freak Day Enterprises, LLC, and Peter Wilder.* Wilder is a professional wrestler known as "Pete the Freak" and, at a staged exhibition, ejected another wrestler into the ringside crowd, striking Fisher. Fisher's neck was broken on impact, resulting in death. During the two-year course of the litigation, Wilder has continued to perform and, during his performances, verbally denounces Marx, even stating that he will "rip out his guts and deep fry them" after he wins his case, because "that's the Freak's way!" These antics have resulted in Marx receiving death threats and being subjected to various forms of harassment. The court has been made aware of these disturbing incidents through formal motions and memorandums by plaintiff counsel. Six months ago, Marx obtained a concealed weapons permit and now carries a firearm for personal protection. On the day trial is to commence, Marx arrives at the courthouse and informs the court security desk that he is armed. The court security officer should

    a. arrest Marx and confiscate the firearm.

    b. admit Marx to the courthouse only if he surrenders the firearm to the court security officer, who will place it in a secured locker.

    c. deny Marx access to the courthouse.

    d. bring Marx before the chief judge for further instructions.

69. The penalty for contempt of court is a jail term of not more than

    a. 30 days and a $250 fine.

    b. 30 days, a $500 fine, or both.

    c. 93 days, a $1,000 fine, or both.

    d. 93 days and a $1,000 fine.

70. The firearms policy was ordered by the

    a. chief judge of the court.

    b. State Supreme Court.

    c. Ninth District Court.

    d. court security desk.

Read the following court officer procedure, then answer questions 71 through 73 based solely on information from the passage.

Court Officer Ethics and Image

Court officers are sworn officers of the court. They are a direct reflection on the image of the judiciary they serve. Therefore, their conduct in and out of the courthouse must be exemplary and not cause embarrassment or disgrace upon the judiciary as a whole.

Court officers should be encouraged to further the positive image of the judiciary through extracurricular community activities that avoid controversy, and emphasize civic pride, dignity, and respect for the community and a dedication to humanity. Some examples are participation in recognized benevolent organizations (e.g., Lions Club, Fraternal Order of Eagles), assistance organizations (e.g., The United Way, American Cancer Fund), and recreational leagues (e.g., Little League, Pop Warner Football).

As sworn officers of the court, court officers are property of no one. The statement of "my court officer" by attorneys or judgment creditors should be immediately and forever discouraged by court officers who are referred to in this manner. Court officers should not accept gifts or other forms of gratuities from anyone. Fee-based court officers will not accept monies over and above allowed statutory fees from attorneys or judgment creditors. They will not tax debtors with excess fees as a form of punishment. Court officers will not provide gifts to public officials, agencies, jurists, or their staffs in return for any type of consideration.

On their oath of office, court officers are expected not only to uphold the law, but also to live under it themselves.

71. Court Officer Jennifer Hill and Senior Court Officer Martin Ryan are field officers, sworn and appointed through the Second Superior Court. On Thursday afternoon, they decide to have lunch at The Old Boys Steakhouse, an upscale eatery located three miles from the courthouse. The restaurant caters to attorneys and business professionals. Hill and Ryan are dressed in business clothes and are seated in the main dining room. They are recognized by Daniel Redford, an attorney with the law firm Redford, Hayes, and Gentry, PLLC, which specializes in creditor law. Hill and Ryan have performed service of process for the firm on a fee for services basis. Redford, without their knowledge, tells the head waiter that he will pay for their meal and to bill his credit card. At the end of their lunch, Hill and Ryan are informed of Redford's actions. Based on the ethics statement, Hill and Ryan should
   a. accept the meal and tip the head waiter the equivalent of the check.
   b. accept the meal and purchase a gift certificate for Redford in the amount of the check.
   c. decline and pay for the meal themselves.
   d. decline and report Redford for attempting to bribe an officer.

72. Court officers' conduct should not cause embarrassment or disgrace to the judiciary. Which of the following is an example of what could be determined improper conduct?
   a. frequenting an adult entertainment club
   b. gambling at the racetrack
   c. being sued in civil court over unpaid credit card debts
   d. failing to pay spousal support (alimony) pursuant to a court order

73. According to the ethics statement, a recognized benevolent organization is
   a. Pop Warner Football.
   b. the Lions Club.
   c. the American Cancer Fund.
   d. Parents Without Partners.

Read the following court officer procedure, then answer questions 74 through 77 based solely on information from the passage.

Policy: Court officers will not serve civil process to a defendant or witness at their place of employment. All process will be attempted at the last known address provided by the plaintiff or party requesting service. If the address is incorrect, the process will be returned unserved. The plaintiff or party requesting service will be responsible for locating the defendant or party's current address. No skip tracing will be performed by court officers.

Criminal process may be effected at a defendant's place of employment and arrest made on a valid warrant.

74. Attorney Henry Sikes requests that civil defendant Marsha Greer be served at her place of employment because he does not have a valid home address. Sikes states he will go with the assigned court officers to identify Greer. Based on policy, the court officers should
  a. refuse the request.
  b. accompany Sikes but have him serve the process to the defendant.
  c. accompany Sikes, wait until Greer leaves work, and serve her off property.
  d. attempt to locate a current address for the defendant.

75. Court Officers Mai and Steinman are assigned a summons and complaint to serve to civil defendant Richard Rolland. At Rolland's home address, the officers are informed by Rolland's mother that Rolland is painting a house five blocks from the home address. Based on policy, the court officers should
  a. leave a notice of attempted service at Rolland's home address with instructions to contact them to arrange service of process at a suitable date and time.
  b. ask Rolland's mother to call him and have him come home and accept service.
  c. travel to the job site and serve Rolland.
  d. make a second attempt later in the week when Rolland is home.

76. David Moss is well known to court officers of the North Bay Municipal Court. Moss has been served with eight summonses and complaints and two writs of execution in the previous six months. Court Officer Tina Kapp is eating lunch at a fast-food restaurant when Moss enters dressed in his work clothes. Kapp is holding a summons and complaint for service to Moss. Based on policy, Kapp should
  a. ignore Moss and finish her lunch.
  b. serve Moss because he is outside his place of employment.
  c. approach Moss, inform him of the process, and arrange a time to serve him at his home address.
  d. travel to Moss's home and post a notice of attempted service.

77. Court Officers Braden and Kreiner hold an arrest warrant for Lawrence Taylor on a charge of jury tampering and obstruction of justice. Taylor is a sales representative for a wholesale food distributor and keeps regular office hours of 9 A.M. to 5:15 P.M. The court officers arrive at Taylor's employment to effectuate the arrest. They discover it is "Bring Your Daughter to Work Day" and Taylor's nine-year-old daughter is present. Taylor informs the officers that he has no family available for several days who can take his daughter, and he does not want to have her placed with Child Welfare Services because of "family issues" with his estranged spouse. He asks the officers to delay the arrest, and he will surrender with his attorney in five days. Based on policy, the officers should

   a. contact Taylor's attorney and arrange his surrender.
   b. allow Taylor to call a friend who can take care of his daughter if no family is available.
   c. accept Taylor at his word and follow up with him in five days.
   d. arrest Taylor and place the daughter with Child Welfare Services.

Read the following court officer procedure, then answer questions 78 through 83 based solely on information from the passage.

Court Officer Uniform Policy

By order of the Uniform Committee of the State Justice Council, all court officers will wear the following uniforms in the performance of their official duties:

Court Security Officers

May 1 through September 30: Short sleeved French blue uniform shirt with navy Class A uniform trousers. Shirts may be unbuttoned at the top collar button only. No ties are required. Regulation black shoes and leather pistol belt and gear. Seasonal outerwear: windbreaker. Shield embroidered navy baseball cap.

October 1 through April 30: Long sleeved navy uniform shirt with navy Class A uniform trousers. Navy tie. Regulation black shoes and leather pistol belt and gear. Seasonal outerwear: uniform blouson jacket or wool uniform sweater. Uniform eight-point hat.

Bailiffs

May 1 through September 30: Light blue two-button blazer, tan plain front trousers, white short sleeved dress shirt, and navy tie. Regulation black shoes and leather pistol belt and gear.

October 1 through April 30: Navy two-button blazer, gray plain front trousers, light blue long sleeved dress shirt, and navy/maroon rep striped tie. Regulation black shoes and leather pistol belt and gear.

Field Officers

May 1 through September 30: Navy short sleeved embroidered polo shirt with navy Class B tactical cargo trousers. Approved regulation black footwear. Ballistic nylon pistol belt and gear. Shield embroidered navy baseball cap. Seasonal outerwear: windbreaker with reflective identification panels or tactical vest depending on weather conditions.

October 1 through April 30: Black long sleeved Class B tactical uniform shirt with black Class B tactical cargo trousers. Approved regulation black footwear. Leather pistol belt and gear. Black patrol cap. Seasonal outerwear: black leather aviator style jacket or black baseball style jacket with reflective identification panels depending on weather conditions.

Approved Regulation Black Footwear

Approved footwear includes 6" or 8" tactical style lace-up boots, or low cut lace-up athletic style shoes in solid black without logos.

Approved Vendors

Approved Vendors are Top Cop Uniforms, Inc.; Gold Shield Law Enforcement Supply Company; LE/MP Enterprises, Inc.; and Hill Street Police Equipment.

78. What is the total number of days bailiffs are required to wear tan plain front trousers?
a. 120
b. 152
c. 182
d. 300

79. The tie color court security officers will wear from May 1 through September 30 is
a. navy.
b. black.
c. navy/red stripe.
d. none of the above

80. According to the Court Officer Uniform Policy, in which of the following shirts may officers have their top collar unbuttoned?
a. the short sleeved blue uniform shirt
b. the long sleeved navy shirt
c. the white short sleeved dress shirt
d. the navy polo shirt

81. The uniform policy was ultimately ordered by the
a. State Supreme Court.
b. State Judicial Council.
c. State Justice Committee.
d. State Justice Council.

82. Which group was NOT issued seasonal outerwear?
a. bailiffs
b. court security officers
c. field officers
d. all of the above

83. Field officers' Class B uniforms are
a. navy.
b. black.
c. olive.
d. charcoal.

Read the following court officer procedure, then answer questions 84 through 86 based solely on information from the passage.

Policy: Orders of Eviction: Manufactured Homes

Manufactured homes are not considered real estate because they are mobile and can be moved from a sitting address.

If the manufactured home is located in a manufactured home community and the community is the plaintiff-landlord, the plaintiff-landlord will be responsible for moving the property from the site after the defendant occupant(s) are vacated from the property.

If the manufactured home is located on private property, the owner shall arrange the removal of the property concurrent with the eviction of the defendant occupants if the owner wants the property moved. It is the responsibility of the plaintiff-owner to coordinate with the court officers the date and time for removal of the property. Rescheduling is highly discouraged because this disrupts the eviction schedule of the court and court officers.

If the plaintiff-owner fails to remove the property at the time of eviction by the court officers and the property is reentered by the defendant occupants or others, the court officer will not return to perform eviction on the satisfied order. All statutory eviction procedures will apply to manufactured housing that remains stationary.

The court officer shall not arrange the moving of the property or make referrals for the removal to the plaintiff-owner/landlord. Court officers shall not change locks or assist in the boarding of doors or windows.

84. Court Officers Hernandez and Green are assigned an order of eviction in the matter of *Landers v. Swartz and All Occupants of 79861 Red Rocks Trail.* The address is ten acres of privately owned land. The officers contact Landers. Landers informs the officers that the manufactured house (trailer) is being donated to a local charity that will remove the trailer at its convenience. Landers wants Swartz and the three occupants evicted immediately, but is fearful they will reoccupy the trailer, and Landers does not want to pay to have the property removed. There is no set date for the charity to haul the property from the land. Based on policy, the court officers should

a. contact the charity and determine what date they will be removing the trailer.

b. evict Swartz and the occupants and leave Landers to tend to his own property.

c. contact Swartz and the occupants and arrange a suitable move-out date with Swartz.

d. wait until the charity provides Landers with a pick-up date and then evict the occupants.

85. The Lush Acres Trailer Park files for an order of eviction in the matter of *Lush Acres Corp. v. Cass and All Occupants of 12 Lush Acres Park.* The order is signed and entered April 2. The order is assigned to Court Officers Harris and Kopakin on April 4. The plaintiff advises the court officers that the defendants moved April 3 and there is no need for their services. The defendants did not return the keys. The court officers should

a. ignore the order and close the file.

b. place the order on the low-priority list and serve it before it expires.

c. serve the order at the address and restore possession to the plaintiff.

d. accept the plaintiff's statements as true and return the order as if served.

86. The Lush Acres Trailer Park files for an order of eviction in the matter of *Lush Acres Corp. v. Phillips and All Occupants of 76 Lush Acres Park.* The order is signed and entered January 11. The order is assigned to Officers Napolitano and Underwood on January 13. The plaintiff advises that the defendant has not paid any rent, and asks the officers to serve the order, but not evict Phillips for up to 30 days as a "scare tactic" to pay the past due rent. The court officers should
   a. accommodate the plaintiff as long as the defendant pays the required service fees.
   b. place the order on the low-priority list and serve it 30 days from January 13.
   c. evict Phillips per established court policy.
   d. inform the plaintiff to withdraw the order if he or she does not want the defendant evicted.

Read the following court officer procedure, then answer questions 87 through 90 based solely on information from the passage.

Policy: Judicial Threats
Court officers assigned to the investigations section of the Office of Court Administration will be responsible for the investigation of any threats to employees of the state judiciary. These employees include judges, magistrates, court administrators and managers, court clerks, court reporters, and court officers.

   Standard and special investigation procedures will apply. Special security measures (SS-911) will apply and be implemented as circumstances dictate.

   Threats will be investigated for credibility and severity. A Threat Assessment Code (TAC) with a range of 1 (low) to 10 (high) will be assigned to each investigated incident based on the initial investigated facts and may be revised as facts warrant. The investigating officer will

have full latitude in the investigation of all incidents. All law enforcement agencies are expected to cooperate with the Office of Court Administration. Prosecutions will be handled by the Office of the Attorney General.

87. Threats made against members of the judiciary and judicial employees are investigated by the
   a. FBI.
   b. state police.
   c. Office of Court Administration.
   d. county sheriff.

88. All threats are assigned a rating between 1 and 10 based on severity and credibility. The rating system is known as the
   a. Incident Response Code (IRC).
   b. Threat Assessment Level (TAL).
   c. Threat Assessment System (TAS).
   d. Threat Assessment Code (TAC).

89. What is the internal code for special security measures?
   a. SS-911
   b. SSM-01
   c. SSM-9-11
   d. SS-9000

90. Prosecutions of judicial threats are handled by the
   a. Department of Justice.
   b. Office of Court Administration.
   c. Office of the Attorney General.
   d. Supreme Court.

Clerical Ability

Answer questions 91 through 97 based on typical clerical duties of a court officer.

91. Compare the sets and select the answer from the following choices.

94726179   j94726179   94726179

   a. All three names or numbers are exactly alike.

   b. Only the first and second names or numbers are exactly alike.

   c. Only the first and third names or numbers are exactly alike.

   d. Only the second and third names or numbers are exactly alike.

92. Compare the following sets.

94726179   j94726179   94726179

The difference between the sets would best be described as which of the following?

   a. The middle combination begins with a letter and the others do not.

   b. The last two digits of all three are different.

   c. The first two numbers of all three are different.

   d. None of the statements is correct.

93. Compare the sets and select the answer from the following choices.

   Rodriquez24
   Rodriquez24
   Rodrigues24
   Rodriques24

   a. All four names or numbers are exactly alike.

   b. Only the first and second names or numbers are exactly alike.

   c. Only the first and fourth names or numbers are exactly alike.

   d. Only the second and third names or numbers are exactly alike.

94. Court Officer Sampson has been asked to alphabetize some contact cards. She must place the name in capital letters in the correct place in the files.

   RICHOT, ALLAN

Names already in the file are:

   Rachot, Allen
   Riache, Allan
   Ricehot, Alain
   Ricehot, Allen

Where in the card file will Court Officer Sampson place *Richot, Allan*?

   a. before all the other names

   b. between *Rachot, Allen* and *Riache, Allan*

   c. between *Ricehot, Alain* and *Ricehot, Allen*

   d. after *Ricehot, Allen*

95. Court Officer Kruter has been asked to alphabetize some contact cards. He must place the name in capital letters in the correct place in the files.

   SARGANT, SUSAN

Names already in the file are:

   Saegent, Suzie
   Sergent, Susie
   Sergent, Suzannie
   Sugant, Sally

Where in the card file will Court Officer Kruter place *Sargant, Susan*?

   a. after *Saegent, Suzie* but before *Sergent, Susie*

   b. after *Sergent, Susie* but before *Sergent, Suzannie*

   c. after *Sergent, Suzannie* but before *Sugant, Sally*

   d. after *Sugant, Sally*

96. When Court Officer Kruter begins to actually file the cards he has alphabetized, he learns that *Sargant, Susan* is an incorrect name and that the name of the contact is actually

SARGANTE, SUSAN

Based on this new information, where will he now file the card?

a. before *Saegent, Suzie*
b. before *Sergent, Susie*
c. after *Sergent, Suzannie*
d. after *Sugant, Sally*

97. Court Officer Kruter has discovered yet another error. The correct spelling of *Sargant, Susan* is actually

SAREGANTE, SUSAN

Based on this even newer information, where will he finally file the card?

a. before *Saegent, Suzie*
b. before *Sergent, Susie*
c. after *Sergent, Suzannie*
d. after *Sugant, Sally*

Answer questions 98 through 100 based on the following document.

OFFICE OF COURT ADMINISTRATION
PROFESSIONAL STANDARDS BUREAU

2009 ANNUAL REPORT OF COURT-RELATED DISCIPLINARY ACTIONS

CASES INVESTIGATED: 193
INVESTIGATIONS CLOSED: 191

CASES RESULTING IN CHARGES: 112
INVESTIGATIONS OPEN: 2

EMPLOYEES TERMINATED: 17
REINSTATED: 0

EMPLOYEES SUSPENDED 90 TO 180 DAYS: 28
EMPLOYEES SUSPENDED 30 TO 89 DAYS: 12
EMPLOYEES SUSPENDED 30 DAYS OR LESS: 52
EMPLOYEES REPRIMANDED NO TIME OFF: 3
EMPLOYEES CRIMINALLY PROSECUTED: 9
CONVICTIONS: 7

VENDORS INVESTIGATED: 6
VENDORS TERMINATED: 2
VENDORS CRIMINALLY PROSECUTED: 0

98. How many employees were criminally prosecuted in 2009?
- **a.** seven
- **b.** eight
- **c.** nine
- **d.** twelve

99. How many vendors were terminated in 2009?
- **a.** one
- **b.** two
- **c.** five
- **d.** six

100. How many employees were suspended 30 days or less in 2009?
- **a.** 40
- **b.** 45
- **c.** 52
- **d.** 66

Answers

1. **c.** This suspect lost his eye in an industrial accident. Another suspect lost his thumb, but that was the result of a car accident.
2. **b.** Manuel Martinez has family in the Dominican Republic.
3. **a.** Only James Beckham has green eyes.
4. **c.** David Torsiello is wanted for rape and has confronted victims outside their residences before forcing them inside.
5. **c.** Suspect David Torsiello is 43 years old.
6. **d.** Fernando Gomez has a tattoo of the Mexican flag, so you can assume that he is of Mexican heritage.
7. **a.** James Beckham has a tattoo of a woman's face on his left shoulder.
8. **d.** Fernando Gomez, who is wanted for murder, is missing his thumb from a car accident.
9. **a.** James Beckham has a heroin habit.
10. **b.** Fernando Gomez was last seen in a stolen black 1998 Nissan Altima.
11. **b.** The vehicle would need to go up around the circle (north), and then continue west.
12. **c.** You would need to go down around the circle (south), and then continue east.
13. **b.** Court Officer Gates is entering from the right and must drive north because of the direction of the arrows in the traffic circle.
14. **c.** Rhode Island Avenue does not run directly north and south, so choices **a** and **b** can be eliminated. Rhode Island Avenue runs south on the bottom of this map, but it runs northeast on the top of this map. Therefore, Rhode Island Avenue runs south *and* northeast, not south *to* northeast.
15. **a.** New York Avenue is a two-way street, as indicated by the map's key.

16. **c.** Public opinion is not stated as a reason why the ordinance was passed.
17. **d.** The court stated that the statue was vague (lacked clarity) and that it could result in arbitrary (also known as capricious) enforcement.
18. **a.** The author's feelings about the law can be inferred from the last sentence of the passage: "The court has ignored the rights of residents in favor of the rights of gang members."
19. **a.** Loitering allowed gang members to establish areas of control in certain neighborhoods (territorial boundaries) which enabled them to intimidate residents.
20. **b.** The dissenters stated that "there is no fundamental right to loiter." The other three answers may all be true, but they were not listed as reasons by the dissenters.
21. **b.** "Loitering and the Vagueness Doctrine: Can the Court See the Fear on Our Faces?" is the best title for this passage, considering the statute was struck down for vagueness and the author is clearly in favor of the statute.
22. **c.** The passage clearly states that a police officer may stop a car based on reasonable suspicion that a traffic violation has occurred.
23. **b.** The passage clearly states that the Supreme Court did not rule against pretextual stops; such stops were not found to violate the Fourth Amendment.
24. **d.** Cops can pull over a vehicle based on reasonable suspicion that a traffic violation occurred, such as a broken taillight or failure to signal. They cannot pull over a vehicle just on the basis of suspected criminal activity.
25. **a.** The blue Toyota, owned by Mrs. Kelleher, suffered front-end damage when Mr. Gudio's car crashed into it.

26. c. The gray Honda Civic, driven by Peter Gudio, was its way to the local grocery store.

27. b. The red minivan, driven by Mark Walters, swerved to avoid hitting Max but subsequently crashed into Peter's car.

28. d. Mr. Baxter, Mrs. Kelleher's neighbor, was the one who called for help.

29. a. Since she "jumped" out of bed and noticed the time was 2:15 A.M., it can be inferred that she was most likely sleeping.

30. d. From the passage, it can be inferred that the car Robert saw speeding away was being driven by the burglars who broke into his garage and stole Antoinette's birthday present.

31. d. He reached directly for the phone upon entering the kitchen, so it can be inferred that the telephone was his main reason for walking toward the kitchen.

32. a. Since Katherine made a left turn out of her room to go toward the master bathroom, it would only make sense that Robert, who was going in the opposite direction, would make a right turn into the hallway toward the kitchen.

33. d. This is sort of a trick question, so you have to read the question carefully. We know that Robert, Antoinette, and Katherine were all present in the house. However, the question asks how many people were in the house *all together* at the time of the burglary. This would therefore include the burglar(s). Hence, the answer has to be more than three.

34. d. The reason the burglars chose this particular home is unknown. There is not enough information about the thieves to infer a reason why they targeted this particular home.

34. d. The last sentence of the passage says that no arrests were made.

35. d. The passage presents two reasons for punishment. The second sentence notes a view that "some people" hold. The first line of the second paragraph indicates "another view."

36. b. This is the main idea of the first paragraph.

37. a. The deterrence theory promotes punishment to discourage future crimes.

38. c. The first sentence indicates that the passage is about punishment. The first paragraph is about retribution; the second is about deterrence.

39. d. The second paragraph notes that one reason behind the deterrence theory is the effect of deterring not only criminals, but also the public.

40. d. This idea is stated in the second sentence and discussed throughout the passage.

41. b. Proof of guilt is the whole point of gathering evidence, but this is never referred to in the passage.

42. c. This is stated in the third sentence. Choice **a** is incorrect because, although rules of evidence protect the accused, that is not the reason the passage gives for why an officer must know them.

43. a. The pragmatic, or practical, intent the author refers to in the second sentence is the purpose of shaping police procedure before arrest.

44. d. The bank manager appears to be a reliable complainant with credible information about the crime. Choices **a** and **b** are incorrect because, although the conduct could raise a reasonable suspicion, the conduct more than likely had an innocent explanation. Choice **c** is incorrect because the intoxicated person's complaint, without further information, appears farfetched.

45. d. Running from the police under these circumstances satisfies the standards of probable cause to make an arrest. Choice **a** is incorrect because reasonable suspicion alone is not enough to make a lawful arrest. Choice **b** in itself is not reliable. Choice **c** is incorrect because a reputation for criminal conduct does not amount to a crime.

46. a. Braverman entered the school unlawfully because she was not licensed or privileged to enter the school. Choice **b** is incorrect because parents must stop at the security desk. Choice **c** is incorrect because Stoker was not physically injured. Choice **d** is incorrect because Braverman did not have the intent to commit a crime when she entered the school.

47. b. This is the only choice that provides an incorrect charge, because Braverman remained in the school with intent to commit a crime therein. Choices **a**, **c**, and **d** are correct answers because she unlawfully entered and she unlawfully remained with the intent to commit a crime therein.

48. b. This is the only choice that provides an untrue charge; Braverman is not guilty of assault because Stoker was not physically injured. Choice **c** is true because Braverman entered the building with the intent to commit a crime therein. Choices **a** and **d** are also true.

49. c. The traffic system can work only with the public's cooperation and voluntary compliance. Not enough officers are available to issue summonses for every violation, so choice **a** is incorrect. Choice **b** is incorrect because officers should not ignore the less serious violations when they are committed in their presence. Choice **d** is incorrect because revenue is not the primary consideration.

50. d. This is the best answer because all laws are qualified by the need to act in genuine emergencies. Choice **a** is incorrect because traffic laws are designed not only for intentional violators, but also for negligent or careless violators. Choice **b** is incorrect because traffic laws are enforced against all citizens to encourage them to drive carefully. Choice **c** is incorrect because looking both ways does not excuse the violation.

51. b. A constructive eviction requires *extraordinary circumstances*, such as when there is no utility service or when the property becomes uninhabitable through owner neglect.

52. c. The term has no gender identification. Choice **a** is an outdated term that was used to identify women who were probate administrators.

53. b. The Allen charge was named for the Supreme Court case *Allen v. Gainer*.

54. a. This is the most common type of restraint on alienation. Choice **b** is illegal, as well as unenforceable. Choices **c** and **d** are unenforceable and unreasonable.

55. c. Redaction applies to *sensitive* information such as Social Security numbers, and in sexual assault cases, names of victims are often redacted when the reports are requested by news agencies or the general public.

56. d. This is direct supply from the manufacturer to it own dealerships. There is no "middle man" as in the other choices.

57. b. This person is known as the accomplice.

58. c. The *future* list of cases is known as the docket, choice **a**.

59. a. Concurrent sentencing allows one prison term for all convictions. Choice **b** requires that each conviction be served independently.

60. b. "Shoplifting" is the common name for this criminal act.

61. c. The unauthorized taking and driving of an automobile without the intent to steal the vehicle is commonly referred to as joy riding. It is a misdemeanor offense.

62. b. This is distinguished from choice **a**, which refers to "motive and opportunity" in a criminal act.

63. c. A bank customer inside the bank is not participating in criminal activity. If the police officer enters the bank and solicits sex from the customer, this is entrapment.

64. a. A returned check is explainable and is not a criminal act *unless* the person writing the check knew at the time there were no funds to cover the check.

65. b. A commutation of sentence does not nullify the original conviction but provides a humanitarian option for prisoners who have shown a significant contribution to society or require care that exceeds that available through the penal system.

66. c. Henderson is a police officer, but he is not on duty and has no official involvement in this action. Choice **d** is too extreme. Choice **b** would violate court policy because Henderson's vehicle is in the court parking lot located on courthouse grounds.

67. a. McKay is a federal law enforcement officer and is exempt from the court policy.

68. d. This is a unique situation that requires some initiative on the court security officer's part. The court is aware of the situation involving Marx. Very likely, the court would allow Marx to carry the firearm onto the courthouse grounds, but he would be required to surrender the weapon at the court security desk before entering the courtroom, and then claim it at the conclusion of the trial's daily activities.

69. c. The court has the option of a jail sentence and a fine, or either at their discretion. Choice **d** is incorrect because it levies a jail sentence *and* a fine. In choices **a** and **b**, the penalty is incorrect.

70. b. The first sentence of the policy identifies who has made the order.

71. c. While there likely is no nefarious motive on Redford's part, the officers should not accept gifts or other forms of gratuities.

72. d. An order of the court must be obeyed. Court officers are expected not only to uphold the law, but to live under it themselves. Choice **c** is a dilemma of a personal nature and,

depending on the court officer's assignment, should not impact the judiciary. Choices **a** and **b** are both legal activities.

73. b. The Lions Club is identified in the statement as a recognized benevolent organization. Choice **a**, Pop Warner Football, is a recreational league, and choice **c**, the American Cancer Fund, is an assistance organization. Choice **d**, Parents Without Partners, is not mentioned anywhere in the statement.

74. a. There is no exception for service of civil process at a defendant's place of employment. Choice **b** is incorrect because Sikes could serve Greer himself and should not have an escort from the court officers that implicates color of law. Choice **c** is also incorrect because this is time-consuming and outside policy, as is choice **d**.

75. a. Choice **c** is incorrect because the job site is Rolland's place of employment for the day. A place of employment is not restricted to a physical structure. Choice **b** is unreasonable, and choice **d** will be accomplished if choice **a** is correctly performed.

76. b. This is acceptable practice because Moss is away from his employment location and on his own time.

77. d. This is a criminal matter. Taylor should be taken into custody and the child referred to the appropriate social service agency for further care and custody. Choice **a** is incorrect because Taylor's attorney is not responsible for his client. Choices **b** and **c** are also incorrect because these are improper procedures.

78. b. There are 152 days from May 1 through September 30.

79. d. No tie is required for court security officers in the spring/summer period of May 1 through September 30.

80. a. The uniform policy states that officers are allowed to have their top collar button unbuttoned when wearing the short sleeved blue uniform shirt.

81. d. The first sentence identifies who has ordered the uniform policy. Choices **b** and **c** are variations on the correct answer. Choice **a** does not appear in the sentence.

82. a. There is no mention of seasonal outerwear for bailiffs in the written uniform policy.

83. b. Class B uniforms are ordered to be worn from October 1 through April 30 and are black. No other colors are mentioned for Class B uniforms.

84. b. The order of eviction commands the officer to remove the occupants. Landers will be responsible for securing the property from reentry until it is removed from the land. Choice **a** violates policy because this would be considered making arrangements for the removal of the property. Choice **c** is improper procedure, as is choice **d**, because both are disruptive to the court schedule.

85. c. The statutory requirements of the order are to return peaceful possession to the plaintiff. Peaceful possession is attained when the locks are changed and the defendant cannot enter with a breach of the peace. Choices **a**, **b**, and **d** are incorrect and improper procedure.

86. d. The plaintiff is obviously not serious in his or her intent to evict the defendant. The order should not be used as an intimidation tool by the plaintiff. Choices **a** and **b** are incorrect and improper procedure.

87. c. The Office of Court Administration investigates such threats.

88. d. The Threat Assessment Code (TAC) is the rating system for these threats.

89. a. Paragraph 2 states that special security measures are also known as SS-911.

90. c. The final sentence states that prosecutions will be handled by the Office of the Attorney General.

91. c. The first and third numbers are exactly alike.

92. a. All the numbers are the same; the difference is that the middle combination is preceded by the letter *j*.

93. b. The first and second names and numbers are exactly alike.

94. d. When the first letter is the same, names are alphabetized based on each succeeding letter. In this example, the first names are not relevant.

95. a. When the first letter is the same, names are alphabetized based on each succeeding letter. In this example, the first names are not relevant.

96. b. When the first letter is the same, names are alphabetized based on each succeeding letter. The *e* added to *Sargente* does not change the name's place in the alphabetical listing.

97. b. When the first letter is the same, names are alphabetized based on each succeeding letter. The *e* added in the middle to create *Saregent* does not change the name's place in the alphabetical listing.

98. c. Nine employees were criminally prosecuted.

99. b. Two vendors were terminated in 2009.

100. c. All together, 52 employees were suspended for 30 days or less.

12 ▶ PRACTICE TEST 4

This is the fourth and final practice test in the book based on the most commonly tested areas on the court officer exam. The practice test consists of 100 multiple-choice questions in the following areas: memory; reading text, tables, charts, and graphs; legal definitions; court officer procedures; and clerical ability. The number of questions and the time limit in the actual court officer exam can vary from region to region.

Set aside three hours to take this practice test.

1. ⓐ ⓑ ⓒ ⓓ
2. ⓐ ⓑ ⓒ ⓓ
3. ⓐ ⓑ ⓒ ⓓ
4. ⓐ ⓑ ⓒ ⓓ
5. ⓐ ⓑ ⓒ ⓓ
6. ⓐ ⓑ ⓒ ⓓ
7. ⓐ ⓑ ⓒ ⓓ
8. ⓐ ⓑ ⓒ ⓓ
9. ⓐ ⓑ ⓒ ⓓ
10. ⓐ ⓑ ⓒ ⓓ
11. ⓐ ⓑ ⓒ ⓓ
12. ⓐ ⓑ ⓒ ⓓ
13. ⓐ ⓑ ⓒ ⓓ
14. ⓐ ⓑ ⓒ ⓓ
15. ⓐ ⓑ ⓒ ⓓ
16. ⓐ ⓑ ⓒ ⓓ
17. ⓐ ⓑ ⓒ ⓓ
18. ⓐ ⓑ ⓒ ⓓ
19. ⓐ ⓑ ⓒ ⓓ
20. ⓐ ⓑ ⓒ ⓓ
21. ⓐ ⓑ ⓒ ⓓ
22. ⓐ ⓑ ⓒ ⓓ
23. ⓐ ⓑ ⓒ ⓓ
24. ⓐ ⓑ ⓒ ⓓ
25. ⓐ ⓑ ⓒ ⓓ
26. ⓐ ⓑ ⓒ ⓓ
27. ⓐ ⓑ ⓒ ⓓ
28. ⓐ ⓑ ⓒ ⓓ
29. ⓐ ⓑ ⓒ ⓓ
30. ⓐ ⓑ ⓒ ⓓ
31. ⓐ ⓑ ⓒ ⓓ
32. ⓐ ⓑ ⓒ ⓓ
33. ⓐ ⓑ
34. ⓐ ⓑ ⓒ ⓓ
35. ⓐ ⓑ ⓒ ⓓ

36. ⓐ ⓑ ⓒ ⓓ
37. ⓐ ⓑ ⓒ ⓓ
38. ⓐ ⓑ
39. ⓐ ⓑ ⓒ ⓓ
40. ⓐ ⓑ ⓒ ⓓ
41. ⓐ ⓑ ⓒ ⓓ
42. ⓐ ⓑ ⓒ ⓓ
43. ⓐ ⓑ ⓒ ⓓ
44. ⓐ ⓑ ⓒ ⓓ
45. ⓐ ⓑ ⓒ ⓓ
46. ⓐ ⓑ ⓒ ⓓ
47. ⓐ ⓑ ⓒ ⓓ
48. ⓐ ⓑ ⓒ ⓓ
49. ⓐ ⓑ ⓒ ⓓ
50. ⓐ ⓑ ⓒ ⓓ
51. ⓐ ⓑ ⓒ ⓓ
52. ⓐ ⓑ ⓒ ⓓ
53. ⓐ ⓑ ⓒ ⓓ
54. ⓐ ⓑ ⓒ ⓓ
55. ⓐ ⓑ ⓒ ⓓ
56. ⓐ ⓑ ⓒ ⓓ
57. ⓐ ⓑ ⓒ ⓓ
58. ⓐ ⓑ ⓒ ⓓ
59. ⓐ ⓑ ⓒ ⓓ
60. ⓐ ⓑ ⓒ ⓓ
61. ⓐ ⓑ ⓒ ⓓ
62. ⓐ ⓑ ⓒ ⓓ
63. ⓐ ⓑ ⓒ ⓓ
64. ⓐ ⓑ ⓒ ⓓ
65. ⓐ ⓑ ⓒ ⓓ
66. ⓐ ⓑ ⓒ ⓓ
67. ⓐ ⓑ ⓒ ⓓ
68. ⓐ ⓑ ⓒ ⓓ
69. ⓐ ⓑ ⓒ ⓓ
70. ⓐ ⓑ

71. ⓐ ⓑ ⓒ ⓓ
72. ⓐ ⓑ
73. ⓐ ⓑ ⓒ ⓓ
74. ⓐ ⓑ
75. ⓐ ⓑ ⓒ ⓓ
76. ⓐ ⓑ ⓒ ⓓ
77. ⓐ ⓑ ⓒ ⓓ
78. ⓐ ⓑ ⓒ ⓓ
79. ⓐ ⓑ ⓒ ⓓ
80. ⓐ ⓑ ⓒ ⓓ
81. ⓐ ⓑ ⓒ ⓓ
82. ⓐ ⓑ
83. ⓐ ⓑ ⓒ ⓓ
84. ⓐ ⓑ ⓒ ⓓ
85. ⓐ ⓑ ⓒ ⓓ
86. ⓐ ⓑ
87. ⓐ ⓑ ⓒ ⓓ
88. ⓐ ⓑ ⓒ ⓓ
89. ⓐ ⓑ ⓒ ⓓ
90. ⓐ ⓑ ⓒ ⓓ
91. ⓐ ⓑ ⓒ ⓓ
92. ⓐ ⓑ ⓒ ⓓ
93. ⓐ ⓑ ⓒ ⓓ
94. ⓐ ⓑ ⓒ ⓓ
95. ⓐ ⓑ ⓒ ⓓ
96. ⓐ ⓑ ⓒ ⓓ
97. ⓐ ⓑ ⓒ ⓓ
98. ⓐ ⓑ ⓒ ⓓ
99. ⓐ ⓑ ⓒ ⓓ
100. ⓐ ⓑ ⓒ ⓓ

Memory and Observation

You will have ten minutes to read and study the following passage. Then, answer questions 1 through 11 without referring back to the passage.

The Stolen Honda

At 10:45 A.M. on Saturday, March 27, Karyn Albino contacted the 46th Precinct and stated that her car had been stolen. Two officers, Patrol Officer Thomas and Patrol Officer Randall, arrived at her home (2048 Davidson Avenue, Apartment 4B, in the University Heights section of the Bronx), at 12:30 P.M. Upon arriving at the scene, both officers noticed a significant amount of broken glass on the street and the sidewalk in front of Ms. Albino's home.

Ms. Albino waited by the window; when she saw the two officers standing in front of her apartment, she grabbed her red sweater and went outside to greet them. Officer Randall immediately started collecting information about her, such as her name, how long she had resided at her current residence, and the make and model of her car. Officer Thomas asked when she noticed that her car was missing and if she noticed anyone unusual in the neighborhood.

In response to Officer Randall's questions, she told him her full name and stated that she had lived at 2048 Davidson Avenue for five years. However, she had lived in Apartment 4B for only the past year; previously, she had lived one floor down in Apartment 3C. She upgraded her apartment from a one bedroom to a two bedroom to accommodate her five-year-old daughter, Annie. Her car was a two-door, silver 2002 Honda Civic. There was a large scratch on the rear bumper from a previous accident that occurred up the street in the Fordham shopping district. The back passenger window was cracked, although she was uncertain when or how this crack occurred. She told Officer Thomas that she had looked out her window that morning and seen that her car was missing; she called the police station within seconds. Officer Thomas asked her if she could have mistakenly parked on another street (a common occurrence in the city), such as Grand Street, but she adamantly stated that she was certain she had parked in front of her house.

She told the officers that it was pouring outside when she came home from work at 6:00 P.M. the previous evening. She distinctly remembers her neighbor, Ms. Keri, telling her, as soon as she walked into the building, how lucky she was to find a spot directly in front of their apartment. It was unusual to find parking on her street, which is why she was certain of her car's location.

When she came home, she noticed two young men standing on the opposite side of the street. It was difficult for her to see, but she noticed that one of them was wearing a blue baseball hat and a black hooded jacket. She could not clearly see the other individual.

Officer Thomas completed the police report. Officer Randall told her to go down to the precinct in two days to pick up a copy of the report. The case would be handed over to their detective squad and she would receive a call from Detective Joseph or Detective Anthony within 48 hours.

1. What is Ms. Albino's address?
   a. 2048 Davidson Avenue
   b. 2048 Grand Street
   c. 2084 Davidson Avenue
   d. 2084 Grand Street

2. Ms. Albino moved from Apartment _____ to Apartment _____ in order to accommodate her daughter.
   a. 4B; 3C
   b. 4C; 3B
   c. 3C; 4B
   d. 3B; 4C

3. What time did Ms. Albino call the police?
   a. 10:45 A.M
   b. 12:30 P.M.
   c. 6:00 P.M.
   d. She never called the police.

4. What day was she told to go to the precinct to pick up a copy of the police report?
   a. Friday
   b. Saturday
   c. Sunday
   d. Monday

5. Which of the following questions was not asked by Officer Randall?
   a. her name
   b. the length of time she lived at her current residence
   c. the make and model of her car
   d. when she noticed her car was missing

6. What color sweater did Ms. Albino grab prior to going outside to meet the officers?
   a. black
   b. blue
   c. red
   d. silver

7. Why was Ms. Albino certain of where she parked her car?
   a. She never parks on Grand Street.
   b. It is unusual to find parking on Davidson Avenue.
   c. It is unusual to find parking on Grand Street.
   d. It was raining and she uncertain where she parked her car.

8. When Ms. Albino came home from work, she noticed two young men standing on the opposite side of the street. One of the young men was wearing a _____ jacket.
   a. blue
   b. black
   c. red
   d. silver

9. Which detective should Ms. Albino expect to receive a phone call from regarding her stolen vehicle?
   a. Thomas
   b. Joseph
   c. Randall
   d. Keri

10. What was the make and model of the car that was stolen?
    a. two-door, silver 2002 Honda Civic
    b. two-door, black 2002 Honda Civic
    c. two-door, silver 2003 Honda Civic
    d. three-door, black 2003 Honda Civic

11. Ms. Albino's car had a scratch from a previous accident. Where was this scratch located?
    a. front bumper
    b. rear bumper
    c. passenger window
    d. driver window

You will have ten minutes to read and study the following passage. Then, answer questions 12 through 15 without referring back to the passage.

Memorandum

Date:	**December 12, 2010**
From:	**Chief Judge Caesar Chamby**
To:	**All Court Officers**
Subject:	**Service Weapons**

Effective February 1, 2011, all court officers will exchange issued service weapons. The current carry firearm will be replaced with a Glock Model 22 .40 semiautomatic pistol. All court officers will qualify with this weapon prior to February 1, or they will not be allowed to carry a firearm and will be relieved of their present duty assignments. Upon entry into service, the weapon will be carried on the strong side in a Level II retention basket weave leather holster on the basket weave standard duty belt. The duty belt will also be fitted with a magazine pouch carrying two fully loaded high-capacity magazines, dual handcuff case, baton carrier, mini-flashlight case, latex glove pouch, and radio carrier, all in basket weave pattern. All currently issued leather will be returned along with the obsolete service firearm to the executive officer upon qualification with the new weapon. Upon read of this memorandum, contact Lieutenant Alden, executive officer, to confirm your qualifying schedule with the rangemaster.

12. The current carry firearm is
   a. a Glock Model 22 .40 semiautomatic pistol.
   b. a Glock Model 17 9-mm semiautomatic pistol.
   c. a Smith & Wesson Model 19 .357 magnum revolver.
   d. not identified by make and model.

13. Based on the date of the memorandum, what is the number of days the court officers have to qualify with the new service weapon?
   a. 30
   b. 35
   c. 40
   d. 45

14. What is the number of items to be carried on the newly issued duty belt?
   a. seven
   b. six
   c. five
   d. eight

15. The executive officer is
   a. Lieutenant Allen.
   b. Lieutenant Alden.
   c. Lieutenant Altadonna.
   d. Lieutenant Alisi.

Reading Text, Tables, Charts, and Graphs

You will have ten minutes to read and study the following passage. Then, answer questions 16 through 25 without referring back to the passage.

Memorandum

To: **All Officers**
From: **Anthony Ellie, Captain**
Re: **Clothing Standards**
Date: **May 1 2009**

Starting May 1, 2010, all officers will receive uniform clothing at no cost. Specific clothing is required to perform certain job functions. Department-issued uniforms will ensure that officers dress professionally, appropriately, and safely. The following will be provided to officers on a yearly basis:

2 Short Sleeve Shirts
2 Long Sleeve Shirts
2 Pairs of Wool Pants
2 Pairs of Cotton Pants
1 Pair of Boots
1 Hat
2 Winter Sweaters

The following items will be issued every 5 years:

1 Winter Coat
1 Windbreaker
1 Raincoat
3 Sweatshirts
3 Sweatpants

Every 10 years, officers will receive:

1 Kevlar vest

Only clothing authorized by the Department will be worn while officers are on duty. Officers will not wear clothing that display logos or promotes products. All undergarments must be black. All undergarments must remain hidden. It is the officer's responsibility to purchase such garments.

Please be advised that the Department has the legal authority to change, modify, or discontinue such issued clothing at any time. If Department-issued clothing is modified, all officers will be required to have all of their current clothes tailored at Dry Clean Express, which is located at 224 East Main Street, 1st Floor. All alterations will be paid for by the Department. Tailoring is available every Monday, Tuesday and Wednesday from 8:00 A.M. to 4:00 P.M. It is also available every Thursday afternoon from 1:00 P.M. to 10:00 P.M. No tailoring is done on Fridays, Saturdays, or Sundays. All tailored clothing must be picked up on Saturdays before noon; they are closed on Sunday. If the Department issues a memorandum for clothing modification, all officers have 30 days to comply. Failure to comply will result in a seven day suspension without pay and a *notice of discipline* in the officer's file. Please be advised that such notices remain on file for three years and can effect evaluations, merit raises, and promotions.

All shirts should be in compliance with Department standards. All State Patches will be worn on the left sleeve. All American Flags will be worn on the right sleeve, stars facing forward. Any specialty patches must be approved by the Department Supervisor. Patches should be centered on the sleeve, professionally sewn, and be one inch below the shoulder seam. Please see Directive 200-42A for further information on clothing guidelines.

16. When will officers begin to receive Department-issued uniforms for free?
   a. 5/1/10
   b. 5/1/11
   c. 1/5/10
   d. 1/5/11

17. Which of the following will not be provided to all officers on an annual basis?
   a. 2 long sleeve shirts
   b. 2 pairs of wool pants
   c. 2 pairs of cotton pants
   d. 3 sweatshirts

18. Which of the following will not be issued to all officers every five years?
   a. 1 winter coat
   b. 1 Kevlar vest
   c. 1 raincoat
   d. 1 windbreaker

19. Department-issued uniforms will ensure that officers dress
   a. professionally.
   b. appropriately.
   c. safely.
   d. all of the above.

20. If Department-issued clothing is modified, all officers will be required to have all of their current clothes tailored at_____.
   a. Dry Clean Express
   b. Cleaning Express
   c. Drying Express
   d. Expressly Clean

21. The dry cleaning establishment where the officers must bring their uniforms for alterations is located at
   a. 242 East Main Street.
   b. 224 East Main Street.
   c. 227 East Main Street.
   d. 210 East Main Street.

22. On which of the following days can officers have their uniforms tailored?
   a. Thursday
   b. Friday
   c. Saturday
   d. Sunday

23. Once the Department issues a memorandum for clothing modification, how many days do officers have to comply with the order before receiving a suspension?
   a. seven
   b. fourteen
   c. twenty-one
   d. thirty

24. All state patches will be worn on the _____ sleeve. All American flags will be worn on the _____ sleeve.
   a. right; left
   b. left; right
   c. right; right
   d. left; left

25. Patches should be sewn _____ the shoulder seam.
   a. one and one-half inches below
   b. one and one-half inches above
   c. one inch below
   d. one inch above

Read the following passage, then answer questions 26 through 30 based solely on information from the passage.

EMPLOYMENT APPLICATION OF RACHEL BURNS
FINANCIAL INFORMATION

Are you currently named as a party in any lawsuits? NO

Have you ever been named as a party in a lawsuit? YES

If Yes, explain:

In 2002, I was named as a defendant in the matter of *Bank Holding, Ltd. v. Burns*, 13th District Court Case # 02-1551-GC. I was sued for a loan default in the amount of $6,000. The case was settled prior to trial for $4,500 and was dismissed with prejudice. In 2003, my husband and I initiated a lawsuit against Westbrook Builders, LLC, in the 13th District Court, *Burns and Burns v. Westbrook Builders, LLC,* case # 03-280-GC. We sued the defendant for defective home repairs for $23,000. The defendant filed Chapter 7 bankruptcy and was discharged. The action was administratively dismissed.

List all outstanding debts, including student loans, which you are obligated to repay.

CREDITOR	DATE OPENED	LOAN AMT./BAL.	PAYMENT
Mortgage Americana	4/2009	$225,000/$220,000	$1,800
1st Auto Finance	5/2001	$23,000/$2,350	$383.41
Credit Card #1	10 yrs.	$15,000/$13,400	$335
Credit Card #2	5/2003	$10,000/$8,500	$225
Home Improve Loans	7/2003	$11,000/$1,200	$200
Casey Dept. Stores	10 yrs.	$4,000/$1,560	$175

Are you delinquent with any of your credit obligations? NO

Have you been delinquent with any of your credit obligations in the past 12 months? YES

If Yes, explain:

In July 2005, we were 60 days late on a car loan to Lark Financial, Inc. The loan was paid current in August 2005 and paid in full October 2005. In February 2006, Credit Card #2 was paid 30 days late and is now current.

Situation: Sergeant Barrett has reviewed the Financial Information Section of Candidate #2, RACHEL BURNS's employment application. The application is 125 days old. Burns advises that the financial obligations are joint with her husband, John Burns, who is a special agent with the State Department of Treasury Criminal Enforcement Bureau. Burns attributes the financial distress to two significant events. In 1999, she began an e-commerce business selling a line of women's wear that was manufactured in Brazil. The business failed to thrive over the Internet, and in an effort to maximize sales, Burns opened a retail store in 2001. The venture was financed with a loan through Bank Holding, Ltd., which Burns personally guaranteed. The venture failed in late 2001 and the store closed. She defaulted on the loan and was sued in 2002. The case was settled prior to trial and dismissed.

The second incident involved a home improvement company, Westbrook Builders, LLC, which the Burnses hired to remodel two bathrooms and the basement of their home. The work was performed in a slipshod fashion and required a complete rebuild by another builder. The Burnses paid Westbrook a total of $5,000 on an $8,675 invoice. They refused to pay the balance and sued for $23,000 to recover the amount paid, the amount of the subsequent repairs, and their attorney's fees. They obtained an $11,000 loan through Home Improve Loans to finance the repairs and litigation expenses. Westbrook filed Chapter 7 bankruptcy after being sued by Burns and eight other plaintiffs. After Westbrook was discharged, the case was administratively dismissed by the court.

Sergeant Barrett questioned Burns about the two payment delinquencies in 2005 and 2006. Burns stated that the vehicle financed through Lark Financial, Inc., is five years old and needed a transmission. The cost was $755. Burns was unable to obtain additional credit and used the car payments to repair the vehicle. The loan was in the end stage and was retired in October 2005. Burns stated that the credit card payment was late because of an oversight. She stated that she is current with all financial obligations.

Burns has two children, ages 10 and 7. She wants to return to work after ten years for financial reasons and personal growth. She informs Sergeant Barrett that she attempted to return to the Eighth Superior Court, where she was previously employed as a probation officer, but there are no current or anticipated openings. The court administrator suggested she apply as a court officer trainee.

Sergeant Barrett reviews the court cases at the 13th District Court and verifies the information. She obtains a credit report and confirms that Burns is now paying all debts in a timely manner. She marks the financial section of the interview report as acceptable, writing a side note that the financial distress is an isolated incident and the financial situation will improve with the addition of a second income.

26. John Burns is employed as a special agent with the
   a. Federal Bureau of Investigation.
   b. Internal Revenue Service.
   c. Office of the Attorney General.
   d. State Department of Treasury Criminal Enforcement Bureau.

27. Rachel Burns was previously employed as a
   a. probation officer.
   b. police officer.
   c. court clerk.
   d. special agent.

28. The Burnses sued Westbrook Builders for $23,000. What amount was recovered?
   a. $11,000
   b. $15,000
   c. $23,000
   d. $0

29. The lawsuits involving Rachel Burns were filed in the
   a. Eighth Superior Court.
   b. Tenth District Court.
   c. 12th Municipal Court.
   d. 13th District Court.

30. Burns applied as a court officer trainee on the
suggestion of the
a. court administrator of the Eighth Superior
Court.
b. court clerk of the 13th District Court.
c. chief judge of the 13th District Court.
d. husband, John Burns.

Read the following document, then answer questions 31 through 44 based solely on information from the document.

SCJC No. 83
In the Matter of
Honorable Elizabeth A. Shanley, Justice of the Esopus Town Court, Ulster County,
Petitioner,
For Review of a Determination of State Commission on Judicial Conduct,
Respondent.

Joseph R. Pisani, for plaintiff.
Gerald Stern, for respondent.

PER CURIAM:
Petitioner, a Justice of the Esopus Town Court, Ulster County, seeks review of a determination of the State Commission on Judicial Conduct sustaining one charge of misconduct and imposing the sanction of admonition (see NY Const, art VI, §22; Judiciary Law §44). The charge contains two separate allegations, both involving petitioner's campaign activity while running for her present position. The first asserts that petitioner circulated campaign literature stating that she was a "graduate" of "Judicial Law Course[s]" at Albany Law School, St. Lawrence University, and Columbia/Greene Community College. In actuality, petitioner has a high school diploma. The courses referenced in her campaign literature were related to the court clerks' continuing education program sponsored by the Office of Court Administration. She had taken the courses at the college campuses in conjunction with her job as a court clerk.

The second allegation charges her with using campaign literature in which she identified herself as a "Law and Order Candidate." In the Commission's view, that phrase committed, or appeared to commit, petitioner to a pro-prosecution bias in criminal cases.

The referee who heard the complaint determined that petitioner misled voters by misrepresenting herself as a "graduate" of judicial law courses at Albany Law School, St. Lawrence University, and Columbia/Greene Community College. The referee determined, however, that the allegation as to her "law and order" campaign literature could not form the basis for any disciplinary action. In the referee's opinion, the phrase *law and order candidate* is "subject to several interpretations," and as such did not constitute an improper pledge or promise.

The Commission affirmed, and petitioner does not challenge, the referee's findings as to petitioner's misrepresentation of her academic credentials. The Commission, however, rejected the referee's finding on the "law and order" charge. In the Commission's view, the phrase created the appearance that petitioner would favor the prosecution, and amounted to an impermissible pledge as to how she would decide cases. The Commission contends that petitioner's campaign posture was inconsistent with the neutral administration of justice and is prohibited by the impartiality requirements of the Rules Governing Judicial Conduct (see 22 NYCRR 100.5 [A] [4] [d] [i]; [ii]). We disagree with petitioner's contention that the Commission lacks jurisdiction to evaluate the campaign practices of non-judge candidates for judicial office. We have already permitted the Commission to discipline a judge for conduct occurring prior to taking office (see *Matter of Nicholson v. State Commission on Judicial Conduct,* 50 NY2d 597, 605 [1980]. We disagree, and conclude that simply using the phrase *law and order* in judicial campaign literature does not amount to misconduct.

In pertinent part, the Rules Governing Judicial Conduct require that candidates for elective judicial office shall not

"(i) make pledges or promises of conduct in office other than the faithful and impartial performance of the duties of the office;
"(ii) make statements that commit or appear to commit the candidate with respect to cases, controversies, or issues that are likely to come before the court; or
"(iii) knowingly make any false statement or misrepresent the identity, qualifications, current position, or other fact concerning the candidate or an opponent"
(22 NYCRR 100.5 [A] [4] [d] [i]; [ii]).

The Commission argues that by holding herself out as a "law and order candidate," petitioner violated subsections (i) and (ii).

According to the Commission, the phrase promises stern treatment of criminal defendants when interpreted in light of its "widely held perception." The Commission cites the popular origin of the phrase in a political context, referring to President Richard Nixon's promise that, if elected, he would appoint "law and order" judges to reverse what he and others regarded as unwarranted judicial leniency toward criminal offenders.

The Commission argues that petitioner's invocation of "law and order" was meant to, and did in fact, convey the image of petitioner as a criminal law conservative. We need not determine whether this was petitioner's intent, or whether a reasonable person viewing the advertisements would have seen it that way. Even under its own interpretation, the Commission has not shown that the phrase carries a representation that compromises judicial impartiality. *Law and order* is a phrase widely and indiscriminately used in everyday parlance and election campaigns. We decline to treat it as a "commit[ment]" or a "pledge[] or promise[] of conduct in office."

Petitioner has conceded that it was improper for her to refer to herself as a "graduate" of the judicial law courses that she took in her capacity as court clerk. While petitioner urges us to dismiss her public admonition, we consider her misrepresentation serious enough to justify it. Reasonable voters viewing petitioner's advertisements would be led to believe that the courses trained enrollees in judging, and voters would not have suspected that the last formal educational institution to have graduated petitioner was her high school. The Commission's determined sanction is appropriate in light of the unchallenged finding that petitioner misrepresented her educational background (see 22 NYCRR 100.5 [A] [4] [d] [iii]).

Accordingly, the determined sanction should be accepted, without costs.

Determined sanction accepted, without costs. Opinion *per curiam.*

Chief Judge Kaye and Judges Smith, Levine, Ciparick, Wesley, Rosenblatt, and Graffeo concur.

Decided July 1, 2002

We disagree with petitioner's contention that the Commission lacks jurisdiction to evaluate the campaign practices of non-judge candidates for judicial office. We have already permitted the Commission to discipline a judge for conduct occurring prior to taking office (see *Matter of Nicholson v. State Commission on Judicial Conduct,* 50 NY2d 597, 605 [1980]).

31. The New York State Commission on Judicial Conduct filed how many charges against Shanley in the initial complaint?
   a. two
   b. three
   c. four
   d. five

32. Elizabeth Shanley holds judicial office as a(n)
   a. Supreme Court justice of the State of New York.
   b. administrative law court judge of the State of New York.
   c. civil judge for the City of New York.
   d. Justice of Esopus Town Court, Ulster County, New York.

33. Shanley is a graduate of Albany Law School. This statement is
   a. true.
   b. false.

34. Prior to being elected town justice, Stanley was employed as a
   a. paralegal.
   b. court clerk.
   c. court officer.
   d. legal secretary.

35. The court clerk's continuing education program is sponsored by the
   a. New York Supreme Court.
   b. State of New York Department of Education.
   c. Office of Court Administration.
   d. State University of New York.

36. The first stage of the SCJC proceedings were heard before a(n)
   a. administrative law judge.
   b. civil judge.
   c. mediator.
   d. referee.

37. Who is listed as the respondent for this case?
   a. Elizabeth A. Shanley
   b. State Commission on Judicial Conduct
   c. Joseph R. Pisani
   d. Gerald Stern

38. The referee determined that the phrase *law and order candidate* suggested Shanley was pro-prosecution and would appear biased in criminal matters.
   a. true
   b. false

39. The Court of Appeals' review of the SCJC ruling on the use of the phrase *law and order candidate* found that it
   a. is an everyday phrase widely used in election campaigns.
   b. is used recklessly by judicial candidates and should be used sparingly.
   c. is rooted in the 1970s and was originally used by (then) President Richard Nixon.
   d. should be reserved for judicial candidates with a proven track record of criminal prosecutions.

40. The Court of Appeals affirmed the SCJC-imposed sanction of
   a. suspension without pay for 60 days.
   b. removal from office.
   c. admonition.
   d. a $250 fine.

41. An alternative for admonition in this matter is
   a. endorsement.
   b. censure.
   c. impeachment.
   d. disparage.

42. The chief judge of the Court of Appeals is
   a. Judge Wiseman.
   b. Judge Bill.
   c. Judge King.
   d. Judge Kaye.

43. The decision from the Court of Appeals was
   a. appealed by Shanley to the New York Supreme Court.
   b. appealed by Shanley to the U.S. District Court Eastern District of New York.
   c. accepted by Shanley.
   d. No final decision is mentioned.

44. What was the amount of costs assessed to Shanley by the Court of Appeals?
   a. $0
   b. $100
   c. $250
   d. $500

Read the following document, then answer questions 45 through 50 based solely on information from the document.

Sergeant Hakim is assigned to the Court Professional Standards Bureau. Sergeant Hakim has served as a court officer since 1995 and is currently in his 14th year of employment. His previous assignments include beginning his career as a court security officer, then working as a field officer and supervisor after being promoted to sergeant in 2004. He undertook his current assignment three years ago. His duties include investigating complaints of court employee misconduct, conducting preemployment background investigations, investigating accident and injury claims involving court personnel, investigating damage and theft incidents involving court property, and conducting confidential investigations on behalf of the

Office of Court Administration.

In the three years he has conducted preemployment background investigations, Sergeant Hakim has discovered many truths and untruths about the people he is investigating. What has surprised Sergeant Hakim most is the lengths people will go to in attempting to hide their pasts, or creating a past when none exists. People lie, but their fingerprints never do. An applicant for a court accounting manager position listed an impressive record as a financial manager for a well-known international nonprofit foundation from 2000 to 2006. He claimed to have managed a pension fund in the $100 millions. The fingerprint check revealed that the applicant had never applied for a securities license. He had never even had a passport, let alone traveled abroad. His only experience in securities trading occurred as a contestant in a ten-week stock market game sponsored by a local newspaper. He failed to finish in the top 25. This is just one of the many discoveries Hakim has uncovered during his career.

45. Sergeant Hakim was promoted to his current rank after how many years of employment?
- **a.** seven
- **b.** eight
- **c.** nine
- **d.** ten

46. Sergeant Hakim's job description does NOT include which of the following duties?
- **a.** investigating complaints of employee misconduct
- **b.** investigating complaints of judges' misconduct
- **c.** investigating damage to court property
- **d.** investigating court employee injury claims

47. Sergeant Hakim is assigned to the
- **a.** Court Professional Standards Bureau.
- **b.** Bureau of Court Administration.
- **c.** Internal Affairs Bureau.
- **d.** Professional Conduct Section.

48. Confidential investigations are conducted on behalf of the
- **a.** Supreme Court.
- **b.** Office of Court Administration.
- **c.** Office of the Chief Justice.
- **d.** Professional Standards Bureau.

49. In conducting a background investigation, the most irrefutable confirmation source is
- **a.** former employers.
- **b.** fingerprints.
- **c.** public records.
- **d.** acquired knowledge.

50. The accounting manager applicant claimed he was previously employed as a
- **a.** pension fund manager for a nonprofit organization.
- **b.** controller for an oil company.
- **c.** securities manager for an international brokerage firm.
- **d.** vice president of fiscal management for a university.

Legal Definitions

The following questions deal with legal terms court officers might come across during their official duties. Answer questions 51 through 65 based on the definitions.

De novo: Latin for "anew." A form of appeal in which the appeals court holds a trial as if no prior trial had been held. A trial *de novo* is common on appeals from small claims court judgments.

De facto: Latin for "in fact." It is often used in place of the word *actual* to show that the court will treat as a fact authority being exercised or an entity acting as if it had authority, even though the legal requirements have not been met.

De jure: Latin for "lawful," as distinguished from *de facto* (*actual*).

Legal citation: The style of crediting and referencing other documents or sources of authority in legal writing.

Ex post facto **law:** Latin for "from something done afterward." It is a law that retroactively changes the legal consequences of acts committed or the legal status of facts and relationships that existed prior to the enactment of the law.

Blended fee: An average fee that is charged for a project based upon the attorneys who worked on the project and their experience.

Contingency fee: A method that allows many individuals who have been injured or seeking damages, such as those resulting from an auto accident or a medical malpractice case, to obtain legal representation even if they do not have money to pay a lawyer at the outset of a case.

Plea bargain: An agreement in a criminal case in which a prosecutor and a defendant arrange to settle the case against the defendant.

Demurrer: A pleading by the defendant that contests the legal sufficiency of the complaint.

Actus reus: Latin for the "guilty act," which, when proved beyond a reasonable doubt in combination with the *mens rea,* i.e., the "guilty mind," produces criminal liability in common law-based criminal law jurisdictions.

Intentional tort: An intentional breach of duty that results in damages to an individual.

Punitive damages: Damages not awarded in order to compensate the plaintiff, but in order to reform or deter the defendant and similar persons from pursuing a course of action such as that which damaged the plaintiff.

Negligence: Failure to exercise the care toward others that a reasonable or prudent person would do in the circumstances, or taking action that such a reasonable person would not.

Pro se **litigant:** A person who chooses to, or who must, represent himself or herself in legal proceedings without a lawyer.

Petitioner: A person who initiates a lawsuit.

Extradition: The official process by which one nation or state requests and obtains from another nation or state the surrender of a suspected or convicted criminal.

Implied consent: Consent when surrounding circumstances exist that would lead a reasonable person to believe that this consent had been given, although no direct, express, or explicit words of agreement had been uttered.

Defamation: Communicating statements that may harm an individual's reputation or character.

Intimidation: An attempt to frighten by speaking or acting in a dominating manner, often with the goal of making a person or people do what the intimidator wants.

Truth-in-Lending Act: A federal statute that requires a commercial lender (bank, savings and loan, mortgage broker) to give a borrower exact information on interest rates and a three-day period in which the borrower may compare and consider competitive terms and cancel the loan agreement.

Fair Credit Reporting Act: An American federal law that regulates the collection, dissemination, and use of consumer credit information.

Injunction: An equitable remedy in the form of a court order that either prohibits a party from continuing, or compels a party to continue, a particular activity.

Temporary restraining order (TRO): Prohibits a person from an action that is likely to cause irreparable harm. This differs from an injunction in that it may be granted immediately, without notice to the opposing party, and without a hearing. It is intended to last only until a hearing can be held.

Personal protection order (PPO): An order that can protect you from being hit, threatened, harassed, or stalked by another person. The PPO may stop someone from coming into your home or bothering you at work. It can stop them from buying a firearm or finding your address through school records. It can also stop them from taking your minor children unless required by the court.

Preponderance of the evidence: The greater weight of the evidence required in a civil (noncriminal) lawsuit for the trier of fact (jury or judge without a jury) to decide in favor of one side or the other.

***Prima-facie* evidence:** Latin for "at first view." It is evidence that is sufficient to raise a presumption of fact or to establish the fact in question unless rebutted.

Caveat emptor: Latin for "let the buyer beware."

Corpus delicti: The body of the offense; the essence of the crime.

Mala prohibita: Those things that are prohibited by law and, therefore, unlawful.

Stare decisis: Latin for "to stand by that which is decided." It is the principle that the precedent decisions are to be followed by the courts.

51. A *per curiam* opinion of the court refers to the opinion of the entire court. Which of the following is an example of a *per curiam* opinion?
  a. a municipal court judge who decides only civil matters
  b. a court of appeals panel of three judges in which two judges concur and one concurs in result only
  c. a court of appeals panel that presents the opinion to the full court for consideration
  d. an opinion of a state supreme court that has concurring and dissenting results

52. Latin for "to start fresh," which of the following is regularly used by appellate courts in reviewing lower court decisions?
  a. *de novo*
  b. *de facto*
  c. *de minimis*
  d. *de jure*

53. Which of the following is a reference to a source of legal authority and a direction to appear in court?
  a. case law
  b. citation
  c. *ex post facto*
  d. holding

54. Intangible assets are nonphysical items as bank accounts, stock certificates, bonds, and pension benefits that have value. An example of a tangible asset is a(n)
  a. real estate deed.
  b. life insurance policy.
  c. automobile.
  d. real estate limited partnership.

55. Which of the following an attorney fee based on recovery of damages that is commonly used in personal injury actions?
  a. a flat fee
  b. a blended fee
  c. a statutory fee
  d. a contingency fee

56. They are legal transactions based on the notion of "judicial economy" and are mainly used in criminal cases. The most common is
  a. sentence reduction.
  b. plea bargaining.
  c. demurrer.
  d. *actus reus.*

57. An intended breach of duty that results in harm or damages to a person is
  a. negligence.
  b. punitive damages.
  c. intentional tort.
  d. consequential damages.

58. A party who opts for self-representation is known as a
  a. *pro se* litigant.
  b. nominal party.
  c. respondent.
  d. petitioner.

59. The process by which one jurisdiction surrenders to another jurisdiction a person accused or convicted of a crime in the other state is known as
  a. concurrent jurisdiction.
  b. implied consent.
  c. extradition.
  d. transitory.

60. An oral communication made to a third party that is intended to harm a person's reputation or to keep others from associating with that person is known as
a. defamation.
b. disparage.
c. intimidation.
d. oppression.

61. Passed by Congress in 1969, which of the following ensures that consumers are provided with sufficient factual information to enable them to make an informed decision about financing?
a. the Fair Credit Reporting Act (FCRA)
b. the Federal Consumption Protection Act (FCPA)
c. the Truth-in-Lending Act (TILA)
d. the Uniform Commercial Code (UCC)

62. Based on the TILA definition, which of the following is NOT subject to TILA regulations?
a. a credit union that makes loans exclusively to its depositors
b. a used car dealership that offers in-house credit ("Buy Here, Pay Here")
c. a furniture store that offers interest-free in-house credit for 90 days
d. a doctor who advertises and makes private real estate loans to individuals

63. An immediate court order that prohibits an action that is likely to cause irreparable harm is known as a(n)
a. injunction.
b. temporary restraining order (TRO).
c. personal protection order (PPO).
d. peace bond.

64. Greater weight of evidence, or evidence that is more credible and convincing to the mind, but not necessarily the greater number of witnesses, is
a. binding instruction.
b. *prima-facie* evidence.
c. holding.
d. preponderance of evidence.

65. Based on a nineteenth-century rule of law, which of the following translates as "let the buyer beware"?
a. *corpus delicti*
b. *caveat emptor*
c. *mala prohibita*
d. *stare decisis*

Court Officer Procedures

Use the following court officer procedure to answer questions 66 through 74.

Fees of Court Officer
COA# 174473
Released: March 14, 2009
Panel: Gribbs, Markey, Kavanagh

Courts—Officers—Fees—Entitlement
A sheriff or court officer has no common law right to charge fees for performing his or her public duties. Any right to compensation beyond the officer's normal salary is statutory, and statutory fees are generally minimal. However, an officer may be entitled to additional compensation for the performance of services outside his or her statutory duties.

Judgments—Execution—Fees—Statutory/
Additional—Recovery—Procedure
A controversy regarding an officer's charge of
fees for performing separate investigatory services in the pursuit of a judgment debtor may
be resolved through a suit for breach of contract separate from the proceeding for determining the proper statutory collection fees that
may be assessed. In this case, the trial court
improperly adjudicated the parties' disputes
regarding both statutory fees and additional
fees in the same proceeding. Remand for determination of the statutory fees and dismissal of
the ancillary claims is appropriate.

Judgments—Execution—Fees—Process Service
Fees may be imposed for process served by
any authorized person, in the amount provided by statute and dependent upon the type
of service made. Statutory fees may be added
to a judgment.
MCL 600.2559(1), MCL 600.2559(2), MCL
600.2559(3), MCL 600.2559(4), MCR
2.625(A)(1)

Judgments—Execution—Levy—Fees
For a levy under a writ of execution, a court officer may recover $20 plus mileage, and the actual
and reasonable expenses of taking, keeping, and
sale, plus, if the judgment is satisfied before sale,
7% of the first $1,000 in receipts and 3% of
receipts exceeding the first $1,000. For a sale on
levy in a case of execution, the officer may
recover 7% of the first $1,000 in receipts and 3%
of receipts exceeding the first $1,000. In this case,
the plaintiff obtained a judgment for $170,564
against the defendant, which the defendant
failed to pay. The plaintiff initiated collection
efforts, including execution of levy by the appel-
lee court officer. The officer located a boat
owned by the defendant and attached a writ of

execution to it, gave a copy to the manager of
the marina at which the boat was stored, seized
the ship's log, and prepared a notice of sale.
However, plaintiff's counsel later learned that
the defendant had transferred ownership in a
boat to his daughter on the day before the judgment was entered. The plaintiff then asked the
officer to cancel the sale. Under the circumstances, the officer had constructive control of
the boat sufficient for a levy, and was entitled to
the fees assessable for execution of a levy.
MCL 600.2559(1)(j), MCL 600.2559(k)

Judgments—Execution—Levy—Validity—
Return—Failure to File
A return of execution is part of the execution
procedure, but a levy occurs when the property
is seized. The failure to return a writ does not
invalidate a levy upon which a sale was not
made. In this case, the officer's failure to file a
return did not invalidate the levy; the officer is
entitled to the statutory fees applicable to levies.
MCL 600.2559(1)(j), MCL 600.2559(k)

Judgments—Execution—Return—Timeliness
Executions must be made returnable not less
than 20 nor more than 90 days from the date of
receipt by the officer. However, when an officer
has begun to serve an execution issued out of
any court, on or before the return day of the
execution, he or she may complete service and
return after the return date. Thus, a return may
be filed after the 90-day period if the execution
is pending within the return period. In this
case, a sale was never made and thus a return
certifying that a sale satisfied or failed to satisfy
the judgment was not possible. The failure to
file the return within the return period did not
invalidate the levy.
MCL 600.6002(2), MCL 600.6002(3)

Commercial Transactions—Debtor/ Creditor—Fraudulent Conveyance—Remedy
Under the Uniform Fraudulent Conveyance Act, when a conveyance or obligation is fraudulent as to a creditor, the creditor may, as against any person except a purchaser for fair consideration without knowledge of the fraud at the time of the purchase, or one who has derived title immediately or mediately from such a purchaser, have the conveyance set aside or obligation annulled to the extent necessary to satisfy his or her claim, or disregard the conveyance and attach or levy execution upon the property conveyed.
MCL 566.19(1)(a), MCL 566.19(1)(b)

Judgments—Execution—Security
Under the Revised Judicature Act, whenever there is reasonable doubt as to the ownership by a judgment debtor of any personal property, or as to its liability to be taken upon an execution, the officer holding such an execution may require of the judgment creditor sufficient security to indemnify him or her for taking the personal property.
MCL 600.6009

Judgments—Debtor Examination—Privilege
Under the Revised Judicature Act, a party or witness examined under the provisions relating to examination of persons holding property of the debtor may not be excused from answering a question on the grounds that his or her answer will tend to show him or her guilty of the commission of a fraud, or prove that he or she has been a party or privy to, or knowing of, a conveyance, assignment, transfer, or other disposition of property for any purpose.
MCL 600.6110(3)

Judgments—Execution—Levy—Validity—Fraudulent Conveyance—Effect
A judgment creditor who reasonably treats goods as fraudulently conveyed by the judgment debtor is stopped from claiming that the officer who levied against the property acted improperly. In this case, after his or her attempts to collect on his or her judgment, the plaintiff filed a suit to set aside several transfers made by the defendant as fraudulent conveyances. In his or her dispute with the court officer regarding the collection fees due to the officer, the plaintiff cannot claim that the officer acted improperly in levying upon the fraudulently conveyed property.

Judgments—Execution—Levy—Fees—Calculation—Value of Property/Recovery
An officer who levies against property in execution of a judgment is entitled to a percentage of the total recovery, regardless of the value of the property levied. In this case, after the court officer made collection efforts and the plaintiff filed his or her fraudulent conveyance suit, the parties agreed to compromise the claim upon the defendant's payment of $100,000. The officer is entitled to a percentage of the total settlement amount.

Judgments—Execution—Fees—Statutory
Reasonable expenses may be awarded to a court officer executing a judgment for the taking, keeping, and sale of levied property. Such expenses may be awarded only regarding property that is taken, kept, or sold, and does not include costs incurred in investigating property, including property never located or seized. In this case, the officer may not recover for expenses incurred in the investigation of stocks and other property never found.
MCL 600.2559(1)(j)

Judgments—Execution—Writ—Service—Authority
Only court officers and sheriffs may serve writs of execution.
MCL 600.6001, MCR 3.103(D)

Judgments—Execution—Fees—Additional—Payment—Procedure
A judgment debtor who uses a court officer to perform judgment collection duties beyond the scope of the statutory duties is obliged to pay the officer for the extra services, including the officer's services as negotiator, messenger, and investigator. An officer's claim for payment for the extra services should be pursued through a suit in contract or quasi-contract.

66. A court officer may be entitled to fees for investigatory services in pursuit of a judgment debtor. The correct procedure for the court officer to recover fees is to
a. show cause against the judgment debtor before the jurisdictional court.
b. show cause against the judgment creditor before the jurisdictional court.
c. file suit against the judgment creditor for breach of contract.
d. file suit against both parties for breach of contract.

67. Statutory fees may be added to a judgment upon recovery pursuant to a writ of execution. Pursuant to statute, what is the percentage taxable for recovery more than $1,000?
a. 3%
b. 5%
c. 7%
d. 10%

68. The court officer located a boat that was property of the judgment debtor at a local marina. The court officer did not remove the boat from the marina, but attached a copy of the writ to the boat, served a copy to the marina manager, and seized the ship's log. The procedure is referred to by the court as
a. maritime execution.
b. constructive control.
c. procedural levy.
d. admiralty levy.

69. The Michigan execution statute requires that a return be filed by the court officer
a. within 180 days of the date of issue by the court.
b. no less than ten and no more than 60 days from date of receipt by the officer.
c. no less than 20 and no more than 90 days from date of receipt by the officer.
d. A return is not required if no recovery is made.

70. The failure to file a return voids a successful execution levy. This statement is
a. true.
b. false.

71. A court officer may require an indemnity bond or sufficient indemnification security from a judgment creditor if there is reasonable doubt as to property ownership. The procedure is governed by the
a. Uniform Commercial Code (UCC).
b. Revised Judicature Act (RJA).
c. Uniform Fraudulent Conveyance Act (UFCA).
d. Statute of Frauds.

72. A party or witness who holds property of a judgment debtor or who has transacted a conveyance of property with a judgment debtor has qualified immunity from self-incrimination when deposed or examined during discovery proceedings. This statement is

a. true.

b. false.

73. The judgment creditor recovered $100,000 from the judgment debtor. Excluding fees for service, mileage, and keeping of property, what is the statutory fee the court officer was entitled to?

a. $3,040

b. $3,200

c. $3,500

d. $5,000

74. A court officer may not recover for "dead end" investigations or for property never recovered or seized from a judgment debtor during the execution process. This statement is

a. true.

b. false.

Use the following court officer procedure to answer questions 75 through 90.

Service of Post-Judgment Process—Special Civil Part
Directive #6-01 April 23, 2010
Issued by: Richard J. Williams, Administrative Director
Special civil part officers who serve post-judgment process shall comply with the following procedures:

I. Execution Sales
Special civil part officers should not post execution sale notices unless they intend to actually hold such a sale. Officers shall not threaten to hold a sale of a debtor's personal property when one cannot be held, or when a sale can be held but there is no real intention to do so.

The notices authorized herein should conform substantially to those in Attachments A and B to this directive. Both notices should contain the seal of the Superior Court. The purpose of these notices is to stimulate the debtor to contact the special civil part officers to arrange to make payment, without making idle threats.

Neither such notice is a substitute for the notice to debtor prescribed by *Rules* 4:59-1(g) and 6:7-1(b), which is served on the debtor and filed with the clerk of the court when the levy is actually made, nor are they a substitute for the notice of sale indicating the time and place of the intended sale that is to be posted in the sheriff's office pursuant to N.J.S.A. 2A:17-33.

II. Communication with Creditors and Creditors——Attorneys

Special civil part officers should notify the judgment creditor or the judgment creditor's attorney when a writ has been received for his or her case. Requests from judgment creditors or their attorneys for information regarding the status of a writ should be responded to within 15 days. Writs should be returned to the clerk of the court upon request by the judgment creditor or judgment creditor's attorney to do so. The return of the writ is without prejudice to the special civil part officer's right to collect fees and dollarage that may be due.

III. Resolution of Disputes Regarding Fees and Dollarage

The special civil part officers' Advisory Committees appointed in each vicinage pursuant to Directive # 4-01 shall each establish an informal procedure to resolve complaints by special civil part officers regarding their fees and dollarage. A special civil part officer is conditionally entitled to his or her fee or dollarage when the effective cause in producing payment or settlement of a judgment is any overt act by the officer toward execution of the writ, including any contact with the judgment debtor or any asset of the judgment debtor, or in the case of a wage execution, any contact with the judgment debtor or his or her employer. Special civil part officers retain the right to collect their fees or dollarage through a civil lawsuit.

IV. Outstanding Checks

A party or attorney named as the payee on an outstanding check issued by a special civil part officer from his or her trust fund that remains outstanding for more than three months shall be contacted by the officer to ensure that the check has been received and the address of the party or attorney is valid. Further checks shall not be issued to that payee until this assurance has been made.

If a check remains outstanding for a period of one year, the amount of the outstanding check shall be deposited in an escrow account maintained by the Administrative Office of the Courts for court officer outstanding checks. Following the expiration of a period of ten years, that amount shall escheat to the State Treasury. After either transfer of the outstanding amount to the escrow account or escheatment, the payee nonetheless still may file a claim for such money, supported by such records or documents as appropriate.

These transfers would eliminate old checks from appearing on the reconciliation. The Administrative Office of the Courts will maintain a record detailing what amounts comprise the balance in the court officer outstanding checks escrow account. Interest earned on such money shall be credited to the Administrative Office of the Courts for one year. Thereafter, interest shall accrue to the State Treasury for monies placed there through escheatment.

ATTACHMENT A
SUPERIOR COURT OF NEW JERSEY
LAW DIVISION, SPECIAL CIVIL PART
_____ COUNTY

Plaintiff v. Defendant

Docket No.

NOTICE TO DEFENDANT

On the _____ day of _____, _____, a judgment was entered against you by this court. A copy of the writ of execution is attached showing the total amount due.

The following steps or any one of them can and will be taken to collect this judgment and may result in additional costs unless you contact the undersigned court officer immediately and make satisfactory arrangements to pay the total due.

- Except for public benefits such as welfare, Social Security, S.S.I., Veterans, unemployment, and workers compensation, your cash assets may be seized.
- Your personal property may be seized and sold.
- You may be entitled to an exemption of $1,000 in cash and personal property.
- Goods that were part of the transaction that led to this judgment may be seized regardless of value.
- A portion of your wages more than $154.50 per week may be paid to plaintiff.
- A lien may be placed against your real estate.

_____

Dated:

Special Civil Part Officer:

Telephone No.:

ATTACHMENT B
SUPERIOR COURT OF NEW JERSEY
LAW DIVISION, SPECIAL CIVIL PART
_____ COUNTY

Plaintiff v. Defendant

Docket No.

NOTICE TO DEFENDANT

On the _____ day of _____, _____, a judgment was entered against you by this court in the amount of $_____ plus costs and fees of $_____, for a total due of $_____.

To date, this judgment remains unpaid. Unless you contact me immediately and make satisfactory arrangements to pay the total due, I shall apply to the court for an order permitting me to enter your home to levy on your household goods and furnishings, inventory them, and have them appraised so that the value in excess of $1,000 may be sold at public auction to the highest bidder to satisfy the judgment.

Dated:

Special Civil Part Officer:

Telephone No.:

75. A special service part officer is required to notify which of the following when a writ has been received for his or her case?
   a. the administrative director
   b. the judgment creditor's attorney
   c. the court officer
   d. the debtor

76. Special civil part officers should NOT post execution sale notices until
   a. the property has been appraised and the value exceeds the statutory exemption limit the defendant is entitled to.
   b. the property is in sale condition.
   c. the debtor has indicated that the property will not be retrieved.
   d. the officers actually intend to hold an execution sale.

77. Civil part officers are encouraged to arrange payments with judgment debtors by use of approved demand letters and notices. The notices should
   a. contain the seal of the Superior Court.
   b. inform the judgment debtor of his or her legal rights.
   c. advise the judgment debtor to obtain an attorney.
   d. provide names and addresses of credit counseling services.

78. Execution sale notices should be posted in
   a. the court lobby.
   b. the U.S. Post Office nearest the judgment debtor's home.
   c. the sheriff's office.
   d. City Hall in the city where the judgment debtor resides.

79. Special civil part officers should notify the judgment creditor and the attorney for the judgment creditor, if applicable, upon receipt of a writ of execution. All status requests should be answered by the officer within
   a. five days.
   b. seven days.
   c. ten days.
   d. 15 days.

80. When a judgment creditor or attorney has the right to request a writ be returned to the court clerk, the special civil part officer must return the writ. All fees due for services are
   a. terminated.
   b. not affected by the return of the writ.
   c. reduced by 50% if returned within 30 days, 25% after 30 days.
   d. to be determined by the court on a petition by the officer.

81. Disputed special civil part officers fees must first be processed through an informal dispute resolution process. If unresolved, the officer's available remedy is
   a. binding arbitration.
   b. state bar grievance procedure.
   c. commencing a lawsuit in civil court.
   d. resubmitting the dispute to a new resolution dispute panel.

82. Special civil part officers must maintain a trust account for all monies collected on wage or property executions. This statement is
   a. true.
   b. false.

83. Unpaid trust account checks must be confirmed as received by the payee by the officer
after
   a. 60 days.
   b. 90 days.
   c. 180 days.
   d. one year.

84. An officer's trust account check that remains
unpaid after one year must be
   a. stop paid by the officer and recorded as void.
   b. stop paid and forfeited to the officer.
   c. paid into the Administrative Office of the
   Court's escrow account.
   d. escheated to the State Treasury.

85. What is a judgment debtor's personal property
exemption valued at?
   a. $1,000
   b. $1,500
   c. $2,500
   d. $0; there is no exemption pursuant to state
   statute.

86. Special civil part officers may break and enter
the home of the judgment debtor without an
Order of the Court for purposes of effecting a
personal property levy. This statement is
   a. true.
   b. false.

87. Certain payments and wages are exempt from
wage execution. Which of the following is NOT
exempt from attachment by the officer?
   a. workers' compensation payments
   b. wages above $220 per week
   c. Social Security retirement benefits
   d. unemployment compensation payments

88. Goods that were part of the transaction that led
to judgment are subject to seizure regardless of
value. This property would be termed as
   a. nonexempt property.
   b. conditional property.
   c. secured property.
   d. security property.

89. Notice to debtor is served to the debtor when
levy is made and
   a. the judgment creditor is also served with a
   copy of the notice.
   b. posted in a conspicuous place near the
   debtor's residence or business.
   c. filed with the clerk of the court.
   d. posted in the sheriff's office.

90. Procedure for service of post-judgment process
was issued by
   a. Richard J. Williams, Administrative
   Director.
   b. the clerk of the Supreme Court.
   c. the chief justice of the Supreme Court.
   d. the Superior Court Office of Court
   Administration.

Clerical Ability

Study the form below and answer questions 91 through 100 based on the form content and use.

Docket No. 604853-91

County: Bergen

Plaintiff: Bayonne Hospital

Defendant: Vasquez, Giovanna H.

Plaintiff's Attorney: Pressler & Pressler, 64 River Road, East Hanover, NJ

Date of Report: 9/15/2010

Type: Garnish

File 3: 12629

POB: Marriott Corp.

Date Received: 1/25/09

Date Returned: 5/17/10

How Returned: Satisfied

Total: $3,293.42

Dollarage: $299.41

Date	Check #	Action	Amt. Rec. $	Balance Made	Made B
1/25/09		Docket Entered/Amount Already Paid			Admin
2/19/09	Credit	Cash Receipt from Defendant	20.91	3,100.08	Admin
2/19/09	Credit	Cash Receipt from Defendant	230	2,870.08	Admin
3/19/09		Docket Information Modified			Admin
3/19/09		Docket Information Modified			Admin
5/31/09	1029	Cash Receipt from Defendant	12.49	2,857.59	Admin
6/05/09	4111	Cash Receipt from Defendant	37.90	2,819.69	Admin
6/11/09	8526	Cash Receipt from Defendant	32.36	2,787.33	Admin
6/15/09	3258	Disbursement to a Lawyer	11.24		Admin
6/18/09	4272	Cash Receipt from Defendant	21.62	2,765.71	Admin
7/02/09	5030	Cash Receipt from Defendant	21.26	2,744.45	Admin
7/02/09	5031	Cash Receipt from Defendant	11.24	2,733.21	Admin
7/15/09	3411	Disbursement to a Lawyer	19.46		Admin
7/15/09	3411	Disbursement to a Lawyer	29.12		Admin
7/15/09	3411	Disbursement to a Lawyer	34.11		Admin
7/16/09	5699	Cash Receipt from Defendant	62.21	2,671.00	Admin
7/23/09	1334	Cash Receipt from Defendant	31.46	2,639.54	Admin
7/30/09	6118	Cash Receipt from Defendant	24.84	2,614.70	Admin
8/06/09	1801762	Cash Receipt from Defendant	41.53	2,573.17	Admin

Date	Check #	Action	Amt. Rec. $	Balance Made	Made By
8/13/09	6857	Cash Receipt from Defendant	56.65	2,516.52	Admin
8/15/09	3562	Disbursement to a Lawyer	55.99		Admin
8/15/09	3562	Disbursement to a Lawyer	10.12	19.13	Admin
8/15/09	3562	Disbursement to a Lawyer	28.31	10.12	Admin
8/15/09	3562	Disbursement to a Lawyer	28.31		Admin
8/15/09	3562	Disbursement to a Lawyer	22.36		Admin
8/20/09	2310	Cash Receipt from Defendant	65.11	2,451.41	Admin
8/28/09	7428	Cash Receipt from Defendant	69.57	2,381.84	Admin
9/12/09	7743	Cash Receipt from Defendant	86.18	2,206.03	Admin
9/15/09	3706	Disbursement to a Lawyer	50.98		Admin
9/15/09	3706	Disbursement to a Lawyer	58.60		Admin
9/15/09	3706	Disbursement to a Lawyer	62.61		Admin
9/15/09	3706	Disbursement to a Lawyer	37.38		Admin
9/25/09	1633	Cash Receipt from Defendant	97.73	2,108.30	Admin
9/26/09	5242	Cash Receipt from Defendant	60.50	2,047.80	Admin
10/02/09	0384	Cash Receipt from Defendant	59.26	1,988.54	Admin
10/15/09	3845	Disbursement to a Lawyer	80.67		Admin
10/15/09	3845	Disbursement to a Lawyer	87.96		Admin
10/15/09	3845	Disbursement to a Lawyer	77.56		Admin
10/15/09	3845	Disbursement to a Lawyer	54.45		Admin
10/19/09	1547	Cash Receipt from Defendant	76.26	1,825.17	Admin
10/26/09	6158	Cash Receipt from Defendant	54.04	1,771.13	Admin
10/30/09	9535	Cash Receipt from Defendant	64.80	1,706.33	Admin
11/09/09	4374	Cash Receipt from Defendant	35.77	1,670.56	Admin
11/15/09	3964	Disbursement to a Lawyer	78.40		Admin
11/15/09	3964	Disbursement to a Lawyer	48.64		Admin
11/15/09	3964	Disbursement to a Lawyer	68.63		Admin
11/15/09	3964	Disbursement to a Lawyer	53.33		Admin
11/15/09	3964	Disbursement to a Lawyer	58.32		Admin
11/19/09	8925	Cash Receipt from Defendant	80.71	1,589.85	Admin
11/21/09	2766	Cash Receipt from Defendant	69.72	1,520.13	Admin
11/30/09	7616	Cash Receipt from Defendant	78.34	1,441.79	Admin
12/10/09	5092	Cash Receipt from Defendant	97.49	1,344.30	Admin
12/13/09	7803	Cash Receipt from Defendant	105.44	1,238.86	Admin
12/15/09	4091	Disbursement to a Lawyer	70.51		Admin
12/15/09	4091	Disbursement to a Lawyer	32.19		Admin
12/15/09	4091	Disbursement to a Lawyer	62.75		Admin
12/15/09	4091	Disbursement to a Lawyer	72.64		Admin

Date	Check #	Action	Amt. Rec. $	Balance Made	Made B
12/20/09	2602	Cash Receipt from Defendant	93.30	1,145.56	Admin
12/31/09	1896719	Cash Receipt from Defendant	73.11	996.42	Admin
1/04/10	1900558	Cash Receipt from Defendant	76.03	1,069.53	Admin
1/11/10	1900558	Cash Receipt from Defendant	85.63	910.79	Admin
1/15/10	4208	Disbursement to a Lawyer	87.74		Admin
1/15/10	4208	Disbursement to a Lawyer	94.90		Admin
1/15/10	4208	Disbursement to a Lawyer	83.97		Admin
1/15/10	4208	Disbursement to a Lawyer	65.80		Admin
1/17/10	1909404	Cash Receipt from Defendant	72.26	838.53	Admin
1/22/10	1914281	Cash Receipt from Defendant	72.01	766.52	Admin
1/28/10	1918051	Cash Receipt from Defendant	95.11	671.41	Admin
2/11/10	1926521	Cash Receipt from Defendant	81.36	497.62	Admin
2/15/10	4329	Disbursement to a Lawyer	65.03		Admin
2/15/10	4329	Disbursement to a Lawyer	77.07		Admin
2/15/10	4329	Disbursement to a Lawyer	68.43		Admin
2/15/10	4329	Disbursement to a Lawyer	64.81		Admin
2/15/10	4329	Disbursement to a Lawyer	85.60		Admin
2/20/10	1931050	Cash Receipt from Defendant	90.96	406.66	Admin
2/25/10	1935192	Cash Receipt from Defendant	77.68	328.98	Admin
3/20/10	1939315	Cash Receipt from Defendant	64.86	264.12	Mike
3/20/10	1943350	Cash Receipt from Defendant	79.37	184.75	Mike
3/20/10	012947312	Cash Receipt from Defendant	68.40	116.35	Mike
3/28/10	1952329	Cash Receipt from Defendant	78.22	38.13	Mike
4/22/10	1969375	Cash Receipt from Defendant	38.13	0	Beth
4/23/10		Status Updated to Open	0	0	Beth
4/23/10		Docket Physically Returned to Court	0	0	Beth
4/23/10		Dollarage Interest Order	−15.68	172.43	Beth
4/23/10		Judgment Has Been Modified	−172.43	172.43	Beth
4/23/10	1969375	Check Values Modified	38.13	172.43	Beth
4/23/10	1969375	Check Deleted from Database	38.71	211.72	Beth
4/23/10	1969375	Cash Receipt from Defendant	38.71	173.01	Beth
4/23/10	1956986	Cash Receipt from Defendant	79.59	93.42	Beth
4/23/10	1961550	Cash Receipt from Defendant	92.89	0.53	Beth
5/25/10	1988214	Cash Receipt from Defendant	0.53	0	Beth
5/25/10	1988214	Check Placed on Hold	0.53	0	Beth
9/02/10	1988214	Check Released from on Hold	0.53	0	Admin

Dollarage Balance: $0.00

Judgment Balance: $0.00

91. What is the docket number?
   a. 606409-91
   b. 606912-91
   c. 604853-91
   d. 605483-92

92. The case caption is
   a. *Bayonne Hospital v. Giovanna A. Vasquez.*
   b. *Bayonne Hospital v. Giovanna H. Vasquez.*
   c. *Bayonne Hospital v. Giovanni H. Vasquez.*
   d. *Bayonne Hospital v. Gina H. Valdez.*

93. What is the number of checks received from the defendant between 1/25/09 and 7/25/09?
   a. eight
   b. nine
   c. ten
   d. 12

94. What is the number of disbursements to the lawyer during 2009?
   a. 23
   b. 25
   c. 26
   d. 30

95. What is the check number received from the defendant on 3/28/09?
   a. 1983456
   b. 1952329
   c. 1982789
   d. 1923457

96. What is the date with the most posted transactions?
   a. 2/15/09
   b. 11/15/09
   c. 3/20/10
   d. 4/23/10

97. Who is the defendant's employer?
   a. Bergen County
   b. Marriott Corp.
   c. East Hanover, NJ
   d. Pressler & Pressler

98. What is the total amount deleted from the original judgment amount?
   a. $188.11
   b. $226.24
   c. $299.41
   d. $309.91

99. When was the report generated?
   a. 5/17/10
   b. 5/22/10
   c. 9/2/10
   d. 9/15/10

100. On 4/23/10, which of the following was NOT posted?
   a. disbursement to a lawyer
   b. docket physically returned to the court
   c. judgment modified
   d. dollarage interest order

Answers

1. a. Ms. Albino resided at 2048 Davidson Avenue.

2. c. Ms. Albino had lived at her residence for five years. She originally lived in Apartment 3C but upgraded to Apartment 4B to accommodate her five-year-old daughter.

3. a. Ms. Albino contacted the police at 10:45 A.M. when she noticed that her car was missing. The officers arrived at 12:30 P.M.

4. b. Ms. Albino made a report to the police on Saturday about her stolen vehicle. She was told to go to the precinct in two days to pick up a copy of the report, meaning her report would be ready by Monday.

5. d. Officer Randall did not ask her when she noticed that her car was missing; this was a question that was asked by Officer Thomas.

6. c. Ms. Albino grabbed her red sweater prior to going outside to greet the officers.

7. b. Ms. Albino stated that it was unusual for her to find parking on her street, Davidson Avenue.

8. b. One of the young men was wearing a black jacket; his baseball hat was blue.

9. b. Ms. Albino could expect to receive a call from Detective Joseph or Detective Anthony.

10. a. Ms. Albino described her stolen vehicle as a two-door, silver 2002 Honda Civic.

11. b. Ms. Albino stated that a previous accident left her car with a scratch on the rear bumper.

12. d. The passage does not identify the make and model of the current carry firearm. Choice **a** is the *replacement* service weapon. Choices **b** and **c** are not mentioned.

13. c. The time from December 12, 2010 to February 1, 2011 is 40 days.

14. a. There is a total of seven items (holster, magazine pouch, dual handcuff case, baton carrier, mini-flashlight case, latex glove pouch, radio carrier).

15. b. Lieutenant Alden is identified in the final paragraph of the passage as the executive officer. The remaining names are not mentioned.

16. a. Starting May 1, 2010 (5/1/10), all officers will receive Department-issued clothing at no cost.

17. d. The three sweat shirts will be issued every five years, not every year.

18. b. The Kevlar vest is not issued every five years; it is issued every ten years.

19. d. The memo states that department-issued uniforms will ensure that officers dress professionally, appropriately, and safely. All of the answers were correct.

20. a. Dry Clean Express is the establishment to which all officers are required to take their uniforms for alterations.

21. b. Dry Clean Express is located at 224 East Main Street.

22. a. Out of the answers provided, Thursday is the only day on which officers may have uniforms tailored. Alterations cannot be made on Friday, Saturday or Sunday.

23. d. Officers have 30 days to comply with the order before facing a possible suspension without pay.

24. b. All state patches will be worn on the left sleeve, while all american flags will be worn on the right sleeve.

25. c. Patches should be sewn one inch below the shoulder seam.

26. d. The passage identifies Burns as a special agent with the State Department of Treasury Criminal Enforcement Bureau.

27. a. Burns's previous employment was with the eighth Superior Court as a probation officer.

28. d. Westbrook filed Chapter 7 bankruptcy and the debt was discharged.

29. d. Both cases were filed in the 13th District Court.

30. a. Burns's former employer suggested she apply as a court officer trainee.

31. a. Shanley is the subject of a one-count complaint containing two separate charges.

32. d. Shanley is a justice of the Esopus Town Court.

33. b. Shanley is a high school graduate. She did not graduate from *any* law school, which forms the basis for the charge of misconduct in the SCJC complaint.

34. b. Shanley was employed as a court clerk as stated in paragraph 1.

35. c. The court clerk's continuing education program is sponsored by Office of Court Administration.

36. d. A referee heard the complaint and acted as fact finder.

37. b. Shanley is listed as the petitioner, Pisani represents the plaintiff, and Stern represents the respondent.

38. b. The SCJC made the allegation that Shanley's campaign slogan made her appear pro-prosecution and that she could not remain impartial in criminal matters.

39. a. The Court of Appeals found no significance in the use of the phrase *law and order candidate* in the instant case.

40. c. The Court of Appeals affirmed the SCJC imposed sanction of admonition.

41. b. In legal disciplinary proceedings, the words are interchangeable.

42. d. Judge Kaye is identified as chief judge.

43. c. Shanley accepted the sanction.

44. a. No costs were assessed to Shanley.

45. c. Sergeant Hakim was promoted in 2004. He was hired in 1995.

46. b. Investigating judges' misconduct is not mentioned in the passage.

47. a. The Court Professional Standards Bureau is identified in the opening paragraph of the passage.

48. b. The final paragraph identifies the Office of Court Administration as being in charge of conducting confidential investigations.

49. b. Fingerprints are like snowflakes: No two are alike. If a person has been fingerprinted (or has not been fingerprinted but should have been) depending on his or her claimed profession, in ink or AFIS (Automated Fingerprint Identification System), there is truth.

50. a. He claimed that he was previously employed as a pension fund manager for a nonprofit organization.

51. c. *Per curiam* opinions are generally reserved for appellate courts and are the opinion of the court as a whole. An alternate term is *en banc* opinion.

52. a. *De novo* is Latin for "to start fresh," and it is regularly used by appellate courts in reviewing lower court decisions.

53. b. Choice **a**, case law, is law based on published judicial decisions.

54. c. A tangible asset refers to personal property that has a physical presence.

55. d. It is contingent or dependent on recovery.

56. b. Plea bargaining is a pretrial process that provides for specific sentencing or disposition in exchange for a guilty plea. Choice **a** is incorrect because it involves post-conviction reduction allowing for good time or to eliminate prison overcrowding. Choice **c** is used in civil proceedings, and choice **d** is Latin for "a criminal act."

57. c. An example of an intentional tort is felonious assault, injury resulting from a drunk driver, or sexual assault. Choice **a** is incorrect because negligence is an unintended act or carelessness.

58. a. *Prose* is latin for "on one's own behalf."

59. c. The process by which one jurisdiction surrenders to another jurisdiction a person accused or convicted of a crime in the other state is known as *extradition*.

60. a. Slander and libel are two types of defamation actions. Libel involves written or printed materials or broadcast materials via television or radio.

61. c. The TILA applies to consumers who seek credit for money, property, or services and regulates creditors, either individuals or businesses, who extend credit on a regular basis that requires a finance charge or is payable in four or more installments. TILA does not cover business, commercial, or agricultural credit.

62. c. The furniture store does not invoke TILA by offering 90 days same-as-cash financing.

63. b. A TRO differs from an injunction, choice **a**, by being a means of temporary relief until a hearing can be held. Choices **c** and **d** are instruments used in domestic actions.

64. d. This is the burden of proof standard by which a civil case is decided.

65. b. *Caveat emptor* translates as "let the buyer beware."

66. c. In the instant case, the court ruled that fees charged for investigatory and ancillary expenses by court officers may be resolved in suit for breach of contract *separate* from proceedings to determine statutory collection fees taxable to the judgment debtor. Choice **d** is incorrect because the judgment debtor is responsible only for payment of statutory collection fees based on recovery in an execution proceeding by a court officer. Choices **a** and **b** are incorrect because a show cause proceeding is not a lawsuit.

67. a. MCLA 600.2559 governs statutory fees pursuant to executions against property.

68. b. The court determined that the court officer had constructive control of the property, which amounted to a successful levy.

69. c. The statute allows a return to be filed after 90 days if successful levy was made and collection activity was completed after the 90-day period.

70. b. This statement is false.

71. b. The procedure is governed by the Revised Judicature Act (RJA).

72. b. MCL 600.6110(3) provides a party or witness may invoke his or her Fifth Amendment privilege in answering questions that may incriminate the party of fraud or being part of a fraudulent transfer of property to defeat a judgment creditor.

73. a. The court officer is entitled to 7% of $1,000 ($70) and 3% of $99,000 ($2,970).

74. a. Fees charged for services relative to pursuing a writ of execution or for services performed outside the scope of an officer's statutory duties are not taxable and may be recoverable under contract or quasi-contract.

75. b. Under the header "II. Communication with Creditors and Creditors—Attorney," it specifically states that the special service part officer should notify the judgment creditor or the judgment creditor's attorney.

76. d. Pursuant to procedure, execution sales are not to be used as idle threats, but as a stimulus to judgment debtors to satisfy the outstanding judgment.

77. a. The seal of the Superior Court is mandatory on all communications. Officers should not provide legal advice or the names of any credit or legal services, making choices **b**, **c**, and **d** improper procedures.

78. c. The sale notice shall be posted in the sheriff's office pursuant to N.J.S.A. 2A:17-33.

79. d. All status requests should be answered by the officer within 15 days.

80. b. The officer is not prejudiced by the return of the writ, and all rights to collect fees are preserved.

81. c. The officer may pursue a civil lawsuit if the Advisory Committee fails to resolve the matter.

82. a. The statute requires that special civil part officers maintain a trust account and make disbursements to the judgment creditor or the creditor's attorney from that account.

83. b. Unpaid trust account checks must be confirmed as received by the payee by the officer after 90 days.

84. c. An amount equal to the unpaid check will be deposited with the AOC in escrow pending escheatment process.

85. a. The state statutory exemption is $1,000 market value on personal property.

86. b. Upon the request of the officer on a showing of noncompliance by the judgment debtor, the court may order the officer to enter the debtor's home and levy all personal property in excess of the statutory exemption limit.

87. b. The threshold for wage execution is $154.50 per week. Amounts in excess of that total are subject to attachment.

88. a. This property would be termed as *nonexempt property*.

89. c. It should be filed with the clerk of the court.

90. a. Williams is identified as issuing Directive #6-01.

91. c. The docket number on this form is 604853-91.

92. b. *Bayonne Hospital v. Giovanna H. Vasquez* is the correct case caption.

93. a. Eight checks were received during this time.

94. c. The number of disbursements to the lawyer during 2009 is 26.

95. b. The correct check number is 1952329.

96. d. There are ten posted transactions on 4/23/10.

97. b. Marriott Corp. is coded as POB (Place of Business).

98. a. Two credits are posted on 4/23/10 in the amounts of $15.68 and $172.43.

99. d. This report was generated on September 15, 2010.

100. a. A disbursement to a lawyer was not posted.

13 ▶ THE INTERVIEW

Passing the written examination is the first step toward becoming a court officer. The interview is often a turning point in the hiring process.

In larger venues, the interview is also known as the oral examination and is typically conducted by two or three court management personnel. The oral examination board will likely consist of a court officer holding the rank of sergeant or greater, a court administrator, and possibly a judge. In smaller venues, the chief judge and the court administrator will conduct the hiring interview.

The interviewers will structure their questions from your employment application. Questions about previous employment will dominate this portion of the interview. Be prepared to explain any termination of employment, gaps in employment, or frequent job changes. Also, be prepared to answer why you made a career change if there was long-term employment with one employer. Courts seek stability from potential employees. Training costs are wasted on those who are here today and gone the next.

The cardinal rule is to be honest. Any adverse information in your background will be discovered and should be addressed. Be prepared to answer the difficult questions with the same candor as the easy questions. Providing false information or embellished information that cannot be verified will prove fatal. Do not believe that it's all right or that everyone lies on his or her resume. Lies will be discovered and will terminate your employment or eliminate you from employment considerations.

Remember that law enforcement agencies can discover information from your past that most other employment organizations would have tremendous difficulty discovering (such as arrests that may have not led to your conviction). Listen to the questions carefully and answer the exact question being asked of you. Do not omit any information, and do not tell them anything extra. Most importantly, when asked a question, **tell the truth**. It is also very important to remain consistent with everything you have stated previously. If you wrote something down on your application and you are asked about it on the interview, your answer should be exactly the same. Review your application prior to the interview, especially all dates of employment and reasons for leaving a position. Inconsistencies in your story could raise questions about your credibility and demonstrate your propensity to lie. It is a good reason for disqualification.

Commonly Asked Interview Questions

Where do you see yourself in five years?

What are your strengths and weaknesses?

Are you willing to work irregular hours to accomplish the job's objectives?

What are your five greatest accomplishments to date?

How do you plan to exceed your current accomplishments?

Many of the questions asked by the panel are standardized, so two different candidates can receive exactly the same questions. Candidates may also have individualized questions that focus on their background, experience, or education. Panelists may probe into one of your responses more deeply, depending on your answer. Panelists can ask you personal questions but cannot ask you questions about religious affiliations, marital status, or ethnic background. Remember, they are bound by Equal Employment Opportunity rules and statutes. Such questions would be illegal and deemed discriminatory.

Most of the questions will focus on your personal character and your ability to perform the job tasks effectively. Reread the job announcement before the interview and familiarize yourself with all the duties of a court officer. You should review legal terminology beforehand as well. Many of the questions will focus on critical aspects of the job. Try to anticipate the questions they may ask you, such as:

- Why do you want to be a court officer? (Note: never say it's because you want to be able to tell people what to do or that you enjoy having power over others; that is an automatic disqualifier.)
- How do you feel your life experiences have prepared you for this job?
- How would you describe your work ethic?
- If there was something you could change about your life, what would it be?
- What makes a good court officer?
- What would you do if someone offered you a bribe?
- What would you do if you knew another officer was engaging in illegal activity?
- Why would you make a good court officer?

In addition to these traditional types of interview questions, behavioral questions are becoming more commonplace during interviews for almost all law enforcement positions, including the court officer position. Responses to such questions should be based on the **STAR** approach (Situation/Task; Action; Result). This approach can be challenging because it requires you to pick events from your past, either professional or personal, that help illustrate your best character traits or work strengths.

Situation or task	Begin answer the question by explaining a past situation you were in or a past task that needed to be accomplished. Be specific about the example and do not speak in generalities.
Action you took	Next, talk about the action that you took to resolve the situation or problem and/or accomplish the task you were given. Again, be very specific about what you did.
Results you achieved	Last, what was the result of your action? Was it positive or negative? What did you learn? Based on the results, if a similar occurrence happened again, would you handle it the same way or differently? Why?

Responses to interview questions using this structure will be more successful than responses that do not utilize this format. Answering all questions in this format will help you to interview better than many other candidates. Always keep the focus on yourself and highlight your achievements. If something did not work the way you planned, talk about the lesson you learned and how this lesson will help you improve the way you handle similar situations in the future. Below is a list of possible questions that could be asked during an oral appraisal exam. Read them over and think about the answers you would give to each question based on the STAR method.

- Describe a situation in which you were able to use persuasion to successfully convince someone to see your side.
- Describe a time when you were faced with a stressful situation that demonstrated your coping skills.
- Give an example of a time when you used good judgment in solving a difficult and complex problem.
- Give an example of a time when you had to adhere to a policy that you did not agree with.
- Tell me about a time when you had to go over and beyond your job duties.
- Tell me about a time when you had to deal with conflict in the workplace.
- Tell me about the most difficult decision you ever had to make.
- Give an example of a time when you tried really hard to accomplish a task but failed.
- Talk about a time where you had to show initiative and take the lead.
- Describe a situation where you were able to have a positive influence on others.
- Give an example of a difficult goal you achieved and how you reached it.

Practice your answers to such questions. Remember, you are training your brain to respond to such questions with plausible and professional answers. If you know someone who is a court officer, they can probably give you a lot of information on which questions will be asked. If you do not know anyone in the field, try coming up with a list of possible questions (like the ones just given) and ask a friend to interview you. This will give you time to practice your answers and "train your brain" to answer appropriately. Failing to prepare properly would be a huge mistake. You will undoubtedly be nervous on the day of the interview, but if you practice your answers to these questions, it will help to alleviate your anxiety. A confident interviewee with great answers will be certain to impress the panel.

Conservative dress is the rule for the interview. Men should wear a dark suit, a white or blue shirt, and a coordinated tie in a solid color or small pattern or stripe. Polished black shoes, a dress belt in excellent condition, and only essential jewelry (e.g., a wedding ring, wristwatch, or tie clasp) should be worn. Do not wear neck chains, earrings, body piercings, bracelets, or flashy jewelry.

Women should wear a navy, black, or dark gray pantsuit, or a blazer with a below-the-knee skirt and conservative dress shoes (no open-toed sandals or stilettos). Only essential jewelry should be worn.

When you are called to enter the room to meet the panel, the panel members will most likely be sitting down. Be polite, say good morning and smile, but do not sit down until you are invited to do so. Besides saying good morning, you should not speak until you are spoken to. Talking too much, talking out of turn, or interrupting a panelist in the middle of his or her questions can be damaging. It may lead the panel members to label you as inconsiderate, overbearing, and rude. These are very difficult labels to overcome.

While the panelists are asking you questions, try to remain relaxed and calm; these are essential qualities of the position. Try not to fidget. Use some hand gestures, when appropriate, while speaking, but don't wave your hands around too much because it could be distracting. However, if you sit with your arms crossed or your hands in your lap the entire time, you may appear too rigid. Body language will weigh into the board's decision making process. Always sit up straight with both feet firmly on the floor. Good posture displays confidence, which is another important quality required of a court officer.

Do not be afraid to take a few seconds to think about the question before you answer. It is better to think about how you want to respond, rather than blurt out an answer that is less than flattering to your character or intellect. On the other hand, do not take too long to answer the question. Again, practicing with a friend should "train your brain" to answer quickly,

appropriately, and enable you to provide an answer that complements both your character and intellect.

Interview Strategies

Be prompt! Arriving even a minute late is a huge mistake. Punctuality is a key requirement for court officers. Be sure to leave extra early in case there is an accident or you have car trouble. You should drive to the testing site before the actual interview, especially if you are unfamiliar with the interview location. You do not want to get lost on the day of the interview; you do not need the extra stress. Map out alternative driving directions in case a street is closed or alternative subway/bus directions in case there is a problem with the line, and find some places to park if you are driving. Running into the interview late will be detrimental. First, it shows that you are not dependable. Second, it looks like you do not really care about the position. Third, it shows the panel that you do not value their time. Fourth, you will be very stressed and anxious and probably will not be able to answer the questions to the best of your ability. If you are more than five to ten minutes late, the panel may cancel your interview and you could be immediately disqualified from the position. If the unforeseen happens, be sure to have a phone number so that you can call and let them know you are running behind schedule. To avoid this from occurring, plan to arrive 20 to 30 minutes early.

When answering the interview questions, choose your words wisely. If answers are in the affirmative, the response is *yes*, not *yeah*, *uh huh*, or *okay*. If answers are in the negative, the response is *no*, not *nope*, *nah*, or any slang. Be clear and concise. Avoid starting sentences with *um*, *here's the thing*, *like*, or *you know*. When answering, take five seconds to think about your response, then answer.

Sit up straight, look forward, and do not fidget. Body language is very revealing.

Do not over-answer the question. Stay focused and on topic.

Practicing with a friend or with someone who has been through the process is invaluable. Tape the practice interview session in either audio or visual format. Replay the tape. Observe and correct weaknesses. You might even consider practicing in front of a mirror.

Generally, the last phase of the interview gives you an opportunity to question the interviewers on the panel. Try to have at least one good question to ask, because saying you have no questions may be interpreted as you have no real interest in the position. If you have nothing specific to ask, ask about the future steps in the hiring process, which shows your interest in continuing as a candidate. You might also consider having a short closing statement that reinforces your interest in the position and your belief that you will be able to fulfill the responsibilities of the position, but you do not want this to sound too rehearsed, as if you'd practiced it word for word for the last month.

When the interview is completed, make sure you thank everyone on the panel. It is good practice to shake everyone's hand before leaving. Make sure your handshake is firm but not too firm—you don't want to hurt anyone!

14 ▶ THE PHYSICAL, MEDICAL, AND PSYCHOLOGICAL EXAMS

The Physical Agility Exam

Physical fitness testing, also known as the physical ability or physical agility exam, is a staple in most court officer selection processes. The physical agility examination will be used to measure your ability to withstand the physical demands of the job.

Tests to measure your physical ability generally take one of two forms: what's known as "job task simulation" and physical fitness. Job task simulation tests, while they may test your physiological fitness, are designed to illustrate your ability in a handful of job areas. Typically, these tests also challenge your motor skills: balance, coordination, power, speed, reaction time, and agility. Physical fitness tests measure your physiological parameters, such as body composition, aerobic capacity, muscular strength and endurance, and flexibility. Physical fitness tests also hint at your medical status and, perhaps more importantly, reveal your ability to perform the potentially hundreds of physical tasks required of a court officer.

You will be tested on leg strength, arm strength, core strength, endurance, and aerobic ability. A typical physical agility exam can consist of a combination of any of the following:

- pedaling a stationary bike
- completing a certain number of sit-ups in one minute
- pumping an arm rowing machine as fast as possible to demonstrate arm endurance and strength
- holding an item steady, such as a simulated firearm, in position for a determined period of time, to verify arm steadiness
- lying on a slanted board and pulling your body upward, utilizing your upper body strength
- stepping up and down on a platform, or climbing stairs, to assess your heart rate and recovery period
- running 500 meters in a certain time
- climbing a six-foot wall
- climbing a five-foot chain-link fence
- dragging 150-pound dummy 100 feet or more
- carrying 45 to 50-pound barbells 100 feet in 30 seconds
- pushing a motor vehicle that is running in neutral 20 feet
- timed 1 mile or 1.5 mile run

Start training as soon as possible. If you are not in the best physical shape, four to six months of training may be necessary. You should familiarize yourself with the agency's physical agility requirements and then you should train expressly for those requirements. Most departments require a timed 1.5 mile run. Do not try to train for the run by engaging in alternative types of exercise such as racquetball or swimming. The only way to prepare for a run is to consistently run. This means you should be running at least three to four times per week. Make sure you practice on a regulation track; do not train for the run by using a treadmill. Focus all of your training sessions on the specific physical agility requirements and nothing else. Furthermore, do all of the requirements in one setting in the exact order you will be tested (e.g., a sprint, sit-ups, push-ups, dummy pull, 1.5 mile run). These tasks may be easy for you to do individually, but when you have to do them all back-to-back, it becomes a bit more challenging.

In order to pass the physical agility component, you must achieve the required number of points on the exam. Each task is scored and each score is based on how well you performed. For tasks such as push-ups or sit-ups, your score is based on the number of reps completed within one minute. Age and gender affect the number you must complete to qualify. Higher points in one category can compensate for lower points in another category; however, you must meet the minimum requirements in each category in order to qualify for employment.

Anyone in reasonable physical condition should successfully complete the examination, which is graded on a pass-or-fail basis.

Important

Regardless of the type of physical test you take, you need to be reasonably fit to complete the test successfully. In addition, it is essential to achieve fitness early and to maintain it for the duration of your court officer career.

Training Tips

In preparing for the physical fitness test, you must plan ahead, taking into account both the timing and content of the test. The short-term objective, of course, is to pass the test. But your greater goal is to integrate fitness into your lifestyle so that you can withstand the rigors of your career.

The first order of business is to determine the type of fitness test you'll have to complete. What you have to accomplish on the test will guide your training program. You can tailor to simulate the test and to train for the test events.

Following some basic training principles will help you create a safe and effective training program. Steady progress is the name of the game. Remember, you don't get out of shape overnight, so you won't be able to change your condition overnight. To avoid injury while achieving overall fitness, balance in fitness training is essential. Work opposing muscle groups when doing strength or flexibility training, and include aerobic conditioning, as well as proper nutrition, in your total fitness program.

The only way to prepare for this exam is to train, train, and train. If you have not exercised in a while or are not in the best shape, now is the time to get healthy. If you fail to prepare adequately for the physical training component, it is unlikely that you will be able to pass the physical agility test. Before beginning any type of exercise program, it is recommended that you see your doctor to make sure that you are physically healthy to undertake an exercise regime. Eating nutritiously by cutting back on fatty foods and increasing your intake of fruits and vegetables will also help you to reach your final fitness goal. On average, people who eat well and exercise regularly have fewer health problems than those who make unhealthy nutritional choices and live a sedentary lifestyle. Exercise can also decrease stress and subsequently improve your overall quality of life.

Start exercising slowly and build upon your strength weekly. If you are not a runner, you should not run an entire mile your first time out. You will tire easily and probably lose some self-confidence. You may also hurt yourself. Start off walking and advance to running. Increase your distance every day until you are able to run the required distance in the required time. Make sure you use a stopwatch to time yourself. The same is true of the sit-ups and push-ups. Start off slowly and increase your reps until you have reached your goal. Use weights to increase your leg and arm strength; this will prove to be particularly important when tested on leg and arm strength/endurance. If you are out of shape, you may notice muscle soreness within a 24-hour time period; this is normal. This soreness should be minimal and should disappear within a day or so. If the soreness continues or the pain becomes severe, contact your doctor immediately. Pay attention to possible injuries and don't push yourself too hard too fast. This regimen should increase your strength and endurance, but it is not supposed to destroy you in the process. Before any type of aerobic or cardio exercise, begin by stretching your muscles to avoid injury.

Finally, don't forget to rest. It allows the body and mind to recover from the challenges of training—and to prepare for another day.

Staying "FITT"

FITT stands for Frequency, Intensity, Type, and Time. FITT simplifies your training by helping you plan what to do and when, how hard, and for how long to do it. Because the four FITT variables are interrelated, you need to be careful in how you exercise. For example, intensity and time have an inverse relationship: As the intensity of your effort increases, the length of time you can maintain that effort decreases. A good rule of thumb when adjusting your workout variables to achieve optimum conditioning is to modify one at a time, increasing by 5% to 10%. Be sure to allow your body to adapt before increasing again.

The following presents some FITT guidelines to help you plan your training program.

Frequency
- Three to five times a week

Intensity
- Aerobic training—60% to 85% of maximum effort
- Resistance training—eight to 12 repetitions
- Flexibility training—just to slight tension

Type
- Aerobic—bike, walk, run, swim
- Resistance—free weights, weight machines, calisthenics
- Flexibility—static stretching

Time
- Aerobic—20 to 60 minutes
- Resistance—one to three sets; two to four exercises per body part
- Flexibility—hold stretch position eight to 30 seconds

A Sample Exercise Program

Physical training begins with a warm-up to increase your core body temperature and to prepare you for a more intense conditioning to follow. Brisk walking or jogging, in place or around a gym, or jumping rope are good start-up options and should be conducted for three to five minutes. This is followed immediately by a period of active head-to-toe stretching to prevent injury.

Basic conditioning in the academy is achieved frequently with calisthenic exercises. Beginners can do sets of ten on a "two count," and those of intermediate or advanced fitness can begin on a "four count" (1, 2, 3, 1; 1, 2, 3, 2, etc.). Running in formation typically follows calisthenic exercises and is done at about a nine- to ten-minute per mile pace. For those who are just beginning to prepare for the fitness test, eight to 12 minutes of running is a safe start; those who are more fit may begin with 25 or more minutes. A three- to five-minute cool-down period to recover and gentle, static stretching from the floor, focusing on the lower legs, will complete your workout.

Simple Calisthenics

Here are some recommended calisthenics to help get you into shape:

- jumping jacks
- half squats
- push-ups
- stomach crunches

And for the more advanced:

- diamond push-ups
- bent leg raises

The Medical Exam

Without exception, all venues require a medical examination. The examination will be conducted at the employer's expense. The exam is thorough, although not extensive. An industrial clinic or independent medical facility under contract to the state or local funding unit (city or county) is the setting.

The exam consists of the following mandatory procedures:

- back X-ray
- range of motion exercise
- blood pressure check
- vision and hearing check
- drug testing

The examination is for insurance purposes as well as to determine your general physical health and ability to perform the required work on a daily basis. The results are forwarded to the hiring unit and remain part of your personnel file. Some venues require an annual medical examination, while in others, this hiring medical exam is the only time you will be examined.

Depending on the department, you may be required to have a physical from your own physician. Your doctor will be required to complete forms that attest to your physical health. Other departments require you to see one of their doctors. If that is the case, make sure you arrive early for your appointment. If you are unfamiliar with the location, drive there beforehand. Being late or missing the appointment could automatically disqualify you from the position.

What to Provide at the Exam

- complete medical history and records, if any conditions are present or if you have a significant medical history
- a list of any prescribed medications
- names and addresses of treating physicians

If you were not tested for drug use during the physical agility portion of the applicant process, it is likely that this will also be done during the medical exam.

The Psychological Exam

The use and method of the psychological examination are varied. Some venues have contracts with local psychologists and psychiatrists and require you to attend an in-person interview. Other venues provide a written examination, which is then evaluated by a private service. Still other venues do not use or rely upon the examination. You may be asked to complete a written exam, in addition to meeting with a mental health professional. Psychological exams can vary. A series of questions regarding your behavior, feelings, beliefs, values and perceptions may be asked. The evaluator may ask you to draw a picture of a person, a tree, or a house as part of your exam, or he or she may ask you to describe a picture or to play a game of word association. While answering questions on the written exam or during the oral exam, be truthful and remain consistent with your answers. You may be asked the same question several different times in various ways. Do not be fooled; this repetitiveness is purposeful—the evaluator is looking for consistency. Inconsistency may indicate deception. Also, if the department you are applying to requires a polygraph exam, you can be asked to verify any of these answers during your polygraph exam.

The examination is *not* a head game or a means of setting you up to fail. It is an appropriate measurement of your mental fitness to withstand the mental stressors of the job. Court officers often see people at their worse, be it in court or in the field, when parties are facing seizure of their property or eviction from their homes. The ability to deal with tense situations rationally is tantamount to officer safety, avoiding liability, and enhancing the positive and impartial image of the court in meting out justice.

The Polygraph Test

A *polygraph* is a device that measures and records several physiological variables, including blood pressure, heart rate, respiration, and skin conductivity, while a series of questions are asked to detect lies. Some venues use the polygraph examination as part of the psychological testing process. In many states, candidates are allowed to decline the polygraph. Check your state law for applicable options.

Polygraphs can be particularly intimidating. Unfortunately, you cannot train for the polygraph exam, and attempting to "beat" the exam will automatically disqualify you from employment. Most court officer positions will not require you to submit to a polygraph. Check the department's website and their list of requirements to find out if you will need to take one. There are plenty of websites that provide information on how to "beat" a polygraph (keeping your body tense through the entire procedure, biting your tongue, moving your extremities, taking deep breathes, fidgeting)—but a trained examiner will know exactly what you are doing. This behavior will unequivocally damage your credibility. The best preparation for a polygraph is to relax, tell the truth, and disclose any information to the examiner beforehand that you think might be problematic. Most importantly . . . **don't lie**. If the polygrapher finds deception in your answers, it could be grounds for disqualification.

The key to the psychological examination is to be honest and relaxed. Unlike the physical agility test, you cannot do push-ups or sit-ups to prepare. During your assessment, it may help to keep in mind that everyone has weaknesses and makes mistakes. The test is less interested in whether you make mistakes than how you handle these mistakes. For example, how and what did you learn from them? As long as you deliver honest responses in a calm manner, you should be successful on the psychological exam.

ADITIONAL ONLINE PRACTICE ▶

Whether you need help building basic skills or preparing for an exam, visit the LearningExpress Practice Center! Using the code below, you'll be able to access additional court officer practice. This online practice will also provide you with:

- **Immediate scoring**
- **Detailed answer explanations**
- **Personalized recommendations for further practice and study**

Log in to the LearningExpress Practice Center by using this URL: **www.learnatest.com/practice**

This is your access code: **7861**

Follow the steps online to redeem your access code. After you've used your access code to register with the site, you will be prompted to create a username and password. For easy reference, record them here:

Username: _____   **Password:** _____

With your username and password, you can log in and access your additional practice material. If you have any questions or problems, please contact LearningExpress customer service at 1-800-295-9556 ext. 2, or e-mail us at **customerservice@learningexpressllc.com**.

NOTES

NOTES

NOTES

NOTES

NOTES

NOTES

NOTES

NOTES

NOTES

NOTES

NOTES

NOTES

NOTES